Mourning, Gender, and Creativity in the Art of Herman Melville

NEAL L. TOLCHIN

Mourning, Gender, and Creativity in the Art of Herman Melville

YALE UNIVERSITY PRESS
New Haven and London

Designed by Nancy Ovedovitz and set in Goudy Old Style type by The Composing Room of Michigan, Inc. Printed in the United States of America by BookCrafters, Inc., Chelsea, Michigan.

Library of Congress Cataloging-in-Publication Data

Tolchin, Neal L., 1952–
    Mourning, gender, and creativity in the art of Herman Melville.
    Bibliography: p.
    Includes index.
    1. Melville, Herman, 1819–1891. 2. Death in literature. 3. Mourning customs in literature. 4. Grief in literature. 5. Sex role in literature. 6. Novelists, American—19th century—Biography. 7. Mourning customs—United States—History—19th century. I. Title.
PS2388.D4T6 1988   813'.3   87–18968
ISBN 0–300–03975–1 (alk. paper)

The paper in this book meets the guidelines for permanence and durability of the Committee on Production Guidelines for Book Longevity of the Council on Library Resources.

10   9   8   7   6   5   4   3   2   1

To Susan,
for her living stories of wisdom and beauty,
with deepest affection.

And to my parents,
for all of their encouragement
and support

Say, Pierre; doth not a funerealness invest me?
Was ever hearse so plumed?
—Isabel, in Melville's *Pierre, or The Ambiguities*

Contents

Acknowledgments

For Ishmaelian conversation about Melville and Ahabian responses to my writing, I wish to thank David Leverenz, who guided me through the dissertation out of which this book grew. I am indebted to Michael Rogin's generosity of spirit in illuminating some of the deeper levels of my material. While serving as dissertation readers, Alice Crozier and Catharine Stimpson gave me wise counsel. I have benefited from the insights of Joyce Sparer Adler, Evan Carton, T. Walter Herbert, Sandy Marovitz, J. Hillis Miller, and Lee Mitchell, each of whom read either portions of or the entire manuscript. However, the critical risks I venture in this study are my sole responsibility. The faculty of the Graduate English Program at Rutgers University, New Brunswick, have been generous in their support, especially George Levine, Richard Poirier, Barry Qualls, Carol Smith, and Nancy Sommers. I am deeply grateful to Walter Bezanson, in whose graduate seminar I first sailed the seas of Melville scholarship and learned an appreciation for the richness of Melville's imagination. To the Berkshire Athenaeum and the New York Public Library I am grateful for permission to quote from their holdings. I am also indebted to Ellen Graham and Carl Rosen of Yale University Press.

An earlier version of Chapter 4 appeared in *Studies in the Novel* 18 (1986):157–76.

My greatest debt is to my wife, Susan Danoff. My conversations with her often clarified what I was learning from my research, and the manuscript has benefited from her editorial skill. Her presence in my life has made this project possible.

Introduction: Primal Ground

Saw a burial. . . . Nearby, saw a woman over a new
grave— . . . Such abandonment of misery! Called
to the dead, put her head down as close to it as
possible. . . . —"Why don't you speak to me?
My God!—It is I!" . . . . All deaf—so much for
consolation. —This woman & her cries haunt me
horribly.

Herman Melville, *Journal of a Visit to Europe
and the Levant*

This book traces the emergence of unresolved grief in Herman
Melville's fiction. By examining texts from *Typee* to *Pierre,* I argue
that the conflicting images of Allan Melvill in his wife Maria's Calvinist and genteel style of bereavement crucially influenced the outcome of Melville's adolescent mourning. To make this case, I study
the social history of mourning in antebellum America and bring to
bear on Melville's life and art recent findings in the psychology,
sociology, and anthropology of mourning.

While earlier studies of Melville have drawn attention to his
"search for the father," I frame this quest in terms of blocked mourning.[1] My case is built out of an analysis not only of Melville's fiction
but also of archival materials—family letters and journals—including the recently discovered group of letters from Melville's mother to
her daughter Augusta. To understand the values and concerns relat-

ed to mourning reflected both in Melville's fiction and in the family documents, I place them in the context of antebellum attitudes to bereavement and in relation to the life histories of significant cultural figures in the period.

I argue that a double bind characterized Victorian American mourning rituals, which at once prolonged the process of mourning and blocked the expression of feeling in bereavement. The antebellum mourner suffering from deep conflicts toward the dead found that his or her culture forbade a public expression of these negative feelings. Instead, conflicts were driven underground, thus setting the scene for lifelong chronic grief, in which the mourner often performed a pathological identification with significant behavior of the deceased, especially a last illness.

Studies of antebellum mourning customs, as well as recent examinations of our own cultural styles of handling grief, stress the role of gender. As one student of antebellum mourning observes, "Judging from surviving artifacts and from the literature, the burden of mourning fell primarily on women."[2] The cultural rules governing the social performance of the nineteenth-century mourner—length of bereavement, style of dress, and manner of comportment—were largely addressed to the female mourner, who served as a public symbol of restrained grief. My book demonstrates that Melville largely obeys the cultural codes which assign women the social symbolization of grief: his representations of women are often mourning figures shaped by the genteel codes prohibiting excessive grief. Further, when his male figures express a sense of bereavement, they are also often feminized.

I approach the role of delayed mourning in Melville's art from a psychological as well as a social perspective. Recent studies of bereavement reveal that the surviving spouse's conflicted grief can critically shape the outcome of a child's mourning, as I discuss in Chapter 1. In closely analyzing Melville's fiction, I argue that the influence of maternal bereavement on his adolescent grief affected his lifelong inability to finish mourning for his father. To a greater extent than do previous studies of Melville, I analyze the influence on his art of his relationship with his mother.[3] In arguing that he internalized her cultural style of bereavement, I make the case that Melville participates more deeply in Victorian American values than earlier studies imply. I thus stage Melville's resistance to social codes as an inner as well as an outer conflict.

Although I argue for the powerful role of Melville's buried griefs in his early fiction—*Typee* through *White-Jacket*—the conflicts of grief and the influence of maternal bereavement starkly emerge first in *Moby-Dick* and then more visibly in *Pierre*. This book concludes with *Pierre* because in it Melville comes closest to openly confronting the impact of his mother's bereavement on his own grief. The progress Melville's fiction makes toward the resolution of these conflicts involves his growing recognition of the way social codes shape feeling. From the outset of his career, his social consciousness is highly developed; however, as he writes more deeply into both himself and his time, his fiction shows an intensified recognition of the relationship between private griefs and social grievances.

While Melville did not achieve anything more than momentary resolutions of his chronic grief in his fiction—and I am careful not to reduce the richness of his art to grief work—the novels suggest that he increasingly came to implicate the form of the novel itself and the expectations of his culture's publishers, reviewers, and readers in the social control of feeling. Both *Pierre* and *Moby-Dick* seem to stand beside themselves, while denying and poking fun at their own authenticity as effective vehicles for exploring psychosocial realities. Late in the 1850s, this recognition bitterly characterizes what one critic calls Melville's "quarrel with fiction."[4] Melville's diminished artistic energies after *Pierre* have a great deal to do with the way his fiction had brought the conflicts of grief to consciousness. It is worth keeping in mind, as well, that the period I am considering in Melville's artistic life—certainly his richest period, notwithstanding the important post-*Pierre* texts—only lasted seven years, 1845 to 1851.

I have also sought to draw attention to the ways in which Melville's mourning moves beyond a pathological manifestation in his art.

Throughout his work, the moments when his unresolved grief surfaces are often those textual sites in which he radically critiques social codes. To take just one example, *Redburn's* most effective attacks on commerce and class emerge in relation to the question of grief. Of the steerage passengers devastated by a fever, caused by the inhuman conditions aboard ship, Redburn observes, "But those who had lost fathers, husbands, wives, or children, needed no crape, to reveal to others, who they were. Hard and bitter indeed was their lot; for with the poor and desolate, grief is no indulgence of mere sentiment, however sincere, but a gnawing reality, that eats into their vital beings" (*Redburn*, 290).

While working from an interdisciplinary approach, I have also tried to build into my readings a sensitivity to the metacritical concerns raised by crossing disciplinary boundaries. What sorts of critical issues, for instance, are raised by reading Melville's fiction against the backdrop of social codes that shaped feeling in the period? How do these discursive codes play through his fiction? To what extent does he critique and resist them, and in what ways does he remain unaware of their influence on his imagination? What are the critical problems raised by a reading which seeks to understand a work of art in relation to the culture in which it was produced? In essence, I have sought to remain highly conscious of the methodological problems involved in the critical and biographical texts I construct.

"What may be most insistent in a modern text," Dominick La Capra has argued, "is the way it challenges one or most of its contexts." As a precursor of American modernism, Melville's work bears out La Capra's contention that "The text may . . . be seen not only to exemplify discursive practices or ideologies in a relatively straightforward way but also to engage in processes that, whether consciously or not, render them problematic." Instead of invoking the contextual evidence I have gathered here as a solution to the complexities of the role of mourning in Melville's art, I regard this material as itself a problematic text but one that interacts revealingly with Melville's life and work. However, as Barbara Johnson observes of the text/context problem, "The 'inside' of a text is no more a 'given' than the 'outside,' and what is inside the text is not necessarily accessible to the reader without philological, historical, biographical, etc., research."[5]

In Chapter 1 Melville is situated both in relation to his culture's dominant discourses of loss and with respect to recent mourning theory. In a radical revision of the biographical text, I locate Maria Melville's hitherto marginalized influence at the center of the tensions in Melville's art. Chapter 2 explores Tommo's fascination with Typee mourning customs from the perspective of anthropological models of metaphor proposed by Victor Turner and Mary Douglas. While *Typee* at times seems to be set in a rural cemetery, *Mardi*'s vistas evoke the "water journeys and islandlike afterworlds" anthropologist Arnold Van Gennep found characteristic of funeral symbolism.[6] Chapter 3 argues that *Mardi*'s jeremiad against Manifest Destiny relates to what Babbalanja obsessively returns to throughout the narrative: the nature of the afterlife. On a more intimate level, I analyze the babbling philosopher—Babb-*alan*-ja—as the internalization of the bereaved image of Allan Melvill that Maria Melville deposited in her son's youthful consciousness.

Chapter 4 examines *Redburn*'s deepening insight into the connection between oppressive social values and the inability to complete grief. The St. Bury Blade, Harry Bolton, and the tyrannical sailor, Jackson, each express different aspects of Melville's conflicted mourning. Chapter 5 explores in *White-Jacket* the man-of-war world, in which Melville's father fell, that elicits Melville's powerful indictment for cutting him off from an authentic bereavement. Through each of these novels' complex social personae, Melville stages the conflicts between Christian pieties and social radicalism which illuminate his imagination's conditioning by the contradictory images of his father that Maria Melville's grief bequeathed to him.

Chapter 6 reads *Moby-Dick* as Melville's attempt to rewrite the memory of his father's deathbed mania. In his sane madness, Ahab unites the failed paternal model with the queenly personality of both Lady Macbeth and Maria Melville. At the peak of Melville's confi-

dence in his imaginative powers, he renders his art fluid to his strongest fantasies and to a deep need to work through conflicted grief.
Moby-Dick parries Melville's disruptive grief both by allowing Queequeg—whose name hints at the queenly personality kept on the
novel's margins—to get up from his deathbed so that his coffin life-
buoy can snatch Ishmael from the vortex left in the *Pequod's* wake
and by having the *Rachel* rescue Ishmael, instead of the twelve-year-
old son (Melville's age when his father died) for whom its captain
searches.

Ishmael reveals himself to be conditioned by the ideology that
forbids the public expression of excessive grief. In his parlor theater of
mourning, the side of Ishmael implicated in genteel codes must label
the bereaved whale hunter a monomaniac. This side of Ishmael keeps
Ahab's aggrieved rage within cultural bounds by staging it within
melodramatic genres; he must give Crazy Ahab a queenly personality
because of the cultural rules that burden women with publicly symbolizing grief. Nevertheless, Ahab's transgressive grief subverts Ishmael's genteel narrative strategies. In the imagery of dismemberment
that the Harvard Study of Bereavement finds characteristic of male
expressions of grief, Melville carves out on Ahab's body the rage of
loss his culture kept on the margins of its public discourses.[7]

Chapter 7 analyzes the paradoxical way in which *Pierre* dramatizes
Melville's conflicted grief in his most distorted and complexly mixed,
experimental style. I argue that *Pierre* appropriates and transforms the
early nineteenth-century needlepoint mourning art practiced by
Maria Melville. This art represents a "classically restrained mourning
figure" against the background of a weeping willow or a pine, and a
burial urn.[8] The mournful and gothically wild Isabel steps out of this
handcrafted funerary rite and leads Pierre into a self-destructive revival of grief for his father. In the novel's self-derisive style, Melville
locates his narrative voice in the text of maternal desire into which
he had been sewn by the blurring of the conflicts of his grief into those
of his mother's bereavement. As he, like the mutilated Enceladus,
batters against desire entangled in chronic grief, *Pierre* comes twist-
edly alive to Melville's deepest conflicts.

In the Afterword, I theorize that we gain a rich perspective on the conflicts of mourning by viewing them in terms of Victor Turner's model of ritual as a social process.[9] In a brief analysis of the ritual of mourning in *Billy Budd*, I argue that Melville's art partially transforms the conflicts of his grief into a social critique of cultural textuality in Victorian America.

Abbreviations

BA Melville Collection in the Berkshire Athenaeum, Pittsfield, Massachusetts.

BB *Billy-Budd (An Inside Narrative)*. Eds. Harrison Hayford and Merton Sealts.

BP *Battle-Pieces and Aspects of War*. Ed. Sidney Kaplan.

C *Clarel: A Poem and a Pilgrimage in the Holy Land*. Ed. Walter Bezanson.

CM *The Confidence-Man: His Masquerade*. Ed. Elizabeth S. Foster.

CP *Collected Poems of Herman Melville*. Ed. Howard P. Vincent.

GLA Gansevoort-Lansing Addition, Rare Books and Manuscripts Division, The New York Public Library, Astor, Lenox and Tilden Foundations.

GLC Gansevoort-Lansing Collection, Rare Books and Manuscripts Division, The New York Public Library, Astor, Lennox and Tilden Foundations.

HHM "Hawthorne and His Mosses" in *Moby-Dick*. Eds. Harrison Hayford and Hershel Parker.

IP *Israel Potter: His Fifty Years of Exile*.

L *Melville's Letters*. Eds. Merrell Davis and William Gilman.

M *Mardi and A Voyage Thither*. Eds. Harrison Hayford et al.

MD *Moby-Dick*. Eds. Harrison Hayford and Hershel Parker.

P *Pierre, or, The Ambiguities*. Eds. Harrison Hayford et al.

R *Redburn*. Eds. Harrison Hayford et al.

T *Typee*. Eds. Harrison Hayford, et al.

WJ *White-Jacket, or, The World in a Man-of-War*. Eds. Harrison Hayford et al.

CHAPTER ONE

The House of Mourning: Melville in His Culture

Great geniuses are parts of the times; they
themselves are the times; and possess a
correspondent coloring.
Melville, "Hawthorne and His Mosses"

In these flashing revelations of grief's wonderful fire,
we see all things as they are.
Melville, *Pierre, or, The Ambiguities*

In his journal of July 16, 1843, Melville's younger brother, Allan,
reflected upon the traumatic loss of their father: "I lost my father. Of
my father I have only a faint recollection. I can but bring him to my
mind as associated with three or four reminiscences. Of his general
appearance and character I remember nothing. This now appears
singular to me I being over nine when this beloved parent died."[1]

For Herman, who was twelve when his father died, we have to turn
to his fiction for evidence of the enduring impact of this loss: "But I
must not think of those delightful days, before my father became a
bankrupt, and died, and we removed from the city; for when I think
of those days, something rises up in my throat and almost strangles
me" (R, 36).

Throughout Melville's work, the threatening hand of grief continues to disrupt recollection. In *White-Jacket*, as the protagonist

1

perches aloft, thinking of "things past," his sense of the present slips away and his disturbing memory nearly causes him to lose his balance, until consciousness seizes him "something like a choking hand at [his] throat" (*WJ*, 77). At the climax of *Moby-Dick*, Melville's next novel, just before Ahab strangles himself on his own whaleline, he exclaims, "Oh, now I feel my topmost greatness lies in my topmost grief!" (*MD*, 468). Almost forty years later, as Melville neared his own death, he imagines Billy Budd's "convulsed tongue-tie" when Billy is accused of mutiny in the presence of the fatherly Vere (*BB*, 98).[2]

On January 28, 1832, after more than two weeks of intermittent mania, Allan Melvill died. In his wake, he left behind eight children, a patrician wife, and staggering debts. After a creditor called in his note, Allan, who had overextended not only his own resources but also those of his relatives, lost his import business and declared bankruptcy. While attempting to develop a coat and cap factory in Albany, Allan once more overreached himself. He suffered a psychic and physical collapse after trekking across a frozen Hudson River in subzero temperatures. The ensuing scenario must have been a frightening one for his family. His brother-in-law, Peter Gansevoort, paints the scene:

> He was unwell . . . But persisted in giving attention to his business— He devoted himself so closely and assiduously, as to produce a state of excitement, which in a great measure robbed him of his sleep. It is but a few days since he yielded to the wishes of his friends and remained at home. The excitement could not be allayed and yesterday he occasionally manifested an alienation of mind. Last night he became much worse—and today he presents the melancholy spectacle of a deranged man.

The "heart-rending intelligence" was intensified when the attending physicians advised Allan's brother Thomas that if their patient survived "he would live, *a Maniac!*"[3]

In *Pierre*, Melville's strange parody of sentimental fiction, the memory of Allan's mania seems blasphemously brought before the public eye. But the terror of the scene dissolves in sentimental retelling: "His father had died of a fever; and, as is not uncommon in such maladies, toward his end, he at intervals lowly wandered in his mind" (*P*, 70). Little Pierre Glendinning hovers by his father's deathbed and listens to his "strange, plaintive, infinitely pitiable, low voice" (*P*, 70). As the shouts of the maniac turn into hushed tones and the mania itself becomes a fever, Melville indicates one strategy for living with the memory of his father's deathbed mania: it becomes something not uncommon in a fever—the deranged shouts become a recollection of how Allan lowly wandered in his mind. In the context of the novel, the memory of Allan's deathbed ravings come to life in the character of Mr. Glendinning's putative, illegitimate daughter, the gothically deranged Isabel, who grew up, if her memory can be trusted, in an insane asylum. Her "mournful face" blurs into the chair-portrait of Pierre's father: "It was loathsome to him, that in the smiling and ambiguous portrait, her sweet mournful image should be so sinisterly becrooked, bemixed, and mutilated to him" (*P*, 197). As the novel unfolds, it becomes apparent that Isabel personifies Pierre's grief for his father, disruptively distorting his experience of both his sexuality and his creative performance. The "death-like beauty" of Isabel's face ushers us into the complexities of Pierre's revived grief (*P*, 112).

Although *Pierre* most intensely dramatizes Melville's buried griefs, throughout his work he crafts rites of bereavement to authenticate the mourning obstructed by social, familial, and emotional forces. While this artistic work of mourning takes complex forms, it centrally attempts to transform the conventions of the cultural discourses in which Melville worked by opening up his art to the conflicts of his disruptive grief. Melville's stylistic experimentation relates to the influence of an obstructed but urgent grief. To render his voice fluid to the conflicts that surrounded the memory of his father, he tried to break through both the forms of Victorian American fiction and the ideologies implicit in them.[4]

His struggle with grief often takes the form of denial. However, his art transforms into rich artistic life the *splitting* which Freud found characteristic of denial. Splitting underlies Melville's susceptibility, long remarked on by his critics, to shift artistic intention in mid-stream of the creative process. *Typee* ruptures its protagonist's response to Marquesan culture into celebration of its free pliant figures and terror of its cannibal urges. In *Mardi*, Melville's performance fractures into romance and political allegory; Ahab and Ishmael fissure *Moby-Dick*'s text; after Melville, midway in the novel, suddenly transforms his protagonist into a serious writer, *Pierre* splits into parody of romance and jeremiad at the strictures imposed on the American writer; in its second half, *The Confidence-Man* problematically changes into the Cosmopolitan's tale. Underlying both the appearance and the reality of Melville's fractured texts is his grief, which links the fissures in his sense of self with the social rifts that intensified in his lifetime, particularly class, sexual, and political tensions.[5]

A thematic reading of Melville must qualify its findings by acknowledging that Melville's fictive voices resist interpretation. Charles Feidelson challenges us to do justice to "the complicated being who moves through the language" of Melville's writing. At times Melville sounds like a radically subversive writer, but he often does so while speaking out of the most conventional of cultural poses. While at his peak, he wrote Hawthorne, "Let us speak, though we show all our faults and weaknesses,—for it is a sign of strength to be weak, to know it, and out with it—not in [a] set way and ostentatiously, though, but incidentally and without premeditation. — But I am falling into my old foible—preaching" (letter of June 29, 1851, *L*, 132). Compare this rhetoric to that of the prig author of *The Young Man's Own Book*, which Melville cites knowledgeably in *Typee*. To hide our "singularity," the etiquette expert advises, would reveal our "weak and pusillanimous temper." A man passes "the whole of his life in opposition to his own understanding, and dare[s] not to be what he thinks he ought to be, in the order of nature." The Melville we have to allow for rebelliously paraded about London in an ostentatious green coat, until he found it played "the devil with my respectability here," and then went out and bought a "Paletot" (*L*, 106 n. 3). Whether Melville pulls our leg in a particular passage, whether he really identifies with the values of Christian gentility he often voices, or whether he manages to do both simultaneously becomes problematic. "With no man do I stand upon any etiquette or ceremony," he boldly writes Hawthorne but then primly adds, "except the Christian ones of charity and honesty" (letter of June 1[?], 1851, L, 126).[6]

That Melville could be speaking in Bakhtinian, double-voiced discourse, in which his inner rebelliousness and his partial allegiance to his culture's codes are at war, complicates any attempt to read authentic expression of emotion in his work.[7] Add to this difficulty of tone what is known about Melville's tailoring of his texts out of multifarious sources, from high to low culture, and some idea of the challenge of voice in Melville can be gleaned. His work demands a thorough examination of the problematic social identity of each of his artfully composed narrative personae.

From the perspective of John Bowlby's revision of Freudian mourning theory, the semiotics of grief in Melville's writing suggests signs of *disordered mourning:* an unresolved experience of bereavement that can lie dormant and revive periodically throughout one's life.[8] According to most mourning theorists, grief becomes *frozen,* or blocked, when one feels a deep ambivalence to the dead. Until the mourner works through the conflicts he or she feels toward the deceased, a full cathartic grief reaction cannot occur. Instead, grief surfaces when the environment or a psychic crisis triggers off long-harbored ambivalent feelings toward the dead.

Commenting on Melville's response to his father's death, one recent scholar observes, "There is agreement that Melville sustained a trauma that he did not overcome by the normal processes of grieving and in the span of time that those processes usually require." Yet the debates among mourning theorists on whether or not the traumas of grief can, or even should, be overcome immediately renders this statement problematic. One widow, the subject of a study on the processes of grief, wisely observes, "Mourning never ends: only as time goes on it erupts less frequently." Bowlby concurs: "an occasional recurrence of active grieving, especially when some event reminds the bereaved of her loss, is the rule."⁹

Recent studies of mourning recognize the complexity and long duration of grief; because it is such a new field, thanatology has yet to produce the studies needed to analyze the tenuous line between normal and pathological mourning. Subtle theorists now argue that the same processes underly normal and disordered mourning. Bowlby identifies the phases of grief in terms of numbness or shock, anger, despair, guilt, yearning and searching, disorganization and re-organization.[10] The model of grief grows complex with the clinical evidence which shows that mourners can experience the phases in hybrid forms: they can leapfrog earlier phases, regress into earlier ones, or experience different emotions simultaneously. In addition, mourning research indicates that cultural codes, especially gender, play a significant role in the fate of grief. In attempting to describe the role of mourning in Melville's fiction, therefore, one must not impose a rigid grid of immutable phases of grief over the complex fluidity of the works' often displaced expressions of bereavement. One must allow for a dialectical process in which Melville's art revises mourning theory both through its subtle insight into the cultural dimensions of emotional processes and through the way Melville's radical intelligence can alert us to our own culture-bound theoretical premises.

Whether one works from the Freudian paradigm of the decathection of or disinvestment of energy in memories of the dead, which comprises what the early Freud called *grief work;* whether one follows Bowlby's information-processing approach, in which patterns of familial development are studied to determine the social texts through which the mourner reads his grief; or whether one applies Paul C. Rosenblatt's reminder theory, which accounts for revived episodes of grief throughout the life cycle by identifying experiential triggers— from the perspective of any theory of mourning,[11] Melville's fluid sense of the life cycle challenges tidy conceptualization.

> There is no steady unretracing progress in this life; we do not advance through fixed gradations, and at the last one pause: —through infan-

cy's unconscious spell, boyhood's thoughtless faith, adolescence' doubt (the common doom), then scepticism, then disbelief, resting at last in manhood's pondering repose of If. But once gone through, we trace the round again; and are infants, boys, and men, and Ifs eternally. (MD, 406)

While for Ishmael memories of the dead seem potentially revivable in bewildering permutations, Melville makes things more difficult for mourning theorists by claiming, "Evil and good they braided play / Into one cord" (C, 418–19). The object relations theory of psycho-analysis supposes that mourning can be finished once the positive internalizations of the deceased are separated from the negative ones. Melville's insight into the possible fusion of opposites offers a for-midable challenge to this theory.

Mourning theory posits that grief becomes disordered when one gets stuck in a particular phase of bereavement, when environmental conditions do not support the expression of the disruptive emotions of mourning, when the conflicts with the deceased are too intense to be confronted openly, and when the surviving parent negatively influences the outcome of a child's grief. Melville's representation of grief as a strangling hand, for example, indicates that his mourning has distorted into "unconscious reproach against the lost person combined with conscious and often unremitting self-reproach."[12] Grief cuts off speech in Melville's protagonists because of the socially unacceptable feelings—especially the anger—it would express. When his characters do melodramatically vent their rage, as is the case with Annatoo, Jackson, Ahab, Pierre, and Clarel's Mortmain and Ungar, Melville writes their death into his cultural script.

> Whatever we seek to do, of our own free will, a
> Dead Man's icy hand obstructs us!
> Holgrave, in Hawthorne's *The House of Seven Gables*

While Bowlby's revision of Freud may be startling news in a field that had taken early Freudian theory—with its implicit notion that normal grief can be worked through within one or two years—as its basis, for many of Melville's contemporaries the durable quality of grief was a given. Orville Dewey, the retired Unitarian minister who in 1850 baptized Melville's children in Pittsfield, eloquently observes, "The world is filled with the voices of the dead. They speak . . . from the private history of our own experiences. They speak to us in a thousand remembrances, in a thousand incidents, events, associations. . . . Though they are invisible, yet life is filled with their presence. . . . Go where we will, the dead are with us." Dewey writes, "One may know the house where death has set his mark long after the time. Traces are left in its affections that are never worn off."13

Melville's fellow literary Young Americans register a sharp protest against what they perceive to be the encroachments of industrial life on private emotion. In his "Tickets for Greenwood," Cornelius Mathews responds acerbically to a public advertisement for stock in a rural cemetery: "We take stock in a graveyard as we do in banks and railway schemes. . . . Hostile systems contend for our living bodies, and we are buried by corporations." In "The Solemn Vendue," Mathews satirizes the commercialization of funerary customs by poking fun at a scam for selling graves in New York City. His "The UnRest of the Age" offers a hyperbolic look at loss: "Ours is the age of suicide and mysterious disappearance." For him, "The truth is custom and social usage sit hard upon men; and they strive to escape them by every possible device and self-delusion." In a passage that foreshadows *Pierre*, Mathews laments,

> Insanity, in many cases—suicide—and other terrible acts of desperation, seem to us the rebellious outbreaks of a nature wronged and tormented by the iron condition in which it is placed. Men know not what deep, overwhelming injustice they do to themselves in neglecting or disdaining the imagination. Slighted or kept under, it proves the most deadly foe of all the human powers, and bodies forth instantly, in vindication of itself, a hell gloomier than Dante's.

For Evert Duyckinck, Melville's intermittent, close associate throughout his career, "Modern society is as ruthless and exacting as an old-fashioned parent in the suppression of weakness and tears. It has no sympathy with sorrow or melancholy; all its cry is action, action; let every thing be onward and successful."[14]

Mourning, mid-nineteenth-century commentators suggest, had become appropriated by the discourse of the age's commercial spirit. In the anonymous parodic sketch "The House of Mourning," we are ushered into a mourning specialty shop's Intermediate Sorrow department, where we are offered a fabric called Settled Grief. The shopman advises his genteel customers that " 'mourning ought not to last forever.' " The Lady scolds her sardonic husband, "what do you know about fashionable afflictions?' " And he retorts, " 'a dry cry is the genteel thing.' " By century's end, A *History of Mourning* can parade in its pages gala funerals with detailed information on who wore what and never once mention the emotion of the bereaved. We are hardly surprised to discover in its last chapter that this is history as commissioned by Jay's London General Mourning Warehouse, unembarrassedly puffing its patron. However, Jay's hack history unwittingly summarizes the ideological forces reshaping the experience of grief: "Private emotion in modern times, like everything else, has been greatly altered and modified, to suit an age of rapid transit and travel."[15]

Mathews and Duyckinck responded to social forces that sought, finally, to control death. As both Ann Douglas and Karen Halttunen have demonstrated, Victorian Americans were obsessed with regulating their response to death. Genteel Christian ideology transformed anguished Calvinistic uncertainties about election into fussy interior decoration of a prospective heavenly home. Death became a halfway house, a bed for the night, on the road to millennialist expectations of rebirth. As a kind of sleep, death no longer seemed quite so mysterious and foreboding. Because of this softening attitude to death, the line between the living and the dead blurred. "The boundaries which divide Life and Death are at best shadowy and vague," Poe's narrator notes in "The Premature Burial." Patents for devices that would open coffins from within, or Rube Goldberg coffins with air-tubes and bells, indicate that Poe's narrator was not alone in his anxiety about being buried alive. Anthropologists have speculated that funerary rites function to clearly demarcate life from death, in order to appease the fears of the mourner that the dead may return. When the bereaved are uncertain of where life shades off into death, they risk an intensification of anxiety and guilt that the dead may punish them for failing to fulfill their responsibilities to them. The cultural fantasy of a death indistinguishable from life thus con-tributed to predisposing the American imagination to disruptive, unresolved grief.[16]

Finding Calvinist mourning customs unsatisfying after the death in 1813 of both his "stern and retributive" grandfather, who had, to some extent, been his surrogate father, and a friend's bride, William Cullen Bryant began to write death poetry. In the antebellum era's best known poem, "Thanatopsis," he closes with the lines, "approach thy death / Like one who arranges the drapery of his couch / About him and lies down to pleasant dreams." Attempting to kill the force of his grief and cover up his conflicted feelings toward his grandfather by deploying an organicist Romantic outlook, Bryant, who grew up across from a graveyard, participated in the burgeoning ideology that sought to deny what Elisabeth Kübler-Ross calls the "unfinished business," especially the conflicts, the mourner must work through with the dying and the dead to finish his or her grief. Bryant influ-enced American life through his poetry and as editor of the New York Evening Post from 1829 to 1878. He helped shape the public imagina-tion of death by eliminating the black borders around newspaper columns, which commemorated an important figure's death. While Bryant can be viewed as sensibly reacting to the excesses of Victorian mourning customs, his ameliorative work overcompensates; it lays the groundwork for what in our century has been called "the dying of death."[17]

Preaching to weekly audiences in excess of twenty-five hundred from his pulpit in Plymouth Congregational Church, Brooklyn, from 1847 to 1887, Henry Ward Beecher advised his parishioners to "talk with death as friend talketh with friend." Echoing Bryant's poetry, Beecher moved out of a gloomy childhood exposure to Calvinism and asked, "Do we call it dying when the bud bursts into flower?" Although his benevolent image was tarnished by Victoria Woodhull's publicization of his putative affair with Mrs. Tilton in 1874, his flower funeral in 1887 symbolized the softening attitude to death, if not to morals, he popularized. His successor, Lyman Abbot, only extended Beecher's ideology, when a title of one of his articles proclaimed, "There Are No Dead."

"Oh, the grave!" Washington Irving pietistically exclaims in a piece from *The Sketch Book* anthologized in *The Mourner's Gift* "—it buries every sorrow—covers every defect—extinguishes every resentment!" In 1809 his nineteen-year-old fiancee, Matilda Hoffman, died, and Irving found himself prone to what he called a "morbid feeling," which plunged him into severe depressions that would now be called chronic grief. In 1817, as he mused on "the agony of her death, the seraphic years of her blessedness," he wrote, "I feel like one withered up & blighted—broken heart is like a desert wherein can flourish no green thing—The romance of life is past." In his mourning manual piece, "Strewing Flowers Upon Graves," Irving fantasizes a power to control his disruptive grief: "The sorrow for the dead is the only sorrow from which we refuse to be divorced . . . this wound we consider it a duty to keep open." But his difficulties in resolving his grief begin to surface even as he poses in the "fashionable affliction"; in mourning, he insists, "truly spiritual affection rises purified from every sensual desire."[18]

Recent studies of Hawthorne, Emerson, Thoreau, and Whitman offer insight into their grief work. Disordered mourning plays an important role in motivating the formative influence prominent Victorian Americans exert on American cultural life. Leading innovators in education, Horace Mann and Catharine Beecher, took up their life's work after the loss of, respectively, a bride and a fiancée. Mann experienced *anniversary reactions*, or disruptive manifestations of grief during the time of year when his loss had been suffered. The severity of these attacks and the depressiveness they imbued caused him to renounce his political ambitions and attempt to revitalize himself through involvement in educational reform. After the loss of

her fiancée, Catharine Beecher suffered from the acute restlessness
characteristic of conflicted grief, which both drove her on to champion the cause of training and placing women in education and to
leave most of her projects unfinished.[19]

The preeminent chronic griever of the period was also its most
prominent symbolic figure, Queen Victoria. For twenty-two years
after Prince Albert's death, Victoria had his clothes laid out each
evening with hot water and a clean towel. Immediately after his
death, she had his room carefully photographed, hung his wreath-
draped portrait over his empty pillow, slept with his nightshirt in her
arms, and had a plaster cast made of his hand, which she kept within
reach by her bedside. Like many mourners, Victoria feared that her
intense grief would drive her insane. Her lethargic depression after
Albert's death has been linked to both her deep dependence on him
and to her anger at his "desertion" of her. In her conflicted grief, she
prayed for her own death. Behind her disordered mourning echoes
Albert's "Victorian" advice to her: "Your great task in life is to
control your feelings."[20]

Radical psychoanalyst Joel Kovel speculates that "different historical epochs will select different pathologies wherein their characteristic form of domination may be reproduced on intrapsychic soil."
Initially it may seem strange to consider conflicted mourning as a
form of domination, but considering the rhetoric and the life histories surveyed above, one begins to see how the attempt to control
death translated into rigid formalization of emotional response,
which prolongs mourning while blocking feeling. Although many of
the figures touched upon both seem to impose this form of domination on themselves and to inflict their pathology on their culture,
when looked at in more detail their regulatory attitude to mourning
becomes symptomatic of more powerful social constraints which give
shape to their identities. One returns to Mathews's jeremiad against
capitalism: "hostile systems contend for our living bodies." One
needs to direct attention, Raymond Williams has incisively argued,
at "how particular social orders . . . select certain faculties and prac-

depraved Ahab, Maria wrote Augusta: " 'In the midst of life we are in death,' may all have wisdom to realize this awful truth, to live prepared to die. "[29] One imagines poor Augusta acting on the conflicting maternal instructions: freeing up her stiff and constrained manners, cavorting in the country, and singing happily of the death-in-life Maria's polyphonic discourse intoned. Out of similar tensions, Melville fashioned *Moby-Dick*'s double-voiced discourse: the life-affirming exhilarations of Ishmael and Ahab's death-obsessed rant.

According to Calvinist doctrine, as T. Walter Herbert points out, Allan's manic end portended his damnation.[30] But the text of grief Maria assembled in her bible indicates that she did not read his death in such a doctrinaire way. "God moves in misterous way," she instead hoped. "The Unpardonable Sin" sketch further suggests that she may have viewed Allan in terms of Mr. L.'s repentance from his moody tempest. Allan went in and out of delirium in his final weeks, but it is not known if his final moments were blissful. It seems probable that even if they were not Maria's family would have comforted her with a white lie.

The Mourner's Book: By a Lady anthologizes the "Account of H. More's Sister Sarah's Death," a good Christian's death, in which Sarah's "strong delirium" mixes with her blessings of Christ. We cannot assume, as Herbert does, that Allan's death was unequivocally viewed by Maria as a sign of his damnation, although she may well have fitfully entertained such notions. Late in life she did invoke the loss of Allan's "Christian example" on pointing "the way to heaven" for his children. Maria's response was probably close to the way that mourning manualist Francis Parkman describes handling a loved one's deathbed mania: "Have you known the light of reason extinguished; . . . the imagination darkened or presenting only images of despair. . . . Then you have known something of the sorrows by which the heart may be overwhelmed." Parkman focuses not on whether the delirium damned the loved one; rather, he addresses the anxieties of the mourner who wonders, "is it permitted to the Christian to yield to overwhelming grief. . . . And must there not be a criminal defect of faith and hope in yielding thus to heartbreaking sorrow?" Antebellum mourning, as Halttunen observes, shifted its focus from the dead to the mourner.[31]

Parkman also addresses the feelings of the child witnessing his parent's deathbed mania: "sad and unnatural reverse, because it violates the order of nature, here is a conscientious child put to shame and confusion by the unworthiness of a parent. These are pangs, only the sharper, because they are secret; in which, as the grief may not be uttered it cannot ask for solace." To Herman, Maria's decision to formally join the Dutch Reformed Church must have seemed a repudiation of his father's Unitarian values. It seems likely that the Melville boys refused to follow their mother and sisters into the Reformed faith because they wished to defend their father's memory, to keep alive their masculine role model. Further, the outcome of their grief must have been adversely influenced by gender codes that "would regard the tenderness of grief as unmanly weakness," in Parkman's words. They would have found little support for their grief's "shame and confusion" from the contradictions of Maria's mixed Calvinism or from the priggish, genteel Christian mourning customs that would have cautioned them not to "murmur" but to weep genteelly, if at all, on the "refuge and defence" of "'the Rock'" of religious piety.[32]

In short-circuiting the conflicts of her response to Allan's death, Maria could not have fully escaped the anger that the etiquette of grief sought to deny. Indeed, her renewal of Calvinist faith after Allan's death may have been motivated by her anger towards him. Calvinism's damnation of the deathbed maniac may have attracted Maria because of her bereaved rage toward her husband. Allan had not only abandoned her for death after his fall from prosperity, but he had gone through more than his share in his father's will and had drawn against Maria's legacy in her mother's estate. She still had capital to invest in the faltering coat and cap company Allan left behind, but she would have had difficulty reconciling Allan's Christian gentility with the details of his devious manipulation of capital in a fatal secret partnership scheme, if it came to her attention.[33]

What would have been more shocking still, had she gotten wind of it, was Allan's probable premarital sexual liaison. After Allan's death and his father's death later in the same year, two women appeared at Major Thomas Melvill's home to claim a share in Allan's putative legacy in his father's will. Judge Lemuel Shaw, the executor of the will and Melville's future father-in-law, queried Allan's brother, Thomas, Jr., several times about these claimants. Thomas could only recall "having paid some money to Mrs. B.—what the amount was, I do not remember," nor could he recollect if he was paying "what she may have claimed as her due." Thomas refers to the younger woman, Mrs. A. M. A., as "quite an interesting young person," and he feels "that it was most unfortunate she had not been brought up different." Apart from his mother and his sister Helen, who were on the scene, Thomas presumes that the other members of his family "are to this day . . . ignorant of her existence"; and were they to learn of it, he "had strong reasons" to believe that they would refuse her claims though they "might have means."[34] While there is no evidence to suggest that Maria learned of what appears to be the emergence of Allan's illegitimate offspring and her mother, the plot of *Pierre* suggests that the gossip reached Herman. In any event, the circumstances in which Allan's death left Maria provided enough tinder to spark the ambivalence of her grief.

Clinical psychoanalyst Vamik Volkan proposes that when a mourner experiences deep conflicts toward the dead, as a way of managing these painful feelings they can turn an inanimate object or a person close to them into a *linking object* or a *living linking object*: a mediatory zone on which the mourner seeks to control his negative feelings toward the dead. Volkan describes the mother as " 'depositing' in her child's self-system the concept that he is the dead person's representative." The child thus harbors within himself a "meeting ground" on which the mother's image of his father fuses with his other self-representations. In struggling to come to terms with the conflicts of his grief, the child confuses his own mourning with maternal bereavement. The linking object's "main function is to provide an illusion of being able to keep or 'kill' someone now dead with whom the ego perceives the mourner has unfinished business." When the child's obstructed grief disrupts his life in adulthood, he often enacts, literally or symbolically, the symptoms of his father's last illness. Identifying with the maternal image of his father, the child "becomes" him as he struggles, not only with his own memory of the dead but also with the conflicts of grief he has internalized from his mother's bereavement.

While Volkan's theory was formulated in relation to childhood grief, the biographical and textual evidence I present suggests that something comparable to the living linking object configuration was operative as a result of the influence of Melville's mother's grief on him. I extend and modify, then, Volkan's theory to account for an early adolescent blocked grief. Yet I do not minimize the conflicts, apart from those bequeathed to him by his mother's grief, Melville himself felt toward his deceased father. Losing one's father on the crest of adolescence certainly complicates the development of masculine identity. And given the economic hardship Allan's death caused his family, Herman surely felt his own anger toward Allan for the humiliation to which this exposed his family and himself, as well as for shrinking the horizon of educational and career options available to him. However, as Bowlby observes, "a substantial proportion of the special difficulties which children experience after the loss of a parent are a direct result of the effect that the loss has had on the surviving parent's behavior toward them."[35]

Writing in 1846 to Lemuel Shaw, Maria observed of her husband's death, "His gigantic efforts to overcome more than ordinary obstacles, his too long & continued exertion both bodily & mental—I have no doubt occasioned his early and melancholy death." In eerily similar terms, Maria describes the state of Herman's health in 1853: "this constant working of the brain, & excitement of the imagination, is wearing Herman out." Maria's anxiety must have been intensified by the way her eldest son, Gansevoort, died in 1846, after a nervous breakdown resembling the one which victimized his father. For her fears that her sons were liable to their father's tendencies, Maria would have found support in religious writers such as Orville

Dewey: "Now I suppose it is obvious, that if anything is hereditary; if influence, temperament, character, the very life-blood, flows down from sire to son; if good or bad name descends, then some evil must pass on along with the good . . . his children may inherit his passions, his vices, his diseases." It is in her letters to the child who bore Allan's name that we find the strongest evidence for Maria's tendency "to regard the child as the incarnation of the dead person."[36]

Allan, Jr., had a particularly hard time of it in the aftermath of his father's death. After the Panic of 1837 wiped out the family business entrusted to Gansevoort, a family council pulled the fourteen-year-old Allan out of school and placed him in his uncle Peter Gansevoort's law office. "I may have since had reason to feel dissatisfied with it [being pulled from school]," Allan writes in his journal; "I have waived the right—so to do," he adds in compressed syntax that suggests a censored anger. Sent to board with a distant cousin, Allan found himself living with "a very queer personage with a very suspicious disposition." Her house, which was "not in the most agreeable part of the city," intensified his consciousness of a fall from prosperity.

Allan's buried anger resurfaces in a falling out with his lawyer-uncle:

> when my Uncle wishing to rid himself of all further experiences & responsibility on my account to obtain his object—picked a quarrel with me & my language (which he provoked) not being as he thought the most respectful toward him, he refused to notice me when I afterwards begged his forgiveness if I had offended him—he told me I must leave him.

In what may have been the scenario Melville reversed in "Bartleby," Allan finds himself trapped between his family's dependence on his uncle and the rage his relative triggers off by a lack of sensitivity. Allan swallows his pride after escaping to New York City for a cooling off period, but upon his return he finds his uncle's "conduct toward me remaining the same. I finally packed up what articles I had in the office and without exchanging a word with his lordship I left him."

In commenting on how his family's relocation from Albany to Lansingburgh (in 1837, after the family business failed) had severed his mother's ties to her friends, Allan vents his bitterness and depressed anger: "But what ties are so sacred as not to be broken, or in some manner affected by the agency of gold silver."[37] Obliquely, Allan accuses his uncle of unloading him from his payroll. But what also seems likely is that Allan had overheard his mother's complaints about being forced to move because of their economic crisis.

Maria's letters to Allan indicate that her memory of her husband's overreaching informed her anxious concern about her son: "My dear son I fear you feel too strong a confidence in your own strength— Remember God will be, inquired of." In a mixed tone of depression and concern, Maria advises Allan to model his behavior on her own conflicts. Disappointed with him for failing to visit, she confesses to him that it is "on the whole rather dispiriting to us who have so little to cheer or enliven our reflections." After attempting to manipulate his guilt feelings by exposing him to her low spirits, she offers her depressed self as a source of strength to him:

> My dear Allan while you live ever remember your Mother with *deep enduring affection,* and when you find you are doing something which your inward Monitor Conscience disapproves let the recollection of your devoted Mother and her heartfelt advice come to strengthen your inward monitor, *crush not its voice* & you will triumph over temptations.[38]

Like his father, Allan manifests a tendency to get into debt. After his creditor harasses her for the fifty dollars her son has failed to repay, Maria sternly advises Allan: "be—economical get out of debt, & then you will feel like a true Man, without freedom from debt no man can honestly feel independent . . . Avoid all debt & pecuniary obligation of every kind as you would pestilence."[39] Clearly, Allan's behavior touches a raw nerve of memory. In her advice, Maria implicitly condemns Allan's namesake, who could not, in her terms, be a "true Man" because of his habitual business speculations with his relatives' funds. In attempting to parent Allan, Maria unwittingly superimposes her aggrieved image of her husband over her son's foibles; she thus imbues in the son the conflicts she feels toward his father.

But it was not just carelessness about money that worried Maria; she also fears for Allan's spiritual and emotional health.

> Allan you are from your Mother's anxious, loving, & observing eye, but remember there is a God above . . . who has promised to be a father to the Orphan if he put his full trust in him. Dear Allan kneel before him in the solitude of your Chamber & ask his direction in time of trouble . . . you will be strengthened to resist temptation, and *be a happier Lad than you have ever been—*.

The last phrase suggests that Maria has been concerned about Allan's troubled spirits. Paradoxically, she wishes to save him from the very depression she elsewhere inflicts on him. "Excuse a mother's anxiety & adopt her advice as you would save yourself from unhappiness," she counsels.[40]

Allan's sister Augusta offers a more revealing glimpse of his suscep-tibility to morbidity: "I hope dearest that you feel more quieted & less nervous, you do not know how it pained me to see you in that state, I would willingly have taken those feelings myself to have restored you to your former cheerfulness." Her anxiety indicates the extent of Allan's depressiveness: "do strive to calm your mind"; "it will do no good, to allow yourself to be so unhappy"; "there is no use in those gloomy introspections."[41] Quite possibly, the reason Allan could not recollect his father was that he managed the conflicts of his grief through his conversion into his mother's living linking object. By internalizing her sense of his father, Allan began to act out both his father's tendency to go into debt and the morbidity of his final weeks. In short, he could not form a mental image of his father because he had so closely identified with his mother's image of him.

The mixed messages and anxieties Maria's letters communicate could only have deepened the ambivalence of Allan's continuing work of mourning. In the same letter in which she asks Allan to kneel before his surrogate father, Maria begins her note by describing her desperate financial and emotional situation:

> This is the first of May and no prospect of my Rent being paid, if your Uncle Herman is in town go to him and in the most respectful manner tell him I am presented with bills daily and now my Rent in addition, I am troubled and my present duties, as entertainer of guests, is painfully increased by the necessary exertion requisite to keep up my spirits, and appear cheerful.

Later in the letter, in a tight-lipped tone, she writes that of "your Uncle Peter's indifference on last Sabbath Evening to your situation, I can have nothing to say." But quickly recovering herself, she adds, "May God forgive him as freely as I do, go up some day when your Uncle is not at home and ask Catherine for the ———— and hand-kerchief of Augustas."[42] If Allan were to follow her advice, he would both bury his anger at his uncle under Christian piety and slip like a thief into his house.

More irksome to Allan must have been his mother's encourage-ment to freely open up to her, while at the same time she seeks to turn him into her gentleman-puppet: "Bear in mind that to a devoted mother a Child can not write too much about himself and it is not considered Egotism or even felt as such when your letters are filled from one end to the other with your own thoughts . . . nothing relating to yourself can weary me or be disagreeable to me." While asking him to tell all, she also, seemingly, offers him her uncon-ditional, parental support: "send me a Catalogue of your re-sponsibilities, I shall look them over & perhaps be able to advise you let there be no reserve for it shall all be between you & me and no other person know aught about it." However, she also exacts a price for this offer of motherly guidance: "I forgot to mention that you mustn't speak about your Uncles strange condition nor ever allow yourself to speak of him when you are angry, when you meet him bow to him politely but do not speak unless he first speaks to you, bear him no ill will, make it a principle to forgive others as you wish God to for-give you."

In a series of postscripts, Maria's anxiety about Allan intensifies. She beseeches him "to resist the natural, depraved, & consequently sinful propensities of your nature." After urging him to tamp down feeling by cultivating the "Celestial power" of his reason, she urges her son:

> Make this your aim to be guided through the mazes of this ——— life by this Godlike power, or to be the slave of base passions and unrestrained desires, you have to choose between respectability, the sure reward, of virtuous conduct the approbation of your own conscience, & the contrary results arising from an unrestrained indulgence of your unhallowed impulses and wicked passions, Be wise in time & remember you are fatherless, excuse a mothers anxiety & adopt her advice.

Becoming more demandingly directive as she goes on, in a final addendum Maria now commands him: "Do not go out in the Evening with young men, but stay at home & study, go to bed early, be pure in mind, think finely, and remember that from 'the heart proceeds all evil & learn to keep your heart with all diligence.'"[43]

And how did Allan respond to Maria's concerned parenting? We can infer his reaction from a reply he makes to similar letters from Augusta. Of her "advicegiving epistle," he complains, "I detest them." On another occasion he teases her for sending him "a long, empty letter."[44] One also gathers what Allan's response must have been from the letter his brother Herman writes him parodying the long, empty letters of gentility. "My Dear Sergeant," Herman begins, "How is you? Am you very well," and on in this manner, concluding with the signature, "Tawney," colloquial for Indian or Negro (letter of Dec. 7, 1839, L, 17).

In a letter advising Allan to watch over the precarious health of his older brother, Gansevoort, Maria attributes her late husband's fatal recklessness about his health to her eldest son:

> Be with your Brother as much as possible he is weak, very thin and at present he has no—appetite, he is imprudent in exerting himself when he is unable to bear it, and in exposing himself to the changes of our variable climate without proper attention to his clothing, be attentive

to him my dear Son, and your advice may often be of service to him, cherish and activate an ardent warm attachment to him, you should be much to each other, you must by this time have discovered the cold heartlessness of the world, and this knowledge should make you cling more & stronger to your own flesh and blood, for children born of the same Parents are very, very near, and cannot be really happy when alienated from each other.[45]

Like her husband, whose fatal illness was caused by exposure, her son endangers his health by exposing himself to the climate without warm clothing. Not only are siblings very, very near in Maria's imagination but so are fathers and sons.

At seventeen Gansevoort was asked literally to assume his father's role. His paternal letters to his brothers and sisters indicate that he took this role seriously. For Maria, it must been a nightmarish repetition of her husband's fate when Gansevoort's business bankrupted and his health failed. His illness took the form of a strange leg ailment that incapacitated him for fifteen months. He was so enfeebled that Maria reports he had to be carried about the house. Herman apparently developed a similar leg problem while he was in the Marquesas. In *Typee*, his protagonist suffers a mysterious leg wound while hiding out after jumping ship and escaping to the interior of the island.[46]

As Gansevoort reenacts his father's tragedy, his leg pain can be said to undo his father's fatal walk across the Hudson. In Gansevoort's illness, as in Herman's first novel, the leg ailment symbolizes the conflict of disruptive, unfinished grief. It represents the boys' anger at losing their father while they were on the crest of a sexual awakening into manhood and their fear of turning out like him. In cutting their own legs out from under themselves, they symbolically gesture toward the loss of paternal support. From a classical psychoanalytic perspective, the pain that breaches their psyche's surface through their legs signifies an unresolved oedipal rite of passage and its residue of displaced castration anxiety, intensified by Allan's death during their adolescence.

However, the pattern of marred manhood in Melville, especially leg wounds or, in Ahab's case, the shearing off of a leg, takes on a richer social dimension in the light of the Harvard Study of Bereavement's finding that men describe their experience of bereavement in terms of dismemberment, whereas bereaved women often express their loss in images of abandonment. One must be sensitive to perspectivist issues when invoking a twentieth-century study of bereavement to account for the imagery of Victorian American loss. Yet the analysis of the Harvard Study of Bereavement of what underlies the mourner's gender-specific imagery argues for a continuity in social codes between the two eras. Twentieth-century male mourners viewed their deceased wives as having been "a necessary component of the functioning system they captained, whereas women more than men saw their spouse as providing protection and comfort." This is why men viewed their bereavement as the loss of "part of themselves," while women focused on "having been left" without economic and emotional support. Victorian America's ideology of separate spheres for men and women exacerbated these middle-class gender roles. Wives were rendered even more dependent on their husbands to captain—at least in an economic sense—their families. Nineteenth-century mourning manuals confirm that the gender roles of this period encouraged mourning imagery of male dismemberment and female abandonment.[47]

The roots of Maria's image of her husband and her deployment of it as a linking object stretches back into her relationship with her parents. Allan appeared in her life sometime between 1811 and 1813. Maria's father died in 1812, and by 1814 Allan and she were married. After her father's death, Maria's mother, Caty Gansevoort, nearly died. As the youngest child and the only daughter, Maria was especially close to her mother. Caty, though, became prone to depression after her husband died. Influenced by the conflicts of her mother's grief, Maria could have converted Allan into a living linking object to her father. This transformation would have been facilitated by the fact that Allan and Maria spent the first two years of their marriage in her mother's home. Trying to fill the shoes of Maria's father, who had been a revolutionary war hero and a powerful political and business figure, could have exacerbated Allan's proclivities for self-aggrandizement and so fueled his self-destructive quest for an ever greater business success.[48]

In mourning Allan's death, Maria probably revived the issues surrounding the loss of her father; with the conflicts of the two losses blurring together, Maria's grief must have intensified, and her anxieties about her sons must have sharpened.[49] Caught in the double bind of needing her sons to assume Allan's role as provider yet unconsciously fearing that they would replicate his tragedy, Maria imparted an anxiety to her sons that made their own grief work more complex.

The disruptive effect of Allan's death on the external conditions of his family prepared the ground for disordered mourning. After his death, Gansevoort and Herman were pulled out of school and put to work, the Melvilles moved to a new home, they were forced to economize until Gansevoort began to make his father's business profitable, and they even changed the spelling of their last name— adding an e to help Gansevoort dissociate himself from his father's poor business reputation. The economic instability Allan bequeathed to his family stayed with them for over a decade. After the Panic of 1837 wiped out Gansevoort's business, Maria was forced to move to nearby Lansingburgh to escape her creditors; Allan was sent out to board; Maria was threatened with the loss of her furniture; and at one point she threatened to break up her family. Herman came of age in a tense environment, one likely to freeze his full grief response until it could surface in a more supportive atmosphere. Perhaps it was only in his fiction that such a nurturing environment ever presented itself to him.[50]

Maria and Gansevoort's letters indicate a concern with the adolescent Herman's laziness, a condition that may suggest an underlying depressiveness. In his paternal role, Gansevoort, in 1840, worries over the twenty-one-year-old Herman's "laziness . . . which consists in an unwillingness to exert oneself in doing at a particular time that which ought to be done." Gansevoort implies that he sees Herman as a nascent writer by comparing Herman's lethargy to "that disinclination to perform the especial duty of the hour which so constantly beset one of the most industrious men of the age—Sir Walter Scott."[51]

Maria also worried over Herman's disinclination to rouse himself to action. After he shipped out to Liverpool, in 1839, she spoke with gratification of his aggressive behavior: "I have just written Herman a few lines, his conduct delights me, he has shown himself to possess an independent spirit not deficient in enterprise & willing to exert himself when necessary." Clearly, she perceives Herman in quite different terms than she does the overtly rebellious Allan, Jr., and the overreaching but fragile Gansevoort. To be a "true Man" Herman had to exert his independent spirit a little harder than he might have wanted to. Eight years later, she still views her now famous son as needing a prod to action. Gratified that he has become "at last convinced" he must use "personal exertions" to secure the office he seeks in Washington, she speaks of him in the tones of an etiquette manual: "It is worth a fortune to any man to understand this, and act it out, it is a lesson Herman has been long in learning."

The continuing commentary in early family letters on Herman's spirits lends weight to the link between his laziness and a possible depression. In commenting on Herman's disposition as he embarked on his whaling voyage, Maria reports that "Gansevoort says he never saw him so completely happy, as when he had determined upon a situation & all was settled." In the letter of 1847 cited above, Maria notes that Herman "seems to be in good spirits." The strong possibility that Herman may have been suffering from a depressive obstructed grief in his adolescence revises our sense of his later depression of the mid-1850s and onward. Viewed as disruptive grief, Melville's later depressions begin to make sense in the total context of his life.[52]

In her husband's eyes, "her characteristic fortitude . . . her natural firmness of mind and instinctive sense of propriety" distinguished Maria Melville: "My noble wife [was] a Woman, whose own native good sense dictates the propriety of conduct in every situation." To

her grandchildren, she seemed "stern" and of a "dignified stateliness." *Pierre*'s haughty widow, Mary Glendinning, bears both her
initials and her parodic likeness.[53]

As we have seen, Maria's letters are filled with phrases that read as
though they were copied out of the genteel guides to etiquette which
filled her bookshelves. As discussed above, her formidable personality offers the contradictory image to her sons of anxieties and depressions mixed with piety and motherly comfort. However, the
conflict that deeply shaped her worldview was that between Dutch
culture and genteel Christian ideology. Individualism gave way to
the family unit in Dutch life, Alice Kenney observes. While capable
of lauding Herman's show of independence, Maria was also educating
her offspring in Dutch family solidarity:

> You must recollect the story of an old Man who on his deathbed called
> his Sons around him and handed them a bundle of Sticks, requesting
> them each in turn to endeavor to break them, they all tryed but were
> unsuccessful, he then requested them to undo the bundle & try the
> sticks singly. They were found to break easily, there was then no
> difficulty in snapping them asunder.
>
> You will understand from the above Illustration the great importance
> of unity & attachment between the different one ——— of the same
> family. Eight of you, & acting together, each anxiously & deeply
> feeling towards each other one interest you will be happier & wiser
> then each to ——— separate ways.[54]

This advice sank in and deeply influenced the course of Melville's
literary career. Gansevoort placed *Typee* with an English publisher
and supervised its preparation for publication; after Gansevoort's
death, brother Allan took over some of the management of the
business details of Herman's dealings with publishers; his sisters
served as copyists for his manuscripts; and Maria stroked his ego. In
1854 she advised her depressed son, "my dear darling Herman," on
taking to the lecture circuit: "you are the very man to carry an
audience, to create a sensation, to do wonders. . . . It will bring us
fame and fortune."[55] Notice that she puts the emphasis on "us," as if
to imply that his literary fortunes are really his family's fortunes.

Helen added a footnote to this letter: "You must not make a martyr of yourself."

While the factors leading Melville to renounce the career of a novelist are complexly multifaceted—disenchantment with the socially conditioned form of fiction surely played a part—his family's Dutch ideology must be kept in mind. The deterioration of Herman's health, both physically and emotionally, seemed to his family directly tied to the rigors of his writing habits. They were convinced of his doctors' prognosis, one typical of the age: if he continued his intensive submergence in writing, he risked permanent damage to his health. Given the necessity of his family's emotional support to his literary production, without it, it seems unlikely he could continue to write. In 1861, the family reports that reached Lemuel Shaw on his deathbed caused him to write, in enfeebled hand, to Allan: "I am as deeply impressed as you possibly can be of the necessity of Herman's getting away from Pitts. He is there solitary, without society, without exercise or occupation except that [writing] which is very likely to be injurious to him in overstraining his mind." The family pressure on Melville in this period to abandon his writing motivated him to swear his wife to secrecy about his new vocation as a poet.[56]

Several of Melville's biographers suggest that Maria orchestrated the family strategy that played a significant role in silencing his novelistic voice. "In matters in which a wife's own relatives were associated," Kenney notes of the social role of the Dutch mother, "her influence must have been paramount." Maria gives evidence that it was not simply writing that endangered her son's health: her pressure on him could well have been motivated by outrage at his use of family history in Pierre. In 1855, three years after Pierre's publication, during the interim of which Melville began but either was unable to complete, or, as he put it, was "prevented" from publishing two books ("Agatha" and the "Tortoise" book), Maria offers her plan of action for Herman's future writing: "our dear Herman would be not so dependent on his pen—but go abroad if he wished to & then come home to be at leisure to write all about his travels." With new travel materials at hand, she implies, he would not need to exploit sources of fiction closer to home.[57]

A family legend, reinforced by the plot of *Pierre*, suggests that Maria used a "steering oar" in bringing Lizzie and Herman together. In her Dutch world, Maria was accustomed to marriages that took place within groups of young people who had played together since childhood. Although there is no evidence that Herman had known Lizzie before he returned from the Pacific in 1845, she had been a childhood friend of his sisters and her father had been intimately involved in Melville family affairs. When Herman visits Boston to set the date for his marriage, Maria notes that his trip is "of much importance to himself & to every member of our family." Apparently, Maria has had a hand in planning their domestic arrangements after the marriage: "if Lizzie loves Herman as I do think she does with her whole heart & soul why, she will consent to live here for the present, & she can be happy too." Maria, as it turned out, would remain a part of her son's household until 1855, his penultimate year as a novelist writing for publication.[58]

After Gansevoort's death in 1846, Herman became the putative head of the Melville clan. In the light of his uncertain literary career—*Typee* was not a bestseller—and given the new pressures on him to assume greater responsibility for his mother and his sisters, he probably was susceptible to Maria's possible efforts to unite her family with the prestigious and wealthy Shaw family. If it later began to dawn on him that he had sacrificed himself in his marriage for his family's well-being, one would expect to find in his writings the kind of resentment toward marriage and women that indeed does play through his work. In *Mardi*, the novel he lost himself in after his marriage, Melville imagines his hero's rescue of the mystical heroine, Yillah, from a ritual sacrifice and then his loss of her to the cruel priestess Hautia. In what he himself called a "dose," *Mardi* may dramatize Melville's subliminal perception that somehow the haughty Maria had kidnapped his erotic life.[59]

The influence Maria exerted on her children, especially her bereavement that shaped their experience of grief, extends itself to Melville's art. In his fiction, Melville struggled to untangle his own conflicted grief from the irreconcilable images of his father—both as idealized figure and as possibly damned—he had internalized from Maria's bereavement. His writing's distorted attitude to women relates to the influence of his mother's grief entangled with his experience of sexuality and creativity. Not only are his fictive women either thinly unbelievable stereotypes, nightmarish Gorgons, or simply absent but he also often feminizes his adolescent protagonists and projects imagery of threatening female sexuality onto the natural world. In the complex contexts of his art, the role of gender intimately relates to the experience of mourning.

He implicates nearly every one of his important female or feminized characters in the experience of bereavement. In one of his juvenilia, "Fragments from a Writing Desk," the protagonist quests to the "mournfully interesting" Inamorata. When we last glimpse her, *Typee*'s Fayaway is "speechless with sorrow" (*T*, 250). The feminized Harry Bolton—the "St. Bury Blade"—comes on the scene in *Redburn* after the narrator renounces his aggrieved search for his father in Liverpool. *White-Jacket*'s central woman is Surgeon Cuticle's cast of the horned woman, "wonderfully expressive of a gnawing sorrow, never to be relieved," which Melville saw in the popular press billed as "The Sunday Widow" or "The Horned Mother." *Pierre*'s "mournful" Isabel seems to personify grief itself, while in the short fiction both Hunilla and Marianna are figures of bereavement. The aborted "Agatha" novel told the tale of a widowed Cape Cod woman. *The Confidence-Man*'s chief female character, Goneril, is the object of the Man-With-The-Weed's grief. In *Clarel*, Ruth, who is first seen in a procession of mourners by the Wailing Wall and last glimpsed at her grave after she dies of grief, epitomizes the mourning figure. Finally, in *Billy-Budd*, the feminized protagonist seems constructed out of nineteenth-century mourning customs: he is the flower "nipped in the bud" of the standard mourning poem collected in mourning manuals. His origin—he is found in a silk-lined basket on a door-knocker—evokes the basket of flowers Americans placed on the door-knocker of the house of mourning, in place of the black crape badge used in England.[60]

Recent psychological research into the connection between gender and mourning offers insight into Melville's work. In a study of gender-disordered patients, an unusually high number report an inability to mourn and an intense anger toward the fathers they lost in adolescence. The "increasing cross-gender identification" of these patients seems, in part, an expression of the conflicts of their grief.[61] With this finding in mind, Ishmael can be put in a new context, for in a strange negotiation of grief, he turns into the wife of a cannibal who revises Melville's memory of his father. Unlike Allan Melvill, Queequeg gets off of his deathbed when he recalls his responsibilities ashore. The feminized adolescent protagonist in Melville's fiction points back to the moment when Melville's grief was frozen by cross-gender identification with Maria's bereavement. His feminine men announce the presence of Maria's unintegrated images of her husband. In Melville's imagination, the paternal model had become confused with maternal influence, just as in the momentary wearing of the pasteboard mask of a queenly personality, Ahab symbolically gestures toward Allan's deathbed mania.

The psychoanalytic argument receives support from the influence of nineteenth-century mourning ritual on the outcome of Melville's grief. For the Victorian American, most of the attention in mourning customs was focused on controlling female bereavement: the codes of dress, length of mourning, manner of deportment, etc., were more rigidly enforced on women.[62] Men, typically, went back to work fairly rapidly after a loss, with perhaps a weed in their hatband. Women were perceived as bearing the burden for publically symbolizing bereavement. The social expectations of genteel performance in female mourning directed Melville to channel the conflicts of his grief into his fiction's female mourning figures. From Maria Melville's perspective, the dependent social role of upper-middle-class mother that she was expected to play further encouraged her to "regard the child as the incarnation of the dead person," at the same time as she feared that by converting her sons into surrogate providers they might turn out like their father. Further, given her forceful personality, the culturally prescribed role of lady must have set in motion an intense, but subliminal anger that would have deepened the conflicts of her grief.

In his art, Melville performs a complex work of mourning. On the one hand, there is an urgency in his writing toward subverting his culture's conventions for regulating bereavement. On the other hand, as not only a part of the times but an embodiment of their "correspondent coloring," his work feels the restraining hand of the ideologies of mourning and gender. He participates in nineteenth-century mourning etiquette, for instance, by controlling his displaced grief in the form of the female mourning figure. The experimental energy of his writing moves out of the need for an alternative mourning ritual, even as it falls prey to the hegemony of the etiquette of grief. In the Civil War poem, "The Conflict of Convictions," Melville writes, "I know a wind in purpose strong—It spins *against* the way it drives" (*BP*, 17).

CHAPTER TWO

The Liminality of Grief: Mourning Ritual in *Typee*

We stand upon the borders of two worlds,
and . . . we may gather lessons of profound wisdom
by contrasting the one with the other.
Justice Story, "Address on the Dedication of Mt.
Auburn Cemetery"

In a letter of February 7, 1846, a puzzled Maria Melville comments on her son's recently published first novel, *Typee*, "his book which none of us understand, so contradictory in its information." One wonders if Mrs. Melville associated her son Gansevoort's leg ailment with the mysterious leg injury that the narrative persona, Tommo, suffers and which causes him to be carried about on a native's back. Writing on March 5, 1839, Melville's mother describes how "Gansevoort has still to be carried to the fire and is unable to bear his weight." One further wonders whether the cause of Tommo's disability, his exposure to "death-like coldness" during a rainy night spent in a ravine, triggered for Mrs. Melville a memory of her husband's fatal exposure (46). To explore the social text of Tommo's leg wound and how it relates to Maria Melville's sense of *Typee*'s contradictions, I examine the novel's conflicting *types* and *peeps*, as it links the pain inscribed in Tommo's body to Melville's frozen grief for his father.[1]

THE RAVINE SCENE

The sequence of events during which Tommo contracts his leg pain begins after he and his companion, Toby, have jumped ship in the Marquesas and escaped into the island's interior to hide out until their ship has departed. Wandering in the island's interior, the escapees come upon a mysterious footprint that directs them to "the verge of the ravine" in which Tommo incurs his leg wound (44). (All unidentified parenthetical quotes refer to the novel under discussion in each chapter.) To Toby, a descent into the ravine threatens "a broken neck," but Tommo becomes stubbornly "resolved to find out" why the footpath broke off at its precipice (44, 45).

"To a dead certainty," Toby argues, the ravine bodes ill—"sore throats and rheumatisms"—but to Tommo it offers "shelter . . . from the weather" (45). At the bottom of the gorge, five streams "swelled and turbid by the recent rains," unite together and, "in one mad plunge" and "with wild uproar," rush "into a deep black pool scooped out of the gloomy-looking rocks" (45). "In one collected body," the waterfall "seemed to penetrate into the very bowels of the earth" (45).

The runaways build their night's shelter right at "the foot of the cataract"; however, their makeshift lodging proves porous to the downpour (46). Toby "lay shivering the live-long night like a man afflicted with the palsy" (46). He depresses Tommo's spirits by refusing to chat with him, while for Tommo "the accumulated horrors of that night, the death-like coldness of the place . . . almost unmanned me" (46). Later Tommo will attribute his leg pain "to the exposure" he suffered that night (48). Upon awakening, Toby jokingly intimates that he has expired in the live-long night. After Tommo informs him the sun's come up, Toby acerbically comments, " 'Then, shipmate, my toplights have gone out, for it appears darker now with my eyes open then it did when they were shut' " (46). "In a rage," Toby roars, "It is an insult to a man to suppose he could sleep in such an infernal place as this" (47).

After climbing out of the ravine, the sailors climb a ridge, cover themselves with grass, but once more are drenched by a downpour. "Completely shrouded with verdure," his "limbs buried in the grass," Tommo begins to feel "cold shiverings and a burning fever" (48). He discovers that "one of my legs was swelled to such a degree, and pained me so acutely, that I half suspected I had been been bitten by some venomous reptile" (48). However, he later learns that the Marquesas are devoid of reptiles.

The onset of leg pain, though, abruptly gives way to an infusion of pleasure. In the grip of his "feverish sensation," Tommo brushes aside a branch and exclaims on the scene before him, "Had a glimpse of the gardens of Paradise been revealed to me I could scarcely have been more ravished with the sight" (49). Suddenly, in the midst of the onset of his fever and swollen leg, he "lay transfixed with surprise and delight," as he looks "straight down into the bosom of a valley" (49).

The leg wound sequence begins with the adventurers poised before the edge of a ravine and it ends with Tommo alternately feverish and pleasurably aroused as he looks over a precipice. Toby initially associates the ravine with death: the " 'roar of those waterfalls down there would batter one's brains to pieces' " (44). Yet Tommo finds the ravine irresistible. In paralleling their responses in this way, Melville suggests that Tommo seems attracted to the death that Toby, in a dead certainty, ascribes to the gorge. As the scene unfolds, it is precisely the death-like coldness that threatens to unman Tommo by incapacitating his leg. Strangely, the waterfall in the ravine calls attention to interior bodily spaces, as it smashes into the very bowels of the earth, just as the weather invades Tommo's body. The waterfall seemed to penetrate the earth, in language that associates this action with madness— "wild uproar" and "mad plunge"—but Tommo's exposure evokes death: both the image of Toby dying of palsy and then the death Toby fantasizes awakening into. The death imagery intensifies when Tommo first experiences his leg pain, while lying shrouded and buried in the grass.

The complexity of the scene deepens, as Tommo swings unstably between fever and sexual stimulation. Moving from the ravine's to the precipice's edge, the leg wound sequence entwines teasing suggestions of mimicked deaths with the sexual allure of the landscape. The swelled and turbid streams phallically penetrate the very bowels of the earth, while doubling the leg ailment that will emerge from Tommo's unmanning by subliminal morbidity enmeshed with covert desire. However, to understand fully the resonances of the scene Toby's link to death needs to be explored.

The ravine sequence suggests a connection between Tommo's leg injury and the fatal exposure of Melville's father to death-like coldness. *Typee* deepens the metaphor through Toby's characterization. Tommo imbues Toby with contradictory personality traits which split Melville's grief for Allan Melvill into the scary image of the manic father and into the son's need to gain access to the conflicts of his mourning. On the one hand, Toby was "a strange wayward being, moody, fitful, and melancholy—at times almost morose. He had a quick and fiery temper too, which, when thoroughly roused, transported him into a state bordering on delirium" (32). Toby's "paroxysms" evidence "the power that a mind of deep passion has over feebler natures": stronger sailors quail before "his furious fits," as perhaps the memory of Allan's deathbed mania unsettles his son (32). Just before Tommo approaches him about jumping ship, "Toby's melancholy had greatly increased" (32). In his first image of Toby, he portrays him as "buried in thought" (33). Like Allan Melvill, who once surprised his wife by actually laughing out loud at the theater, Toby possesses an "imperturbable gravity of . . . tone and manner," such that "No one ever saw Toby laugh" (32).[2]

Although Toby seems unstable and untrustworthy, he also appears "active, ready, and obliging, of dauntless courage, and *singularly open and fearless in the expression of his feelings*" (31, my emphasis). Toby's sides evoke Melville's grief reaction: Melville both fears the hair-trigger delirium and envies Toby's access to feeling. Unlike Tommo, who teaches his Marquesan father Marheyo the words *home* and *mother*, Toby "was one of that class of rovers you sometimes meet at sea, who never reveal their origin, never allude to home, and go rambling over the world as if pursued by some mysterious fate they cannot possibly elude" (32). Like Tommo he has fallen in class, but unlike him Toby was "anxious to conceal it" (32). To Tommo, most of the crew "were as coarse in person as in mind," but he admires Toby's "remarkably prepossessing exterior," his "great flexibility of limb" (an important trait in contrast to Tommo's later limp), and he finds romantically attractive the "mass of jetty locks clustered about his temples" that "threw a darker shade into his large black eyes" (32).

What does this mysterious characterization have to do with Toby's real-life model, Tobias Greene, future Buffalo sign painter, who felt no need to conceal his identity under an alias? The shade that has possessed the fictive Toby resembles the chair-portrait of Melville's father, in which jetty locks curl onto the forehead of the prepossessing man of the world. Cut off from origin and home, the image of Allan that flits through Toby becomes doomed to the mysterious fate of the father who abandons his son: the pattern that Toby reenacts with Tommo.

The mad plunge of the streams at the base of the ravine into the deep black pool in the gloomy-looking rocks mirrors the way Tommo's leg wound enters back into the depressive grief buried in Melville's very bowels.[3] Through his association with Allan Melvill, Toby's mimicked death and his evocation of death imagery heighten the relation of the ravine scene to Melville's buried grief. After the sailors fall into the Typees's hands, Toby leaves to procure medicine for Tommo and fails to return. He then seems either to have been cannibalized or to have simply abandoned Tommo. Melville thus directly uses Toby to evoke his sense of loss.

Tommo's leg becomes a mediatory zone on which Melville controls his own depressive rage at being abandoned by his father. But this is an anger that remains unresolved because of the presence in Melville's inner world of the alternately frightening and alluring image of Allan Melvill. Tommo's fears of cannibalism periodically overwhelm him, usually after he has yielded to the pleasures of native life.[4]

Like the Typees, Melville wants to eat and make his own the power of the cannibal victim, but he also wants to bury the internalized corpse of Allan. Melville does not simply deny "his anxiety, help-lessness, and dependency," as one critic argues; rather he taps into them to deepen and enrich his art. *Typee*'s sources of creative power derive precisely from its destructive, cannibalistic urges. They fuel Melville's struggle to resolve his grief as well as his effort to break free from his culture's constricting codes of gender and narrative voice.[5]

"Oh! there is a fierce, a cannibal delight, in the grief that shrieks to multiply itself," *Mardi*'s Babbalanja says of the poet Lombardo's cre-ative process, "We are full of ghosts and spirits; we are as grave-yards full of buried dead, that start to life before us. And all our dead sires, verily, are in us" (M, 594, 593–94). In *Typee*, Melville multiplies his cannibal delight through an energizing but frightening contact with displaced versions of the image of failure and madness of his dying father. If he can master his father's instability by appropriating (can-nibalizing) it into his fictive performance—"the sane madness of vital truth" he later claims for artistic genius—then he can both bury and steal his father's power (HHM, 542).[6]

In his attraction to seemingly fluid, Marquesan styles of ex-pression, Melville moves toward freeing himself from a fear of inher-ited, paternal instability. Melville's fantasy of fluid enactments of power, often performed by *Typee*'s gallery of women, reflects his attempt to both master and transform the disruptive grief that throbs in Tommo's limb. Fayaway and the canoe scene exemplifies this fantasy.

THE RIGID FIGURE IN THE CANOE

Tommo's abrupt mood swings, and the contradictory peeps at Marquesan life he performs in them, must have been in large part responsible for the bafflement with which Melville's family read *Typee*.[7] In one instance, "the violence of my grief" overwhelms Tommo after Mehevi, the most powerful chief in the Typee valley, responds with an "inflexible rigidity of expression" to his desire to

investigate the appearance of a ship in the bay (120, 119). After
sinking "insensibly into that kind of apathy which ensues after some
violent outbreak of despair," Tommo discovers that his leg has "suddenly healed" (123). But during his depressions he views his captors
as "nothing better than a set of cannibals" (118). He finds his own
volatilely shifting reactions to native life perplexing: "I can scarcely
understand how it was that, in the midst of so many consolatory
circumstances, my mind should still have been consumed by the most
dismal of forebodings, and have remained a prey to the profoundest
melancholy" (118). But when his "grievous affliction" eases and his
"agonizing" leg pain vanishes, he sings the praises of the "perpetual
hilarity" of the Typees (118, 126, 119): "There seemed to be no
cares, griefs, troubles, or vexations, in all Typee" (126). Now he sees
all around him a "Happy Valley" and he finds that "beyond those
heights there was naught but a world of care and anxiety" (124).

In these moments of release into the pleasures of cannibal life,
Tommo lashes out at "white civilized man as the most ferocious
animal on the face of the earth" (125). In condemning the "thousand
sources of irritation" of civilized life, Tommo obliquely comments on
the family situation Melville had fled by shipping out (126). In
Typee, there "were no foreclosures of mortgages, no protested notes,
no bills payable, no debts of honor" and especially "no widows with
their children starving on the cold charities of the world"—a con-
ventionalized overstatement of the Melville family status but not by
much (126). With a blindness to the source of his own leg pain,
Tommo exclaims of Typee, "Blue devils, hypochondria, and doleful
dumps, went and hid themselves among the nooks and crannies of
the rocks" (126).[8]

While Tommo's agonizing trek through a series of "black and
yawning chasms" creates the impression that he descends into the
gulfs of his own depressions, the sailors' entry into the Typee valley
almost seems willfully suicidal, as they deliver themselves into "that
fearful death which, under all these smiling appearances, might yet
menace us" (54, 97). In the valley, Tommo's first bout of depression
occurs after Toby fails to return from his trip to procure medicine.

The disappointed Tommo "became a prey to the most gloomy thoughts" and "deep dejection" (104). Tommo seeks "to derive a desperate consolation from dwelling upon the perfidy of Toby," but "at other times I sunk under the bitter remorse which I felt as having by my own imprudence brought upon myself the fate which I was sure awaited me" (109). By performing Allan Melvill's role in Melville's unresolved grief, Toby triggers a grief reaction in Tommo that mixes anger and guilt.

Typee offers Tommo the consolatory circumstances Melville could only have fantasized in his adolescent bereavement. In his adopted Typee home, the house of Marheyo, Tommo discovers rich "sources of consolation" (110). Under the ministrations of his adopted sisters, he "buried for the time every feeling of sorrow" (110): "Nothing could surpass their efforts to minister to my comfort" (113). But Tommo's anxiety and distrust undercut these fantasies of nurture. More specifically, "everything connected with Toby" reignites his suspicion of the real motive behind Typee generosity (140). "All their kindness had terminated in his [Toby's] disappearance," Tommo anxiously reasons, "Might not the same fate await me?" (141) Tommo intuits what a subtle analyst of cannibalism, Eli Sagan, proposes: affection and aggression are intimately intertwined in the cannibal act.[9] To explore this ambivalence, I turn to Tommo's relationship with his favorite Marquesan sister, Fayaway.

Fayaway expresses the "liveliest sympathy" for Tommo (108). In "the attractive cast of her countenance, singularly expressive of intelligence and honesty," Tommo finds both balm for his depression and a sensual allure (108). While approaching the mournful Tommo "with one arm slightly elevated in a gesture of pity, and her large glistening eyes gazing intently into mine, she would murmur plaintively, 'Awha! awha! Tommo,' and seat herself mournfully beside me" (108). Tommo's image of her resembles an eroticized, oral experience: "Her full lips, when parted with a smile, disclosed teeth of a dazzling whiteness; and when her rosy mouth opened with a burst of merriment, they looked like the milk-white seeds of the 'arta,' a fruit of the valley, which, when cleft in twain, shows them reposing in

rows on either side, imbedded in the red and juicy pulp" (85). Com-
mingling the erotic and the cannibalistic, Fayaway's sensuality becomes a mouth that turns into red and juicy pulp, as Tommo's imagery intimates a fearful engulfment in her sexuality. However, her
sexuality turns into the mothering—the milk-white seeds of fruit—
Tommo's depressions elicit.[10]

Fayaway seems to him "the very perfection of female grace and
beauty," but he most admires her "free pliant figure" (85). Early in
the novel, Tommo discovers a similar quality in the sensuality of
the whihenies, the young island women, as he admires their free
unstudied action (15, my emphasis). Tommo's pietistic denunciation
of the "unholy passions" his shipmates exhibit in their orgy with the
whihenies and his concomitant evasion of his own desire come into
sharper focus in his canoe scene with Fayaway's free pliant figure
(15).

Marquesan culture taboos the canoe as a male vessel, and a woman
who violates these strictures meets with death (14). "I was ever
partial to what is termed in the 'Young Men's Own Book'—'the
society of virtuous and intelligent young ladies,'" Tommo explains of
his motivation for negotiating the suspension of the canoe taboo
(132). Ironically, he then proceeds to violate Marquesan "notions of
propriety" by acting out his own culture's sense of decorum (132).
While luxuriating in the canoe with Fayaway, Tommo muses:
"Strange as it may seem, there is nothing in which a young and
beautiful female appears to more advantage than in the act of smoking" (133). By playing off his own culture's female taboo—a woman
smoking—and transforming the etiquette book tone in which he had
earlier narrated into a violation of itself, Tommo collapses
Marquesan proprieties into Western ones.[11]

While canoeing one day, Fayaway "seemed all at once to be struck
with some happy idea. . . . With a wild exclamation of delight, she
disengaged from her person the ample robe of tappa . . . and spread-
ing it out like a sail, stood erect with upraised arms in the head of the
canoe" (134). Tommo exclaims, "We American sailors pride ourselves upon our straight clean spars, but a prettier little mast than

Fayaway made was never shipped aboard of any craft" (134). In possible sexual innuendo, the breeze "distended" Fayaway's sail and "the long brown tresses of Fayaway streamed in the air," while Tommo "directed" the canoe, using his paddle as a rudder, until it "dashed up the soft sloping bank" (134). "Many a time afterwards was this feat repeated," a deadpan Tommo confesses (134).[12]

In its sexual teasings, the scene turns Fayaway into the empowered limb Tommo lacks. Even as he controls the scene, manipulates Marquesan and Western taboos, and directs the canoe, Fayaway dreams up the feat and her sail provides the canoe's locomotion. Of course, this is Tommo's tale, his fantasy of woman-as-sail, and the way he ends the canoe scene reveals his inability to fully open his narrative to a powerful woman. "The declared admirer of Miss Fayaway," Tommo swiftly reappropriates her power into genteel rhetoric (134). He covers up her free pliant figure by making her a dress in which she looked "something like an opera dancer," who only titillates male appetites by revealing a "bewitching ankle" (135).[13]

However, a dark strain underlies the canoe scene. In her pose as *rigid* mast, Fayaway fulfills the penalty for violating the canoe taboo: death. The liberating fluidity Tommo projects onto the whihenies' free unstudied action, momentarily symbolizing a free and powerfully imaginative feat, which subverts and exploits both Marquesan and Western gender taboos, fuels a covert death scene.

Another canoe scene, "within a stone's cast of Fayaway's lake" (171), explains why Fayaway is both phallically erect and symbolically dead in the canoe scene.[14] After confessing his "almost entire inability" to make sense of Typee religious life and doubting "whether the inhabitants themselves could do so," Tommo admits that "one of their superstitious observances with which I became acquainted interested me greatly": "the mausolem of a deceased warrior chief" (171). Tommo lingers over the burial site for several pages, and he rewrites Fayaway's canoe scene, insofar as the death evoked in her rigid pose turns into an actual corpse and her phallicism turns into a male Marquesan authority figure.

ing tone, in which the aggressive exuberance presenting a scenario of exhaustion becomes a masculine identity subtly undermining itself as it emerges from its depleted environment.

In *Typee*'s preface, Melville trusts that "his *anxious desire* to speak the unvarnished truth will gain for him the confidence of his readers" (xiv, my emphasis). In the novel, however, his anxiety and desire turn into a strange attraction to symbolic castration. Tommo's attitude to the male authority figures in the novel further illustrates the self-cannibalistic side to his anxious desire.[20] Mow-Mow only enters the novel in its climactic stages. After a battle with the Happars, the Typees bring their enemy dead to the male taboo Bachelor Hall, the Ti (157). Mow-Mow first appears as the "heavy hand" on Tommo's shoulder which directs him to leave the Ti, so that the Typees can conceal their cannibal feast from him (236). On his next visit to the Ti, Tommo violates a taboo and lifts the cover of a vessel that turns out to contain "the disordered members of a human skeleton" with fresh meat on its bones (238).

"Desponding" with renewed force, Tommo's leg worsens and he sinks into "gloomily pondering over the fate which it now appeared idle for me to resist" (243). During his "long days of suffering and sorrow," he takes "a strange interest in the slightest movements of the eccentric old warrior," Marheyo, his Marquesan father, whom Tommo watches building a hut he seems destined never to complete (243). Earlier, Marheyo perplexed him: "he seemed to be governed by no fixed principles whatever; but acting just according to the humor of the moment, slept, ate, or tinkered away at his little hut, without regard to the proprieties of time or place" (151). Marheyo seems a ludicrous character for much of the novel—he naps in the sun at noon, bathes at midnight, and at one point appears "in the tuft of a cocoa-nut tree, smoking"—but it is Marheyo who intercedes for Tommo at the crucial moment of his escape (151).

The formerly decrepit Marheyo turns into Melville's fantasy of the good father, who unlike Allan Melvill does not overwork himself into the grave but seemingly disregards "fixed principles" and benevolently turns from his work to commiserate with his adopted son and gives him the love that the depressed Tommo craves. During Tommo's escape, Marheyo suddenly materializes by his side after the natives block his route to the beach: "I shall never forget the benevolent expression of his countenance. He placed his arm upon my shoulder, and emphatically pronounced the only two English words I had taught him—'Home' and 'Mother.' I at once understood what he meant, and eagerly expressed my thanks to him" (248). Then, in his only assertion of authority in the novel, Marheyo orders his son, Kory-Kory, to carry Tommo to the beach.[21]

We can read in Marheyo's name—Mar/He/Yo[u]—Melville's covert fear of the inner paternal corpse.[22] Initially, Melville manages the disabling paternal influence by turning Marheyo into an eccentric, senile warrior. But later in the novel, Melville negotiates his anxious desire for confidence by splitting the father image into the loving Marheyo and the deadly Mow-Mow, both of whom lay their hands on his shoulder to vastly different effect.

Yet the real paternal power in Typee resides in the person of the head chief, Mehevi, who virtually disappears during Tommo's escape. Melville brings Mow-Mow on the scene at the end of the novel so that Tommo will not have to do battle with the real heavy of Typee. On his first entrance to the valley, Tommo cannot avoid Mehevi. Tommo and Toby ponder whether they have wandered into Typee or Happar territory, and Tommo feels Mehevi's intense gaze "looking at me with a rigidity of aspect under which I absolutely quailed. . . . Never before had I been subjected to so strange and steady a glance; it revealed nothing of the mind of the savage, but it appeared to be reading my own" (71). Growing "absolutely nervous," Tommo frantically asks himself, "Typee or Happar?" (71). Mehevi seems to have entered into his thoughts: "I started, for at the same moment this identical question was asked by the strange being before me" (71). Immediately winning the natives's approval by identifying with them—keeping in mind that Tommo claims Typee means "lover of human flesh"—Tommo's first experience of the Typee leader consists of Mehevi terrifying him by seemingly giving voice to his own thoughts. In Mehevi—Me/He/Vi[e]—Tommo

confronts a paternal challenge, one which registers Melville's sense
of being held a captive to the threatening memory of his father.[23]

DANCING WIDOWS

In arguing that *Typee* centrally concerns the conflicts of Melville's
unfinished grief, that Tommo's leg wound functions to control these
conflicts, and that this disruptive grief lies just beneath important
images and action in the novel, I suggest that *Typee* invents an
alternative and displaced mourning ritual. However, the cannibalism at the center of Tommo's adventures itself has to do with
mourning customs. According to Eli Sagan, cannibals eat their enemies to incorporate their spiritual power and to revenge their dead
slain in battle, or they eat their dead loved ones as part of a ritual
bereavement. Although Tommo does not realize it, he might be
viewed by the Typees as a part of their mourning for deaths inflicted
in battle with the white man, perhaps even reaching back to Captain
Porter's merciless campaign against them. Sagan illustrates that cannibals often adopt a future victim into their tribe, allow them to
marry, but after several years suddenly take revenge.[24] From this
perspective, the issue becomes not whether the Typees love Tommo
but instead what their affection means in the context of their culture.
In broader view, the question becomes, What does Typee emotion
have to do with Western codes of feeling? And, further, if there is a
disparity between the two, what does this tell us about the social text
of grief? Tommo's fascination with Marquesan funerary rites provides
a clue to some answers to these questions.

Making the best of his captivity, Tommo daily strolls to Mehevi's
palace. Before Tommo's terrors come to a head, he fully enjoys his
lunches with "the bachelor chiefs of the Ti" (151). In this "right
jovial place," "secure from female intrusion, there was no restraint
upon the hilarity of the warriors" (152). But Melville structures the
narrative so that it is female intrusion into the taboo grounds surrounding the Ti that most fascinates Tommo. Melville's description
of Tommo's visits to the Ti leads into four chapters (22–25) devoted

to the Feast of the Calabashes, which occurs on the Ti's " 'hoolah hoolah' grounds," the "Taboo groves" (91). Structurally, the novel subordinates its brief description of Tommo's bachelor pleasures to its more extended treatment of the feast.[25]

While exploring the taboo groves, Tommo comes upon a "pyramidical" monument which looks as though it is made out of "a cenotaph of skulls"; he names this funerary site the "Feast of Calabashes" (160). Later, Tommo borrows the name of the cenotaph for the native festival because the monument "formed so prominent a feature in the approaching revels" (160). After a cursory description of the costumes and food of the festival, Tommo details the ritual at the center of the festivities: the "Dancing Widows" (189).[26] In preparation for this ritual, the men "deserted" the area in front of the Ti, which filled with "bands of females, shouting and dancing under the influence of some strange excitement" (166).

The chief dancers, in what turns out to be a mourning ritual, are

> four or five old women who, in a state of utter nudity, with their arms extended flatly down their sides, and holding themselves perfectly erect, were leaping stiffly into the air, like so many bobbing sticks to the surface, after being pressed perpendicularly into the water. They preserved the utmost gravity of countenance, and continued their extraordinary movements without a single moment's cessation. They did not appear to attract the observation of the crowd around them, but I must candidly confess that, for my own part, I stared at them most pertinaciously. (166)

As if fearful of the ritual, Tommo diminishingly refers to it as a "peculiar diversion," an "indecorous custom," which "amused" him (166). Kory-Kory explains that the "leaping figures" enact grief for husbands "slain in battle many moons previously," but Tommo remains unsatisfied "as to its propriety" (167).

The "afflicted females," like Fayaway in the taboo male vessel, dance their ritual bereavement in a usually taboo male space (167). They provide a cross-commentary on the relation of Tommo's swollen leg to Melville's obstructed grief. Like Fayaway as powerful limb, the widows are perfectly erect as they stiffly leap. Their ritual inverts Tommo's unconscious mourning, as their bereaved dance invigorates the limbs that Tommo's blocked grief cripples.

Tommo admits, "During my stay in the valley, as none of its inmates were so accommodating as to die and be buried in order to gratify my curiosity with regard to their funeral rites, I was reluctantly obliged to remain in ignorance of them" (193). However, he claims to have witnessed Marquesan funerary rites in Nukuheva bay, which he describes in detail. "Two females, of a dejected appearance, watched by" the corpse's side, "plaintively chanting and beating the air" (193–94).[27] "Masters of ceremonies," wearing "head-dresses of beautiful tappa," lead the "entertainment": "With the exception of those who mourned by the corpse every one seemed disposed to drown the sense of the late bereavement in convivial indulgence" (194). The natives mourn by dancing, chanting, smoking, chatting, feasting, "and seemed to enjoy themselves as pleasantly as they could have done had it been a wedding" (194). After the funeral, the Marquesans practice "the art of embalming"; great chiefs are "preserved for many years in the very houses where they died" and heads of enemies are preserved and hung as trophies in the natives' homes (194).

When Tommo appears at his Typee home at just the wrong moment, he sees Marheyo's collection of embalmed heads "in a state of perfect preservation," including, to his horror, one of a white man (232–33). Parrying "the fearful apprehensions that *consumed me*," Tommo's leg pain "nearly unmanned" him, as his inner self-cannibalization finds a corollary in Typee customs (232, my emphasis). Tommo's reactivated depression can not simply be a fear of following the fate of Captain Cook, who was cannibalized, but rather a guilty anxiety aroused by an externalization in Typee behavior of Melville's own desire to cannibalize the internalized corpse of his father. When the Typees mirror back the cannibal impulse he himself feels, Melville intensifies the anxiety of Tommo's guilty self-recognition. The Typee social practice of preserving the dead terrifies Tommo because he enacts on an intrapsychic level the preservation of Melville's conflicted image of his father.

THE LIMINALITY OF GRIEF

Melville fantasizes a resolution of these tensions in the character of the tabooed wanderer, Marnoo. His characterization becomes a veiled self-confession of the hollowness and inauthenticity of Melville's narrative persona—itself the result of his cannibalization of Stewart's and Porter's personae.[28] Marnoo walks into the novel immediately following the canoe scene with Fayaway. His "flexible figure" displaces her free pliant figure (137). Marnoo's "power-ful . . . natural eloquence" captivates Tommo, and within the safety of a male character he explores the social fate of Fayaway's free and powerful energy: "The grace of the attitudes into which he threw his flexible figure, the striking gestures of his naked arms, and above all, the fire which shot from his brilliant eyes, imparted an effect to the continually changing accents of his voice, of which the most accomplished orator might have been proud" (137). The "lively emotion" in Fayaway's eyes, which "beamed upon the beholder like stars," transmutes into Marnoo's fire-shooting brilliant eyes (86). Marnoo's "cheek was of a feminine softness," and like the Marquesan women it is free of tattoos (135–36). This Polynesian Apollo not only melds together gender roles, but he also combines both Marquesan and Western cultural roles—earlier he had worked on a whaler. Further, Marnoo's taboo status enables him to travel with immunity between the warring tribes of the island.

Seemingly all things to all people, Marnoo first poses as Melville's artistic ideal: the unmarred fluidity and adaptability of identity Tommo himself strives for in the contradictory information of the continually changing accents of his voice. The personification of organic art, Marnoo exhibits an artu-tree tattooed on his back: "the best specimen of the Fine Arts" Tommo sees in Typee (116). But Marnoo has polluted the living work of art he embodies by marring his natural eloquence with the duplicity of Western art. He explains he deliberately snubbed Tommo "in order to increase my astonishment, as soon as he should see proper to address me" in English (140).

Marnoo's eloquence epitomizes "the freedom from all restraint"

Tommo thinks he sees in Marquesan manners, and because Marquesan words are polysemic, the natives must use "a variety of gestures and the eloquent expression of the countenance" to inflect their meaning (185, 224–25). What initially seemed *natural* eloquence turns out to be part of the culturally determined language. When Tommo attempts to "read [the] nervous eloquence of their looks and gestures," they remain opaque signifiers (142). Their "wayward and passionate spirits" remain as indecipherable to him as his own depressions (144).

Indeed, Tommo slowly realizes that his captors are as far from being free from all restraint as he is. What initially looks like easy access to emotional expression turns out to be as rigidly controlled as the "stiffness, formality, and affectation" of Western manners from which he thought he had escaped (161). Like the "gallery of coronation beauties, at Westminster Abbey," the "artless vivacity and natural graces" of Typee women are bounded in by their version of etiquette: the "all-controlling power" of the taboo (161, 221).[29]

"How were their passions controlled in their everyday transactions?" Tommo asks (200). When he attacks missionaries, Tommo answers this query by claiming that the Typees have no need for religious colonization because the "grand principles of virtue and honor, however they may be distorted by arbitrary codes are the same the world over" (201). But when Tommo dons a different rhetorical guise and tries to analyze Marquesan manners on their own terms, it appears that their arbitrary codes do far more than simply distort their inherent nobility. Of the taboo, he explains, "The savage, in short, lives *in the continual observance* of its dictates, *which guide and control every aspect of his being*" (221, my emphasis). Taboo is the Marquesan version of the "canons of good breeding" and to violate it is simply "ill-manners" (221): "Anything opposed to the ordinary customs of the islanders, although not expressly prohibited, is said to be 'taboo'" (224).

In reconsidering Marquesan mourning customs—the dead chief's effigy, the Dancing Widows, the formalized wake—from the perspective of the native taboo, they seem as rigidly ritualized as the mutes, weeds, and black paraphernalia of Victorian mourning. Was Tommo witnessing an authentically felt grief in the bereaved widows or in the Marquesan version of mutes (the women who appeared dejected as they wailed outside the house of mourning)? Beneath the electrifying effect of the nervous eloquence of Marquesan manners, Tommo unwittingly suggests, lies their version of Victorian proprieties, and beneath that? This is what terrifies him, as when Mehevi's most cordial manner changes into an inflexible rigidity of expression.

Emotion is in Derridean fashion "always already" scripted into the cultural text, and Tommo's grief most subversively disrupts the narrative when it plays one culture's codes off the other's.[30] After delineating the power of the taboo, Tommo wanders into a scene in which Marquesan women are making the native cloth, tappa: "I regarded them for awhile in silence, and then carelessly picking up a handful of the material that lay around, proceeded *unconsciously to pick it apart*" (221, my emphasis). The women then "scream, like . . . a whole boarding-school of ladies just on the point of going into hysterics" (222). Perplexed, Tommo thinks a "venomous reptile" was concealed in the bark (222). Once more he began "to separate and examine it" and "the horrified girls redoubled their shrieks" (222). Now "actually alarmed" himself, he throws down the bark and begins to flee, when a girl grabs his arm, points to the bark, "and screamed in my ears the fatal word Taboo!" (222). He learns that the bark was intended for use in a female headdress and that "the whole masculine gender" was "interdicted" from its "manufacture" (222).

On a larger level, *Typee* performs the socially symbolic action of picking apart cultural codes—a gesture that Tommo unconsciously signals with the Marquesan tappa-text. Symbolic anthropologist Victor Turner analyzes the ritualistic social drama Melville thus creates in *Typee*. Turner compares metaphor to the *liminal*, which is "a moment [in] ritualized movement" when the subject is free from the "cultural script" or "liberated from normative demands" and situated "betwixt and between successive lodgements in jural political systems."[31]

For Turner, metaphor initiates "a certain kind of polarization of meaning in which the subsidiary subject is really a depth world of prophetic, half-glimpsed images, and the principal subject, the visible, fully known (or thought to be fully known component), at the opposite pole to it, acquires new and surprising contours and valences from its dark companion." Metaphor thus becomes a ritual of meaning-making, insofar as it enacts "the very creative darkness of liminality that lays hold of the basic forms of life." According to Turner, then, subversive writing moves outside of conventional uses of language into the darkness of liminality, and by crossing from one side of the metaphor to the other it draws attention to "new and surprising contours and valences" in accustomed social reality.

What Melville teaches us about the social fate of grief in *Typee* is that culture can exert an all-controlling power on emotional life: each of the Marquesan mourning rituals are prescribed by Typee customs, right down to the ritualized weeping written into the cultural script. Richard Huntington and Peter Metcalf contend in a recent anthropological study of mortuary ritual that "we can assume neither the universality of particular modes of feeling nor that similar signs of emotion correspond to the same underlying sentiments in different cultures. . . . Expressions of sentiment in ritual [are] . . . not merely reflections of feeling, but symbols whose meaning can be discovered through careful analysis." Tommo, though, hardly possesses the conceptual tools to read the Marquesan text of grief, and he intimates that neither do the experts of his day.[32]

THE ISLAND-MOTHER'S GRIEF

To the extent that Melville succeeds in momentarily unpicking both Marquesan and Western codes of feeling, he creates "metamorphic, transformative" metaphors, which deepen our sense of the complexity of grief. "In this gap between ordered worlds," Turner speculates, "almost anything can happen." What happens in *Typee*'s gaps between ordered worlds is that Melville's conflicts toward male authority figures transform into a deeper tension in his relationship to powerful maternal figures. Recall that it is Fayaway—daughter of Tommo's

Marquesan mother, the powerful Tinor—who, after mothering the depressed Tommo, at first occupies the position of power in the canoe, and that it is ultimately bereaved widows who usurp the male taboo space of the Ti.

Helen Petrullo suggests that at the start of the novel, when Tommo's ship sails into Nukuheva bay, he really enters an island-sized woman's body. Flanked by two small islets, the horseshoe shaped bay evokes female anatomy. During his first visit to the island, Tommo bathes in a "verdant recess," in which he "felt as if floating in some new element, while all sort of gurgling, trickling, liquid sounds fell upon my ear" (28). From this amniotic perspective, the island's landscape becomes a womb-like scene of a "narrow valley, with its steep and close adjoining sides draperied with vines, and arched overhead . . . nearly hidden from view by masses of leafy verdure" (28). Later, during his escape, he and Toby hurl their bodies against the thick cane prohibiting their entrance into the "immense arbor" of the island-mother (28).[33]

On this view, Tommo receives his leg wound in a scary, female interior space: the bottom of the ravine, or "the very bowels" of the island-mother (45). According to D. H. Lawrence, by slithering along a river-bed into the Typee valley, Tommo enacts "a bit of birth-myth, or rebirth myth."[34] The conflicted grief I earlier linked to Tommo's leg ailment now can be seen as a maternal inscription that he spends the rest of the book painfully reading.

But why does Tommo need to climb back into the island-mother to evoke Melville's revived grief? The answer lies in Melville's adolescent grief for his father as crucially influenced by his mother's style of bereavement. In name Tommo pastes together the "om" and "mo" of the only words he teaches his Marquesan father. "H-om-e" and "Mother." Through his anxious desire to resolve his grief, Tommo seems to become Maria Melville (home and mother), as he swells out the bosom of his coat with food during his escape, then later dons a petticoat, impersonates a belle, and indulges in fantasies of self-castration (Pedro, Mow-Mow, the leg pain). From this perspective, it seems appropriate that in his most vivid delineation of Marquesan mourning he describes bereaved widows. In the ritual of his fiction, Melville unconsciously picks apart the taboo, maternal text of grief by seeking to turn himself into it, or, as a "lover of human flesh" of another sort, he incestuously attempts to birth himself from his mother's grief.[35]

THE BODY POLITIC

Anthropologist Mary Douglas argues that "the body is a model which can stand for any bounded system. . . . We cannot possibly interpret rituals . . . unless we are prepared to see in the body a symbol of society, and to see the powers and dangers credited to social structure reproduced in small on the body." Tommo's polluted leg signifies the bounded system of the living linking object configuration: the maternally inscribed text of Melville's grief. According to Douglas, "The rituals work upon the body politic through the symbolic medium of the physical body." As a symbol of Victorian American codes for controlling bereavement, which Melville internalized from his mother's grief, the genteel "limb" in its throbbing threatens to release the powers and dangers of conflicted grief that Tommo's society wishes to keep within bounds. "Tommo" as subversive, bereaved text proves out Douglas's contention, "There is power in the forms, and other power in the inarticulate area, margins, confused lines, and beyond external boundaries." In his corporeal and narrative confused lines, Tommo mirrors back to Maria Melville the "contradictory . . . information" of her own unresolved grief as it has been transmuted into and energized her son's fictive mourning rite.[36]

CHAPTER THREE

Isles of the Dead: Dangerous Imaginings in *Mardi*'s Afterworlds

Women sob, and are rid of their grief; men laugh,
and retain it.
Babbalanja, in Melville's *Mardi*

Babbalanja tells of his father being sacrificed on the isle of Maramma:
"And have I not reason to be wary, when in my boyhood, my own sire
was burnt for his temerity; and in this very isle? Just Oro! it was done
in the name of Alma,—what wonder then, that, at times, I almost
hate that sound. And from those flames, they devoutly swore he went
to others,—horrible fable!" (349–50). Maramma parodies the Calvinistic faith of Melville's mother: the island's name condenses *Maria*, *mamma*, and *mar*. *Babbalanja*, the wildly speculative philosopher's
name, has swallowed up within it Melville's father's name: Allan.
The babbling speculator refigures the raving father on his deathbed,
whose financial speculations brought on his ruin. Babbalanja does
most of the talking in the last two-thirds of the book, yet criticism of
the novel has failed to draw attention to what, from his first to his last
speech, Melville's philosopher obsessively returns to: the nature of
the afterlife. "'All thought is a puff,'" the chronicler Mohi claims.
"'But in every puff, there hangs a wreath,'" Babbalanja retorts
(376).[1]

One of the main plot-lines of *Mardi* dramatizes how doubting

Babbalanja is finally saved on the island of Serenia, a land that simply practices Alma's or Christ's teachings without institutionalizing them. His conversion experience there alleviates the main source of Babbalanja's doubts: his anxiety about life after death (633). Although Alma's heaven radically differs from the heavenly home of liberal Victorian Americans—its inhabitants are still "liable to sin" and will "never gain a fixed beatitude" because "theirs is no state complete"; nevertheless, like the dominant ideology of the afterlife in Melville's culture, Alma's heaven offers believers such as Babbalanja "'repose,'" or a kind of sleep from which they may reawaken to a higher state (634, 630).

But what would Babbalanja's father's fate be in this new heaven? The horrible fable of damnation the philosopher earlier rejected has not been eradicated in Alma's afterlife. When Babbalanja asks about the fate of "'those who, living thoughtless lives of sin, die unregenerate,'" his angelic guide cryptically answers, "'they, too, have their place . . . but 'tis not here.'" "'Sin,'" the angel explains, "'is death'" (634). Of the hundreds of pages of his speculation through which the reader has wearily plodded, the philosopher now claims, "'All I have said ere this, that wars with Alma's precepts, I here recant'" (630).

Like the annoyed reader, *Mardi*'s protagonist, Taji, is not having any of Babbalanja's Serenian renunciation.[2] He continues his quest for "the lost one," the maiden Yillah, whom the narrative pervasively associates with the "ultimate" (347, 369). After failing to rescue her from the witch Hautia's whirlpool, Taji heads for his own afterworld. Seizing the helm of the boat sent to rescue him from Hautia, Taji proclaims, "is a life of dying worth living o'er again?— Let *me*, then, be the unreturning wanderer." As Yoomy recognizes, "eternity is in his eye!'" (654).

Taji's angry defiance and Melville's own sense of "a certain something unmanageable," a kind of explosive energy that had made him feel "irked, cramped & fettered" early in the composing process, both speak directly to the disorderly, adolescent energy that infuses *Mardi* (letter to Richard Bentley, June 5, 1849, *L*, 70–71). I argue that these disruptive feelings emerge in the narrative in intimate relation to cultural issues surrounding Melville's unfinished, conflicted grief for or his dangerous imaginings about his father. Babbalanja's obsession about the afterlife exposes Melville's need to exonerate his father from the flames to which Calvinism would have consigned him. "'Better were we all annihilated,'" Babbalanja maintains, "'than that one man should be damned'" (350). However, King Media, who sponsors Taji's Mardian quest, keeps raising the issue of moral accountability in response to Babbalanja's radical speculations about the nature of the afterlife.

Through a pervasive stealing motif, Melville links Babbalanja's critique of Victorian America's need to colonize heaven to a condemnation of similar urges motivating the ideology of Manifest Destiny: "'conquerors sighed for new Mardis; and sages for heaven'" (580). Thus the inset political allegory fits into the discourse on the hereafter that underlies much of Babbalanja's babbling and many of the vignettes that occur along the way. The conflicted, adolescent grief for Allan Melvill evoked by Mardi's discourse on the afterlife is linked to the sexual issues of adolescence and to the need to find a stable center, a viable masculine role model.[3]

The motif of stealing in the narrative links all of these themes: Allan Melvill was involved in an underhanded business scheme whose failure brought on his death; Taji instigates the action of the book when he steals a boat to escape the Arcturion, and the plot thickens when Hautia steals Yillah from Taji; the Parki episode introduces sexual issues into the text through the pilfering Annatoo, of "a lusty frame and a lustier soul," who personifies the disorderly energy about to plunge the narrative into a wild, interminable quest; and the Vivenzian jeremiad-scroll admonishes Jacksonian Americans, "'It is not freedom to filch'" (69, 529).[4]

Melanie Klein's notion of bizarre objects provides a useful perspective on the psychological dynamics of Mardi's multiple worlds. "Bizarre objects . . . are the outcome of pathological projective identification in which the object is perceived as split into minute fragments, each containing a projected part of the self. These bizarre objects are experienced as being charged with great hostility." The object often consists of the self, or parts of the self, which are disintegrated and then projected outward. If one defines self more broadly in terms of the cultural codes that factor into its formation, then Klein's notion can help us to see how *Mardi's* disruptive energy transforms into a critique of a cultural ground of identity. In other words, the conflicts of grief—the hostility that splits apart into the novels's archipelago of worlds—fuels the radical insights of Melville's imagination.[5]

AN AFTERWORLD OF DISPLACED GRIEF

Melville intimates at the outset of the narrative that all of the quest to follow might be the protagonist's fantasy while in a revery aloft after arguing with the *Arcturion's* captain about the latter's breaking of his "agreement": "he was going to detain me unlawfully" (7). The captain has decided to sail northern waters in search of whales in violation of the protagonist's understanding of the voyage for which he signed up. He feels a desire to jump ship that "became little short of a frenzy" (8).

At the outset, Taji tells us that the *Arcturion* sailed from "Ravavai" (3). The opening chapter thus begins by evoking a Raving I and ends with the narrator worked up to a frenzy. Before his argument with the captain, Taji confesses he began to long to escape from the ship while it lay "dead before the equatorial breeze" (4). Of the captain's decision to hunt in northern waters Taji observes, "We were going, it seemed, to illustrate the Whistonian theory concerning the damned and comets;—hurried from equinoctial heats to arctic frosts" (5). As the quest to follow transforms the material evoked in the first chapter—especially Taji's fear that he will turn into the Raving I—it glosses the broken agreement with the fatherly captain and connects it to the unresolved conflicts of Melville's adolescent grief for his father.

JARL

Before the quest through Mardi begins, the narrative takes us through three sequences: the escape with Jarl, the *Parki* drama, and the rescue of Yillah and slaying of the priest Aleema. Each of these narrative units brings us closer to the issues of Melville's conflicted grief before the quest proper translates them into larger cultural terms, especially as they connect with Babbalanja's wild speculations on an alternative to the dominant ideology of the afterlife in Melville's culture.

Prior to the escape, a calm at sea seems to Taji "a state of existence where existence itself seems suspended" (9). As if Taji has suddenly found himself in a kind of afterworld, "Thoughts of eternity thicken. He begins to feel anxious concerning his soul" (10). Immediately after the calm we meet Taji's first comrade, the fatherly Jarl, "a fine old seaman" (12). Jarl's first speech touches upon death: " 'To ourselves, we all seem coeval with creation. Whence it comes, that it is so hard to die, ere the world itself is departed' " (12). Taji, as well, starts talking about death: "Let us compose ourselves to death as fagged horsemen sleep in the saddle. Let us welcome even ghosts when they rise. . . . In heaven, at last, our good, old, white-haired father Adam will greet all alike, and sociality forever prevail" (12–13).

The escape itself is intimately associated with death. While examining their getaway boat, Taji speculates, "But how lower the tackles, even in the darkest night, without a creaking more fearful than the death rattle?" (20). This fear causes Taji to concoct a cover for their escape: they will holler man overboard, pretend that they are lowering to search for the victim, and then hope the captain thinks they were lost at sea while searching. In other words, Taji will feign the death at sea of both the spurious man overboard and then of himself and Jarl. But not only will Taji and Jarl escape by feigning death, but they will also be escaping the death that awaits the *Arcturion*: the ship was never heard from after their escape (25).

Immediately after the escape has been accomplished, their boat sails "right into the darkness, and dead to leeward" (28). Taji has the uncanny sensation of having died. "For the consciousness of being deemed dead, is next to the presumable unpleasantness of being so in reality. One feels like his own ghost unlawfully tenanting a defunct carcass" (29). Their boat rocks on the sea "as from hand to hand lost souls may be tossed along by the chain of shades which enfilade the route to Tartarus"; and they seemed "buried in watery hollows" (30). In mourning manual rhetoric, Taji advises us not to view death as "the last enemy of all" but rather to "regard him as the inflexible friend, who, even against our own wills, from life's evils triumphantly relieves us" (30).[6]

One might think he would go on to other things, but Taji continues his speculations about death—setting the tone for what will turn out to be Babbalanja's obsessive concern. "And there is but little difference in the manner of dying," Taji philosophizes, "To die, is all" (30). But he is not content to let the subject rest here. Geoffrey Hudson (the dwarf), a butterfly, and women "have lived nobler lives, and died nobler deaths, than men" (30). It begins to appear that Taji feels ambivalent about the importance of "the manner of dying," because he next tells us that "To expire, mild-eyed, in one's bed, transcends the death of Epaminondas" (31). Taji avoids addressing directly here what to make of one, like Melville's father, or more recently his brother Gansevoort, who dies after a personal failure and in the throes of mania. More curious is why he even speculates at length on such matters at this moment in the narrative. The reason is that Melville obsessively focuses on death and afterlife from the beginning to the end of *Mardi*, and much of what initially seems unmotivated rambling comes into perspective when viewed in terms of a continuing discourse on these questions.[7]

What motivates this discourse are the conflicts of unresolved grief that slowly emerge as the narrative unfolds, although they never starkly breach Melville's resistance to and denial of them. The amiable but shallow captain who breaks his agreement with Taji is displaced by the loving figure of Jarl: the seemingly good parent. But once alone at sea with Jarl, Taji begins to note some unsettling things about him. As he thinks about him in this new setting the issue of mourning immediately surfaces: "In the tragico-comico moods which at times overtook me, I used to look upon the brown Skyeman with humorous complacency. If we fall in with cannibals, thought I, then, ready-roasted Norsemen that thou art, shall I survive to mourn thee; at least during the period I revolve upon the spit" (34). But what provokes Taji's anxiety is Jarl's deathlike silence (36). A few pages later Taji pauses to note that "the only true infidelity is for a live man to vote himself dead" (39).[8]

In a second calm, Taji's anxieties about death sharpen, and his buried anger at the displaced father figure emerges. During the stillness, gusts of wind seemed "faint as the breath of one dying" (48). As their water dwindles, Taji begins to wish for Jarl's death: "Like a desperado giving up the ghost, I desired to gasp by myself" (50). When the calm abates, their boat "seemed raised from the dead" (50).

After Taji kills a shark, the bereaved pilot fish which had swum beside it transfer their attachment to the boat. The pilot fish have been associated with grief, and by following Taji's boat they deepen the association of his quest with a funeral procession. Later the pilot fish seem to transform into Hautia's messengers, who bring real messages of conflicted grief from the abhorrent Hautia. After the quest gets fully under way, this link is directly made. Taji comments that he and his mates "drooped lower and lower, like funeral plumes; and our gloomy canoe seemed a hearse" (370). King Media asks, " 'Go we to bury our dead?' " (371).[9]

BROKEN BLADES: ANNATOO

The second major sequence of *Mardi*'s first part occurs aboard the *Parki*, a seemingly abandoned ship lost at sea, which Jarl initially insists is "haunted" (57).[10] During the "*Parki* drama," the disorderly, thieving "termagant," Annatoo assumes center stage (88, 81). The emphasis given to her pilfering of the *Parki*'s supplies and to the destructive consequences of her thievery obscures what she more powerfully signifies: the disorderly energy that is about to take over the narrative, motivated in part by Melville's pilfering of the classics he was then first discovering and resulting in the destabilization of the book with uncontrolled and anxious inventiveness. Annatoo's characterization functions to connect these unruly impulses with the sexual issues of Melville's unresolved adolescent grief.

In first exploring the *Parki*'s hold, Taji comes upon a cutlass: "The broken blade of the cutlass was very rusty and stained. . . . It looked so tragical that I thrust it out of sight" (59). Burrowing deeper into the ship, they come upon Annatoo's deserted "lair" (59). Rummaging through her treasures, they find "a queer little hair trunk" securely locked (60). Prying it open, they find "pasted on the inside of the cover . . . a little colored print, representing the harlots, the shameless hussies, having a fine time with the Prodigal Son" (60). As soon as this piece of treasure is opened, Annatoo, from the rigging where she hides, drops "a great top-block," which just misses Jarl (60).

Jarl now becomes more convinced that "piratical ghosts and goblins" inhabit the *Parki*, "a shade of a ship, full of sailors' ghosts" (63). Yet the exploration of the ship assumes another dimension. Sounding the ship's well, Taji comments, " 'Tis like feeling your own pulse in the last stage of a fever" (63). Finding a " 'barge' of biscuit," they gorge themselves, while Jarl starts at "wild shadows" (64). However, this container of food is "an oblong oaken box" or coffin-shaped.

We learn about Annatoo's thieving ways from Samoa's story of the *Parki*'s history, as retold by Taji. After this tale is told, Taji undercuts its trustworthiness: "Though abounding in details full of the savor of reality, Samoa's narrative did not at first appear altogether satisfactory" (89). The tale itself, though, details the duplicities of the Cholos, who deceive the *Parki*'s crew in order to massacre them, and it presents an Annatoo who embodies the suspicious and untrustworthy. Fearing that Samoa will not submit to his authority if he tells him that he jumped ship, Taji himself participates in the theme of distrust by telling Samoa a tailored version of his own story: "I therefore spoke vaguely of our adventures, and assumed the decided air of a master" (90). Taji's anxious sense of his own authority can be understood through a close look at Annatoo's characterization.

Samoa falls for Annatoo after her "first virgin bloom had departed, leaving nothing but a lusty frame and a lustier soul" (69). The narrative deepens her association with desire run amuck. She acquits herself valiantly in defeating the Cholos and behaves like a greedy child who wants all of the *Parki*'s treasures for herself (75). Because her voice was "a park of artillery; her talons a charge of bayonets," she lets Samoa have the captain's "arms and ammunition"; but in fact she has hung a basket of "sundry knives, hatchets, and ax-heads" over the side of the ship (76, 113). While Samoa "assigned" her to amputate his arm wounded in the fight with the Cholos, with "untiring energy" Annatoo thwarts the masculine wills aboard the Parki and, as a result, the narrative associates "the audacious dame" with an unmistakably castrating force: she seems to cannibalize the figure of heroic manhood, Samoa (78, 80).

In this role, she elicits Taji's deepest insecurities about his masculinity. Out of fear of "the outlandish caprices of Annatoo," Taji takes command of the ship "in the mild, firm tone of a superior; being anxious, at once to assume the unquestioned supremacy" (96). But his authority partakes of the presence of "honest old Jarl at the helm, watchfully guiding her path, like some devoted old foster-father" (97).

Annatoo seems to be "possessed by some scores of devils, perpetually inciting her to mischief on their own separate behoof, and not hers" (113). After she steals the ship's compass, Taji decides that the "nightly incarceration" of Annatoo is necessary (114). Ultimately, Annatoo becomes for Taji a figure of "Woman unendurable" (115). But Annatoo seems less a woman than a personification of destructive human urges, which may well be the Victorian American definition of woman uncontrolled by man.

Samoa illustrates the consequences for identity of the presence of such inner devils in human nature. His tattoos cause him to look like "a union of the unmatched moieties of two distinct beings" (99). Because his tattoos cover only half of his body, "When he turned round upon you suddenly, you thought you saw some one else, not him whom you had been regarding before" (99). At once "manly enough, nay, an obelisk in stature . . . a hero," Samoa also turns out to be "a coxcomb" (98): "For myself, I ever regarded Samoa as but a large fragment of a man, not a man complete. For was he not an entire limb out of pocket?" (78) The "broken blade" reappears not only in his fractured identity but also in the form of "the stump [of his] multilated arm" (66). Samoa wears the kind of fine goods—calico and silk—Melville's father dealt in: he appears "theatrically arrayed in kilt and turban; the kilt of a gay calico print, the turban of a red China silk" (66). The kilt, as well, gestures toward Allan Melvill's Scottish ancestry.

Melville picks up on the theme of fractured manhood in a seeming digression on the Indian swordfish. Taji compares his "bony blade" to the "drawn soul of genius" (104). Commiserating with the bereaved pilot fish who are at the mercy of the swordfish, Taji catches the latter and severs "his terrible blade" (105). Claiming the broken blade as a "trophy," he mounts it "over the head of my hammock": "It was an aromatic sword; like the ancient caliph's, giving out a peculiar musky odor by friction" (105).

Prior to this vignette of phallic rivalry, Taji describes his descent into Annatoo's "hiding places": the "midnight hold," which he descends as if entering "old vaults and catacombs" (101). The hull seems "a mine of stolen goods, stolen out of its own bowels" (101). First he finds the captain's "jaunty shore cap"; next, he finds Annatoo's special hiding place: "a huge ground-tier butt, headless as Charles the First," where she was "wont to coil herself away, like a garter-snake under a stone" (101, 102). The phallic victory over the macho swordfish seems motivated by this glimpse into castrating Annatoo's lair: the place where she has secreted the goods she appropriated from the captain's stores, or the bits of masculinity, of patriarchal power, Taji fears she will also steal from him.[11] Later Taji costumes himself in a "free, flowing" manner with goods taken from the same captain's stores (127).

Mardi finally assigns Jarl the task of getting rid of Annatoo. During a storm, "spending in a few, brief blasts . . . [its] concentrated rage," Jarl fells the mainmast in an attempt to save the ship (116). The falling mast knocks a lanyard-block into Annatoo's "forehead," sending her into the "whirlpool under our lea," as if revenging Jarl for Annatoo's earlier attempt to kill him with a "great top-block" (117).

The storm creates a graphically orgasmic scene in which its few brief blasts throw Annatoo's lusty frame into a whirlpool of desire. After the storm subsides, the "wreck" of the ship also intimates a post-orgasmic scene: "With every pitch we lifted our dangling jib-boom into the air; and beating against the side, were the shattered fragments of the masts" (118).

Annatoo's death scene conflates rage and sexuality. And it is rage that underlies the *Parki* drama. Annatoo's initial attempt to kill Jarl externalizes the anger about his fractured sense of manhood that genteel Taji cannot express, except in the displaced broken blade motif.[12] When Jarl dismasts the Parki in an attempt to save it—before he leaves the ship he "buried his ax in the splintered stump of the mainmast"—the mast becomes yet another broken blade: this time one which eliminates the disorderly Annatoo, but which also gestures toward Allan's final dismasted, manic state (120). After the passing of the storm in which Annatoo dies, "every dead dash" of the sea on the Parki's hull seems "like blows upon a coffin" (118). The water turns "a pallid white color," and it casts "a cadaverous gleam upon the boat, so that we looked to each other like ghosts" (121).

Within the *Parki*, Melville pits against the good father, Jarl, disorderly feelings which evoke ambivalence about Allan Melvill, who could have seemed to his son, because of the illicit secret partnership scheme that bankrupted him and his general over-reaching style as a merchant, to have been associated with the pilfering energy of an Annatoo. Annatoo condenses both a veiled allusion to his father and the buried rage of Melville's unresolved grief response. Under the safety of her mask, in displaced form, his anger toward Allan can emerge.

Melville's covert identification with Annatoo's *Explosive I*, the "park of artillery" in her voice, underlies the *Parki* sequence. From this angle, *Mardi* evokes the *Marred I*, the broken blade of selfhood left in the wake of and epitomized by Allan's death. *Annatoo* seems a scrambled version of Allan Too, or Two. In her thievery and irrationality, this refiguration of Melville's memory of Allan registers a son's fears that he too will be victimized by the disorderly energy that turned his father into a maniac. Annatoo obsessing about the captain's goods seems a painful translation and distancing of Melville's anxieties about appropriating his share of valuable masculine treasures from the memory of his raving, bankrupt father. And from this perspective, the broken blade motif also evokes the imagery of dismemberment, which, as we have seen, the Harvard Study of Bereavement finds characteristic of male bereavement.[13]

ALEEMA AND YILLAH

The third and final sequence before the quest proper begins strongly evokes Melville's unresolved grief. After Taji loses Yillah to Hautia, the quest seems one not so much deeper into the ultimate significance of Yillah, as one that distances and distracts Melville from what surfaces in the murder of Aleema. When Taji first approaches Aleema's canoe, he offers the priest silk handerkerchiefs as peace tokens; Aleema ties the handerchiefs on himself "like a brace of Highland plaids" (130). Taji soon learns that Aleema transports Yillah, a sacrificial offering, "from the island of Amma to the gods of Tedaidee" (131). The "invisible victim" hidden in her tent provokes Taji to battle Aleema and his sons for her rescue (131). To win Aleema's confidence, Taji gives the priest "a roll of printed cotton" with a pattern of "sailor boys" climbing the rigging (132). Aleema claims that he had "ascended the shrouds of a ship," and as he says this "his countenance was overcast with a ferocious expression, as if something terrific was connected with the reminiscence" (132).

The murder of Aleema occurs after he inexplicably warns Taji, "'Depart and you live; stay and you die'" (132). After Aleema "flung" Taji "from his side" and menaces him with his dagger with a "thrust and a threat," Taji strikes first and slays him (133). Yet Taji hardly acts but rather reacts: "Ere I knew it, my cutlass made a quick lunge" (133). In the Annatoo episode, Taji's rage against a father figure was projected onto Annatoo. Now his anger hones in on a paternal figure who rejects him. Once more the silk goods and Scottish ancestry of Allan Melvill are evoked in the silk Highland plaids

Aleema seems to wear. But now the innocent adolescent self victimized by grief splits off into Yillah, who is an "offering" from *Amma* (Mama) to *Tedaidee* (To Daddy). The formula here resembles the living linking object configuration, in which the child's grief takes shape from that of the surviving parent's bereavement. In name, *Aleema* seems to conflate not only Allan and Ma, but also the surrogate father of the Melville family Lemuel Shaw, who had recently become Melville's father-in-law.[14]

After slaying Aleema, Taji confronts the intense bereavement of the priest's sons. In their howling, "Rage and grief had almost disabled them" (133).[15] Their "low, piercing wail" profoundly unsettles Taji (134). Turning from his guilt, he approaches Yillah's tent, which seemed "now still as the grave" (135). However, his first glimpse of her mirrors back to him the grief reaction from which he has just turned away. She "looked sadly out from her long, fair hair. A low wail issued from her lips" (136). Her "piercing, bewildered gaze" resembles mourning's first phase (137).

After hearing the fantasic history Aleema has taught Yillah, Taji becomes convinced she was "some beautiful maniac" (137). Not only is Yillah the innocent self sacrificed to Allan's death and the grief reaction Taji cannot experience and that therefore he cannot recover after Hautia (a mask for haughty Maria) steals her from him—a close approximation of how Maria's grief could have subsumed her son's—but she also seems to be a maniac like Melville's father on his deathbed.[16]

Indeed, Yillah is intimately associated with death. Initially, Taji thinks she is a Tulla, or one of an albino race who "die early" (153). Just before he loses her, Taji wonders of her presence, "Did I commune with a spirit?" (193) If Yillah is a figure for grief, within her characterization Melville situates the uninhibited creativity he quests for and fails to open up in *Mardi*, as though his unresolved grief seals within itself full access to his creative energy. Yillah's "witching" hand "seemed no hand, but a touch. Visions flitted before me and in me; something hummed in my ear; all the air was a lay" (144). She becomes his creative landscape (this is echoed in the Mardian poet Lombardo's notion of creating the creative landscape within himself before he can begin to write): "Was not Yillah my shore and my grove . . . and my arbor?" (145).

This configuration assumes a stark formulation for Taji: "As we glided along, strange Yillah gazed down in the sea, and would fain have had me plunge into it with her, to rove through its depths. But I started dismayed; in fancy, I saw the stark body of the priest drifting by" (145). To go into the depths of feeling with Yillah would mean to confront the dead corpse that has not been dealt with there. Aleema's "ghost sunk not in the deep waters of my soul. However in exultations its surface foamed up, at bottom guilt brooded" (140). Unable to expunge Aleema from his own thoughts, Taji nevertheless alleviates Yillah's "dangerous imaginings" (142). He fears that after the loss of her father figure Yillah's bereaved "fancies" will be "all roving through mazes" (142). He quells her fears by substituting himself for the dead father: " 'Think not of him . . . Look on me' " (142). However, the dangerous imaginings of his own conflicted grief continue: "Many visions I had of the green corse of the priest, outstretching its arms in the water, to receive pale Yillah, as she sunk in the sea" (159).

The death of and grief for Aleema and Taji's loss of and bereavement for Yillah neatly bracket the Aleema/Yillah sequence. After returning home to find their "arbor vacant," Taji "raved" (194). After his "Misery became a memory," Taji pauses to comment on the persistence of a deep grief over time:

> The keen pang a deep vibration . . . There are thoughts that lie and glitter deep: tearful pearls beneath life's sea, that surges still, and rolls sunlit, whatever it may hide. Common woes, like fluids, mix all round. Not so with that other grief. Some mourners load the air with lamentations; but the loudest notes are struck from hollows. Their tears flow fast: but the deep spring only wells. (194)

The enduring tearful pearls beneath life's sea become significant in the novel's conclusion because there Hautia and Taji ostensibly dive for pearls in her whirlpools.

AFTERWORLDS OF MASCULINE DECLENSION

Mardi's reader quickly recognizes that its quest hardly has Yillah as its object. Instead, the survey first of the defective manhood of Mardi's kings and then the political allegory of Melville's contemporary scene serve to critique larger cultural formations that make the possession of Yillah or a full grief reaction impossible.[17] Each king portrays another aspect of the Marred I. As a group portrait, the kings comprise an image of masculine identity that conforms to Babbalanja on manhood: "We have had vast developments of parts of men; but none of manly wholes" (593).

Taji himself embodies the flawed manhood he meets with on every island he visits. When he arrives at the first Mardian island, King Media's Odo, its inhabitants mistake him for "a sort of half-and-half deity . . . ranking among their inferior ex-officio demi-gods" (164). A "calm old" king, though, identifies the Taji of their mythology more specifically: " 'Thou wast but a quarrelsome demi-god, say the legends' " (166).

Taji soon fades into the background of the quest, during which he is supplanted by his Mardian host, King Media, and his traveling companions, the humor characters Babbalanja, the diffident poet Yoomy, and the elderly historian Mohi. However, the mechanism by which they displace him involves their growing out of the "small strange voices" that constitute Taji's initial grief for Yillah (194). Each of these characters as well turns out to be deeply flawed. Although Media is eminently levelheaded and graced with an "easy, frank demeanor," he tyrannizes over the disadvantaged of Odo, at one point refusing to grant them trial by jury (182). The chronicler Mohi turns out to be flawed not only by pedantry but also in his fear of approaching death (619). Babbalanja's flaw consists of the inner devil, Azzageddi, who at times seizes control of him and who can be a figure for morality: As-aged-die.

The poet Yoomy's liability is creativity itself and it prepares us for the portraits of the kings and for the deeper implications of the novel. He "was so capricious a mortal; so swayed by contrary moods; . . . so made up of a thousand contradictions, that we must e'en let him depict himself as our story progresses" (197). Yoomy's creative experience as a poet has inverted his sense of gender. "'The air that breathes my music from me is a mountain air! Purer than others am I; for though not a woman, I feel in me a woman's soul'" (438). Like the narrative itself, which splits into a multi-vocal performance once the quest commences, Yoomy "was miraculously gifted with three voices; and, upon occasions, like a mocking-bird, was a concert of sweet sounds in himself" (559–60). "Had kind friends died," Taji asks, "and bequeathed him their voices?" (560).

Of the eight kings who are delineated in detail, the first two, Peepi and Donjalolo, and the last two, Yoky and Abrazza, vividly illustrate the relationship between grief and masculine declension in *Mardi*. The text inserts a vignette about grief into the visit to each of these kings' islands, so that their lack of "manly" wholeness is intimately related to the experience of bereavement.[18] The first king, Peepi, is a ten-year-old whose father died before he was born and bequeathed to him twenty heroes "previously lodged" in himself (202). As a result, "revolving souls," which make him "one of the most unreliable of beings," govern Peepi's consciousness (203).

The narrative pauses only long enough on Peepi's island to discuss teeth as mourning mementoes. While "in all lands, men smite their breasts, and tear their hair, when transported with grief; so, in some countries, teeth are stricken out under the sway of similar emotions" (206). In Peepi's Valapee, "they extract the teeth from the departed, distributing them among the mourners for memorial legacies; as elsewhere [in Melville's Dutch milieu], silver spoons are bestowed" (206).

Before we meet the second king, Donjalolo, Media encourages his party to discourse freely by doing "'away with all rigidities'" (208). As a result, the discourse among the questors that is to carry on for several hundred pages begins. Their chatter commences in earnest after they pass a rock called "Pella, or The Theft," which is believed to be an urn for ten kings (209). Babbalanja's first lengthy speech occurs at this point, and it ushers in the topic he obsessively dwells on throughout the narrative: the nature of the afterlife. Of the kings supposedly buried in the rock, Babbalanja argues, " 'whether they ever lived or not, it is all the same with them now. Yet, grant that they lived; then, if death be a deaf-and-dumb death, a triumphal procession over their graves would concern them not' " (209–10).

"Certain peculiar deprivations, under which he labored" distinguish the second king, Donjalolo, a young man of twenty-five (218). Donjalolo possesses a harem of thirty wives, one for each day of the month; and "it was his harem that did much to stamp [his] character": that of an enervate, feminized youth (241). The spermatic economy that Victorian Americans believed could drain a man of vital force has marked Donjalolo with a "comeliness . . . so feminine, that he was sometimes called 'Foonoo,' or the Girl" (216).[19]

But this gender inversion in Donjalolo has been produced by what looks very much like conflicted grief. The king's ancestor, Teei, defeated his brother, Majora, in a battle for the throne.[20] After Marjori kills Teei, a "sacred oracle" condemns Marjori not to leave the glen where he slew his brother, thus creating a scenario in which the kings of Juam are "buried alive in their glen" (220, 231). Locked within the glen carved inside of a mountain, Donjalolo "wasted the powers which might have compassed the noblest designs" (223). Determined to explore the world outside the glen, his fate is sealed when he prepares to set out on an adventure only to have his questing thwarted by his father, who takes poison in order to force his son to accept the royal legacy.

In his conflicted grief—his anger at his father for dooming him to life within the glen and his guilt at having motivated the paternal suicide—Donjalolo "gradually fell into desperate courses, to drown the emotions at times distracting him" (223). His masculine identity—defined in terms of the aggressive individualism of Victorian America's masculine role—has been turned against itself: "His generous spirit thirsting after some energetic career, found itself narrowed down within the little glen of Willamilla, where ardent impulses seemed idle. But these are hard to die; and repulsed all round, recoil upon themselves" (223). Donjalolo "at intervals . . . was the victim of unaccountable vagaries; haunted by specters, and beckoned to by the ghosts of his sires" (223).

In the visits to the last two kings, Yoky and Abrazza, Melville more intimately explores the relationship between grief and the declension of masculinity. Yoky's Isle of Cripples, Hooloomooloo, is the asylum for the deformed children of the other islands.[21] Yoky himself is legless and "deaf and dumb": "So huge his all-comprehensive mouth, it seemed to swallow up itself" (570). It then becomes intriguing that on this island, which sharply evokes the feeling of being crippled, helpless, and all mouth, *Mardi* situates its most intimate tale of bereavement.

The tale concerns Rozoko, "an old gray-headed Chimpanzee" (571). Yoky's "venerable predecessor" one day found Rozoko "meditating in the woods" (571). The chimp was "very grave, and reverend of aspect; much of a philosopher" and "in love with his Timonean solitude"; however, the king lures Rozoko to his court; and they become "Ardent friends," who confront their imminent deaths together (571).

Due to his love for the chimp, the king orders that at death they be buried together. After the king dies, Rozoko was "reduced to second childhood, wailed most dismally . . . and noisely expired" (572). Years go by, the islanders grow ashamed that their king is buried with a chimp, but when they attempt to separate the remains they are unable to tell the king's from the chimp's bones. On one level, the tale pokes fun at antievolutionists, but something else is going on here. On the isle of cripples, we are told a story of a loving friend who dies of grief for his beloved companion. In the tale of Rozoko, which appears close to the end of the quest, Melville associates fulfilling a need for intimacy and yielding to intense grief with a crippling, deadly threat. Rozoko himself seems to have stepped out of one of Maria Melville's Dutch Calvinist mourning mementoes: the "monkey spoon."[22]

The last king, Abrazza, personifies the alternative to yielding to grief. Just before they reach his island, the questors sail through a Death-cloud (586). This mighty storm sweeps before it a "thousand prows," ships that would have been saved had they not fled their islands in fear of the storm (586). " 'Flying death, they ran to meet it,' " Babbalanja comments (587). But of he who did not flee, Babbalanja notes, " 'tis because he stands the center of a circle; its every point a leveled dart; and every bow, bent back' " (587). This evocation of the immediacy of death ushers us into our visit to the last king, the "care-free bachelor" who has "something sinister, hollow, heartless" about him" (588, 603).

At first sight and sound Abrazza's island seems to evoke grief. It is "overcast with shadows; a shower was falling; and pining, plaintive notes forth issued from the groves: half-suppressed, and sobbing whisperings of leaves" (588). But Abrazza lives on the other side of the island, the "sunny side" (588). The sounds of grief are the voices of his oppressed people, who lurk in the shadows like "some ugly phantom" (590). Although Abrazza " 'vows he'll have no cares,' " the very jewels of his crown cast "sinister" beams: "all present looked cadaverous" in their glow (589). During Abrazza's genial feast, Babbalanja refuses to partake and instead hopes he will meet Abrazza " 'the first midnight after he dies; at the grave-yard corner;—there I'll be, and grin again!' " (610).

AFTERWORLDS AS JEREMIADS

After Melville completed a manuscript of the quest through Mardi, he added several set-pieces. Chief among these is an allegorical tour through his contemporary world scene. The critical consensus on this political insert is that it breaks the unity of the quest and prolongs the agony of an unsuccessful novel. When viewed, however, in the context of the novel's pervasive discourse on the afterlife, one sees that Melville has skillfully illuminated his culture's attitude to the afterlife as the underpinning of its political credo, Manifest Destiny. Melville's contemporaries viewed death as a sleep from which one would awaken after the millennium, which would be brought about after the American political empire triumphed. " 'The grand error' " of Vivenza (America) is the " 'conceit that Mardi is now in the last scene of the last act of her drama; and that all preceding events were ordained, to bring about the catastrophe you believe to be at hand,—a universal and permanent Republic'" (525). " 'Eternity is not ours by right,'" Bardianna, Babbalanja's guru insists, implicitly linking the afterlife to Manifest Destiny (577). Melville thus critiques his culture's urge to colonize—or steal—political and spiritual territory. On a more intimate level, Melville's anger at cultural thievery provides him with a context in which he can exonerate his father's illicit business manuevers and his ultimate fall by viewing them as participating in a cultural norm.[23]

Melville carefully sets up his analysis of the similarity between Victorian American attitudes to the afterlife and to territorial expansion. The "Land of Life," Vivenza, turns out to be a landscape of death. In a *Yankee Doodle*-style jeremiad at Congress, Melville describes the Senate in terms of "catacombs, which seemed full of the ghosts of fat Lamberts [Daniel Lambert was 5 feet 9 inches tall and weighed 739 pounds]" (516).[24] The senators are glimpsed "making a great show of imperious and indispensable business," as they fold scrolls and give them to boys, who "fled as if with salvation for the dying" (515).

Just before he introduces a mysteriously authored scroll containing his critique of the thievery at the heart of the Vivenzian soul, a parody of the expansionist Senator William Allen appears in the person of Senator Alanno.[25] While orating on Dominora's (England's) encroachments on the Northwest, Alanno turns into a "crazy man," "the unfortunate lunatic" (517). "Roaring like a wild beast, and beating the air like a windmill," Alanno delivers his speech in a "delirium" (517, 516).

In a perfect example of how Melville perceived that his father's fall was shaped by larger cultural forces, he blurs Senator Allen together with Allan Melvill as deathbed maniac. "The hostility of the lunatic orator" leads into a consideration of the relationship of America to England insofar as they "stand in the relation of sons to sires" (519). Babbalanja claims that America should maintain " 'a reverential respect for its parent'" (519). In rhetoric that demands the expungement of conflict between child and parent, Babbalanja argues that Dominora should be given confidence " 'that when at last laid in his tomb, he will yet survive in the long, strong life of his child, the worthy inheritor of his valor and renown' " (520). The political allegory turns into behavior manual advice about denying grief's conflicts.[26]

AFTERWORLDS OF CREATIVITY

Babbalanja articulates his most subversive views on death in his discussion of the poet Lombardo's creativity. Although Lombardo initially wrote by "Necessity," something else took over once he got going: "We are full of ghosts and spirits; we are as grave-yards full of buried dead, that start to life before us. And all our dead sires, verily, are in us; *that* is their immortality" (593–94). In this view, the afterworld opens up within the writer's creative experience as his ancestors are resurrected inside him. Immersion in inner conflict spurs the writer to delve into his inner afterworlds: " 'We need fiery baptisms in the fiercest flames of our own bosoms' "; "Oh! there is a fierce, a cannibal delight, in the grief that shrieks to multiply itself' " (594).

Of the form of Lombardo's epic, *Koztanza*, Babbalanja says, " 'its expanding soul, past Mardi does embalm' " (597). This would in-volve a cannibalistic feeding on the awakened dead in one's inner afterworld: creativity as a funerary rite.[27] In another chapter thought to be a late insert, "Dreams," creativity is viewed in similar terms. The dreamer comes upon an inner "Antarctic barrier of ice," which feels "Deathful, desolate" and seems comprised of "frozen cemeteries of skeletons and bones" (366–67). Filled with "many, many souls," not just immediate progenitors but those of the great writers, the dreamer's creative life takes shape out of their conversation within himself (367).

Babbalanja's key speech on the experience of grief occurs just before the questors arrive at Serenia. In "Babbalanja at the Full of the Moon," the philosopher responds wildly to Media's request to laugh and drink. After Media asks, "'Go we to a funeral, that our paddles seem thus muffled,'" Babbalanja acts out this fantasy (612). Pouring wine for his companions, he exclaims, "'And now let us drown away grief. Ha! ha! the house of mourning, is deserted, though of old good cheer kept the funeral guests; and so keep I mine; here I sit by my dead, and replenish your wine cups'" (612–13). As Babbalanja vents his buried griefs, his voice surges out of control: "let us laugh, let us scream! . . . Though wisdom be wedded to woe, though the way thereto is by tears, yet all ends in a shout. . . . Ha! ha! how demoniacs shout" (613).

Significantly, Babbalanja associates lingering bereavement with mania. The babbling philosopher here reveals why his name has cannibalistically incorporated that of Allan: Babbalanja's wild speculations grow out of the instability Melville associates with his own chief masculine model. The babbling, in short, is displaced grief—or a way of talking around but always coming back to Melville's anxieties about his father's fate. To parry the conflicts of his grief in *Mardi*—his sense of a Marred I—he devises a way of identifying with Allan through Babb-*alan*-ja. In fact, as he defines creativity as discourse with the dead reawakened within one's psyche—creativity as the real afterworld, the one lived out in the present—Melville can hardly avoid identifying with his father's deathbed mania and creatively transforming it—or trying to—into Babbalanja's voice.

For Babbalanja, creativity as displaced grief is inescapable: "'there is much to be learned from the dead, more than you may learn from the living, and I am dead though I live; and as soon dissect myself as another; I curiously look into my secrets: and grope under my ribs. *I have found that the heart is not whole, but divided*" (613–14, my emphasis). The writer thus opens up the afterworld of creativity within himself—"'we live in Eternity now,'" Babbalanja claims—that other men project into the heavens (620). Rather than act out the ethos of Manifest Destiny, the writer turns inward—in implicit violation of gender codes, which explains the poet Yoomy feeling within himself "'a woman's soul'"—discovering there the "contrary moods" that Melville's fellow Jacksonians escaped as they enacted an expansionist anxiety (438).[28]

Babbalanja intimately reveals his inner instability after hearing Yoomy's parody of Shelley's "Adonais," " 'a noble monody upon the death of Adondo,' " who died after being "wounded in the head"—a fate that recalls that of Melville's father (453).[29] Babbalanja confesses, " 'I have not yet been able to decide who or what I am' ": "I keep an eye on myself, as I would on a stranger. There is something going on in me, that is independent of me" (456). For Media, these admissions are unsettling: he quickly asks a question he raises throughout the book, one central to Melville's assessment of his father's fall, "have you mortals no moral sense, as they call it?" (456). Although Babbalanja concedes the existence of a moral sense, he argues that men " 'are governed by their very natures. . . . It is easier for some men to be saints, than for others not to be sinners' " (457). This provides a basis for exonerating Allan for his fall, but it also implicates Melville in a possible inheritance of his father's wounded head.

In a revealing narrative sequence, Melville's conflicted grief takes on a sharper definition. The questors visit the antiquarian Oh-Oh's museum and examine books with telling titles: "The Philosophy of Honesty, by a late Lord, who died in disgrace" and "Letters from a Father to a Son, inculcating the Virtue of Vice" (384). These Chesterfieldian titles serve to evoke the fate of Allan Melvill, who owned volumes by Chesterfield. Babbalanja is much more taken by a book by his guru, Bardianna, "A Happy Life." When he begins to read this book we are told: "Bringing forth the treasure he had buried in his bosom, he was soon buried in it; and motionless on his back, looked as if laid out, to keep an appointment with his undertaker" (387). The book turns out to be a behavior manual that spews forth advice immediately relevant to and critical of the way Allan's bankruptcy proved fatal: " 'I would bear the same mind, whether I be rich or poor, whether I get or lose in the world' " (388).[30]

The questors soon visit the ultra-genteel Tapparians, who are

obsessed not only with "amazingly arbitrary" laws but with cloth—
the goods Allan imported—and who disavow their ancestry (399).[31]
From here the questors travel to the Isle of Fossils, where Babbalanja's
demon, Azzageddi, first begins to rave (417). Before the demon's
emergence, Babbalanja, "in sepulchral tones," reads the "picture
petrified" of the fossils (416). He describes "a stately banquet of the
dead," in which "a monarch [was] fossilized in very act of murdering
his guest" (416).

In this narrative sequence, anger at Allan emerges in the Chesterfieldian titles and in Bardianna's etiquette manual, and Allan-like
gentility is lampooned in the Tapparians, but the sequence concludes
with a self-punitive gesture: in the fossilized afterworld the monarch
proves a murderer, an image evocative of Melville's fear of his memory of Allan. This fear then assumes a more overt form when, as if in
imitation of Allan's deathbed mania, Babbalanja's demon rides him.

HAUTIA'S AFTERWORLD OF CONFLICTED GRIEF

Mardi ends with Taji's visit to and then escape from Hautia's isle.
Unable to give over his quest and accept Babbalanja's quiescent
afterworld, Serenia, Taji journeys to his own afterworld, one fraught
with conflict. As Taji first approaches Hautia's island, "conflicting
emotions tore up" his soul "in tornadoes" (643). Instinctively, his
"whole heart abhorred" Hautia (643). She seems associated with
both death (she is "motionless" and "mute") and sexuality (of her
island he says, "No sweets can be sweeter, but no Upas more deadly"
[646, 644]). After Hautia drugs Taji, he turns into " 'my own monument [burial marker?], till Hautia breaks the spell' " (649). The key
image of the Hautia episode is the vortex: she identifies herself as
" 'the vortex that draws all in,' " and she takes Taji to dive for both
pearls and Yillah in "conflicting currents" (650, 653). From the
conflicting emotions her island first evokes in him to the conflicting
currents that prevent him from rescuing Yillah from the vortex,
Hautia's realm stands for the conflict Taji attempts to project outside
of himself.

The cave to which Hautia first takes Taji to dive for pearls "shone like a Queen of Kandy's casket" (651). Finally, she reveals that Yillah is in a vortex-tomb in another cavern (653). Unable to swim to her through "gulfs of blackness," Taji, with "death-glazed eyes" wanders on the beach in his own afterworld (653). " 'Taji lives no more,' " he answers to Mohi's question, " 'Is this specter, Taji? . . . I am his spirit's phantom's phantom'" (653).

Taji seizes "the helm" of the boat sent to rescue him and heads for the " 'deep beyond,' " from which " 'no voyager e'er puts back' " (654). Determined to be the " 'unreturning wanderer, [repudiating] a life of dying,' " Taji commits the " 'last, last crime' " as he aspires to " 'eternity' " (654).[32] The novel ends on a series of staccato images: Yoomy "buoying Mohi up" as they swim away from the mad Taji, "the salt waves dashing the tears" from Yoomy's "pallid face," which gazes "mournfully" on Taji—a split-off image of expressive grief; and Aleema's sons still pursuing Taji, as though they personify a bereaved rage that Taji cannot confront in himself (654).

"Again the buried bard tore at my soul," Taji says of his revived grief, "again Yillah was invoked, but Hautia made reply" (568). In her first appearance in the novel, Taji identifies Hautia as "a spirit, forever prying into my soul" (186). In the context of *Mardi's* action, Hautia seemingly punishes Taji for killing Aleema by stealing Yillah from him. Melville's mother's haughty grief conditioned his own grief for his father, and this grief haunts Taji through Hautia. Taji poised before unattainable Yillah in Hautia's vortex evokes Melville cut off by conflicted grief—his own mixed with his mother's—from full possession of his creativity. To finally recover Yillah, to heal his *Ill I*, Melville has to work through the Marred I that his Calvinist mother superimposed on his memory of his father. "The whole story is told in a title page," Taji claims; and *Mardi* hints at Mar-i-[a]. And, as Alice Kenney observes, *Mardi's* plot derives from one of the few surviving Dutch dialect folk tales, which Melville possibly heard from his mother, or associated with her after hearing it elsewhere in the Dutch milieu of his childhood.[33]

In *Mardi*, Melville stages an elaborate attempt to exonerate his father: by portraying the cultural norm of masculinity in declension and by showing how it could not handle the experience of grief; by critiquing the relationship between the political imperialism of Manifest Destiny and the spiritual imperialism of the dominant view of the afterlife; and by uncovering the instability at the heart of conventional notions of identity. But in the very act of cleansing his father from sin, by conjuring up the "water journeys and island-like afterworlds" of funeral symbolism, including the "symbolic cleansing stream" of his culture's mourning picture, Melville acts out the disorderly adolescent energy springing from the conflation of his own grief's conflicts with those of his haughty mother.[34]

CHAPTER FOUR

Redburn's Mourning Pilgrimage

Never say die, is my motto.
Harry Bolton, in Melville's *Redburn*

COMICAL SADNESS, SUBTERRANEOUS DESPAIR

Redburn addresses Melville's memory of his father more directly than any of his other works. Redburn's father, Walter Redburn, and Allan Melvill are both importers of French goods; both arrive at Liverpool on the same day; both know the same Irish notable; both own the books to which Redburn alludes; and both die bankrupt. Yet the novel's complex tone undercuts one's ability to assess where Melville stands in relation to Redburn and to the emotions Redburn expresses both as narrator and as adolescent protagonist.[1] The challenge posed by *Redburn*'s problematic tone inheres in whether Melville identifies with the rage Redburn exhibits in the opening of the novel and in the extent to which the author shares his narrator's pietistic persona.

If Melville was simply satirizing his youthful protagonist's bitterness and anger, or if he partially or wholly shared in them in his late adolescence, their role in the text is linked to conflicted grief.[2] With Walter Redburn's guidebook in hand, his son searches for his father; however, after he renounces the hunt, Redburn finds Harry Bolton, the "St. Bury Blade"—in whose character Melville attempts to work through the conflicts of his grief. These feelings take a dark form insofar as they are earlier projected onto the dying sailor, Jackson.

Finally, Melville directs the anger of his unresolved grief at a displaced father figure, the duplicitous Captain Riga.

Throughout *Redburn*, the narrator continually turns from burlesque gag to the novel's obsession with death. In Redburn's voice, Melville stages the conflicts—especially the contradictory self-images—he uneasily attempts to tame down into an Irvingesque "comical sadness" (149). The narrator's pieties and social radicalism square off in Redburn's voice, revealing Melville's own self-divisions and the work of the cultural codes that reinforce them. In its darker register, the novel sadistically toys with the painful disillusionment that the narrator at times satirizes in his younger self and in other moments attempts to transform into more mature social criticism. Instead of creating a sense of distance from Redburn's conflicted grief, Melville's self-divided tone enacts this bereavement on a formal level.[3]

THE SAD YOUTH

And I thought how much better and sweeter it must
be, to be buried under the pleasant hedge that
bounded the sunny south side of our village graveyard, where every Sunday I had used to walk after
church in the afternoon; and I almost wished I was
there now; yes, dead and buried in that churchyard.
Redburn, in Melville's *Redburn*

The opening of the novel establishes the adolescent protagonist's depressive rage and links it to the loss of his father:

Talk not of the bitterness of middle-age and after life; a boy can feel all that, and much more, when upon his young soul the mildew has fallen; and the fruit, which with others is only blasted after ripeness, with him is nipped in the first blossom and bud. And never again can such blights be made good; they strike in too deep, and leave such a scar that the air of Paradise might not erase it. (11)

"But these thoughts are bitter enough even now," the narrator confesses, "for they have not gone quite away; and they must be uncongenial enough to the reader; so no more of that, and let me go on with my story" (10). His narrative, though, centers on his depressive rage.

From the outset of the novel, Redburn explains his motivation to ship out in response to the loss of his father. His father, like Melville's, had been "an importer" and had crossed the Atlantic on business (5). When Redburn reads shipping advertisements, he thinks of "cases of silks and satins," the goods Melville's father imported (4). Redburn's "shadowy reminiscences of wharves, warehouses, and shipping" evoke a memory of "standing with my father on the wharf" (4). He feels "fated . . . to be a great voyager" like his father: "and that just as my father used to entertain strange gentleman over their wine after dinner, I would hereafter be telling my own adventures to an eager auditory" (7).

His father has crystallized in Redburn's memory as "a marvelous being, infinitely purer and greater than I was, who could not by any possibility do wrong, or say an untruth" (34). "I had never dreamed of such a thing as doubting him," he confesses (34). His father's death hovers in the background throughout his narrative. "I was so glad and happy then," Redburn reminisces of his childhood: "But I must not think of those delightful days, before my father became a bankrupt, and died, and we removed from the city; for when I think of those days, something rises up in my throat and almost strangles me. . . . I tried to think that it was all a dream, that I was not where I was . . . but that I was at home again in the city, with my father alive, and my mother bright and happy as she used to be" (36).

The close resemblance between Redburn's father's life and that of Allan Melvill, tempts one to read Redburn's feelings for his father as autobiographical. The idealized father, untarnished even by Redburn's disillusioned attempt to follow him through the streets of Liverpool with his old guidebook, is never directly attacked in the novel for abandoning his family to genteel poverty. However, Melville creates a strange tonal effect in *Redburn* by sugarcoating his narrative persona's depressive rage with Christian pieties and the novel of sensibility's "pleasing sadness" (143). Redburn—"the sad youth"—deals in a literary melancholy that undercuts authentic expression of feeling. Instead, Melville mixes Redburn's darker emotions with conventional literary poses, thus keeping his protagonist's buried rage within genteel bounds. Melville's conflicted grief in *Redburn* appears in displaced and disguised manifestations, particularly in the novel's two major characters, Jackson and Harry Bolton.

Redburn's memory of his father has become epitomized in a childhood attachment to an "old fashioned glass ship" which his father originally gave to Redburn's uncle and namesake, Senator Wellingborough, who "died a member of Congress in the days of the old Constitution" (7). Upon the senator's death, the ship came to rest in Redburn's home. The ship, "after being the admiration of my father's visitors," now serves as the "wonder and delight" of his mother's visitors, who come by just to see it (7). The young Redburn fantasizes that the ship contains a hidden treasure, "something wonderful" (8). "And often I used to feel a sort of insane desire to be the death of the glass ship, case, and all, in order to come at the plunder" (8). Fearing "this temporary madness of mine," his mother puts the ship on the mantlepiece out of his reach, "until I should recover my reason" (8).

The ship, named *La Reine*, or *The Queen*, looks as though it has battled its way through wild waves: Redburn "used to be giving her up for lost and foundered every moment" (9). Although "many of her glass spars and ropes are now sadly shattered and broken," Redburn "will not have her mended" (9). The ship's "figure-head, a gallant warrior . . . lies pitching head-foremost down into the trough of a calamitous sea under the bows—but I will not have him put on his legs again, til I get on my own; for between him and me there is a secret sympathy; and my sisters tell me, even yet, that he fell from his perch the very day I left home to go to sea" (9).[4]

In a state of disrepair and in ever-present danger of foundering, the fragile ship tantalizes the young Redburn with a secret treasure that provokes in him an insane desire to be its death. The ship as symbol of Redburn's childhood psychic state embodies the conflicts toward his father that Redburn will reenact during his adolescent voyage to Liverpool in search of his father's legacy.[5] To identify with his paternal inheritance—the ship's treasure—means that Redburn must reenact the deathbed mania—"temporary madness"—of Allan

Melvill. In other words, to be the death of the ship involves performing a pathological identification with the last illness, the mania, of the deceased.

The linking object theory enables us to make sense of both the ship's name, *The Queen,* and the fact that Redburn's mother controls this linking object to the dead by removing it from her son's destructive urges. The ship momentarily functions as a linking object, as Redburn projects onto it his attempt to control his conflicts toward his father.

"More than anything else," Redburn explains, the ship caused him to seek "my fortune on the sea" (7). But to quest after his "fortune" turns into a "search" for his father in Liverpool.[6] The young Redburn cannot gain access to the paternal "treasure" with its promise of resolving conflicted grief. Instead, his adolescent self unearths Jackson, in whose fatal coughing fits Redburn translates the "something" that "rises up in my throat and almost strangles me" when he thinks of his father, and Harry Bolton, the "St. Bury Blade," whom Redburn "finds" in Liverpool after his father's guidebook proves nearly useless.

A MAN RAISED FROM THE DEAD

In every being's ideas of death, and his behavior
when it suddenly menaces him, lies the best index to
his life and his faith.
Herman Melville, *Redburn*

Jackson and Bolton displace the glass ship as linking objects. In their characterizations Melville's conflicted grief surfaces while being controlled and kept at a distance. Jackson comes on the scene after Redburn witnesses a "shrieking man . . . raging mad with the delirium tremens . . . in a fit of frenzy" rush on deck and jump overboard to his death (50). Horrified by this initiation to sailor life, Redburn is more terrified when he discovers that "the suicide had been occupying the very bunk which I had appropriated to myself" (51). This suicide introduces two of the novel's important motifs: the figure of the suicidal maniac that appears several more times in the narrative and the motif of "subterraneous despair."[7] Prior to the shrieking man's appearance, the sailors hear "a horrid groaning noise down in the forecastle" (50). Before Redburn can recover from the shock of learning that he occupies the suicide's berth, Jackson approaches him with a threat: "I had better steer clear of him ever after, for if ever I crossed his path, or got into his way, he would be the death of me" (52).

Jackson thus puts in his first appearance in the novel as a mortal threat to a protagonist who has just experienced a subterraneous identification with a suicide. But everything about Jackson conjures up death. He is "such a hideous looking mortal, that Satan himself would have run from him"; he appears to have "just recovered from the yellow fever" (57, 54). His "most deep, subtle, infernal looking eye . . . so cold, and snaky, and deadly . . . haunts" Redburn "to this day" (57). What most distinguishes Jackson is that he seems marked by "a fearful end nigh at hand; like that of King Antiochus of Syria, who died a worse death, history says, than if he had been stung out of the world by wasps and hornets" (58).

From first to last Redburn regards Jackson as though he resembles a damned man on his deathbed: "And I sometimes fancied, it was the consciousness of his miserable, broken-down condition, and the prospect of dying soon like a dog, in consequence of his sins, that made this poor wretch always eye me with such malevolence as he did" (58). In Jackson, then, Redburn is mortally threatened by a sinner on his deathbed.

Jackson is a melodramatically heightened version of a deathbed victim, and like Melville's father he turns into a deathbed maniac. Redburn shudders when "I caught this man gazing at me, as I often did; for he was apt to be dumb at times, and would sit with his eyes fixed, and his teeth set, like a man in the moody madness" (58). When Jackson sadistically taunts the sailors, who are also petrified of him, he "broke out in such a rage, that his lips began to glue together at the corners with a fine white foam" (61). Like a maniac, Jackson "seemed to be full of hatred and gall against everything and every body in the world. . . . *Sometimes I thought he was really crazy*" (61, my emphasis).

Jackson turns the crew against Redburn: "so that at last I found myself a sort of Ishmael in the ship . . . and I began to feel a hatred growing up in me against the whole crew—so much so, that I prayed against it, that it might not master my heart completely, and so make a fiend of me, something like Jackson" (62). To become a Jackson, for Redburn, means to become "spontaneously an atheist and an infidel," one who tries "to prove that there was nothing to be believed; nothing to be loved, and nothing worth living for; but every thing to be hated. . . . He was a horrid desperado; and like a wild Indian . . . he seemed to run a muck at heaven and earth. He was a Cain afloat: branded on his yellow brow with some inscrutable curse; and going about corrupting and searing every heart that beat near him" (104).

Jackson, then, is Redburn's depressive rage personified and turned into a monstrous presence. Implicit in his characterization is Melville's fear that to deal with his conflicted grief directly would be self-destructive. Melville displaces his rage at abandonment on the figure identified with the damned deathbed maniac. And Redburn fears that to get too close to this figure would involve a pollution by Jackson's corrupted presence. However, Redburn pietistically exonerates even the hideous Jackson: "But there seemed even more woe than wickedness about the man; and his wickedness seemed to spring from his woe; for all his hideousness, there was that in his eye at times, that was ineffably pitiable and touching; and though there were moments when I almost hated this Jackson, yet I have pitied no man as I have pitied him" (105).[8]

The genteel Redburn cannot allow himself to hate or to flirt with the dark vision of Jackson. This heightens Jackson's lurid characterization. As *Mardi* intimates, Melville himself entertained some of the radical doubts he ascribes to Jackson. Mimicking Dutch Max, Jackson comments of a ship littered with dead, "dare is no dood hope for dem . . . dey are drowned and d . . . . d, as you and I will be. . . . Don't talk of heaven to me—it's a lie—I know it. . . . you'll find, that by dying, you'll only go from one gale of wind to another'" (104). Jackson, though, has been poisoned by his negative feelings: he "seldom spoke, but to contradict, deride, or curse" (104). The disease that eats away at him is rooted in conflicted feeling. As his face thins, "his eyes seemed to kindle more and more, as if he were going to die out at last, and leave them burning like tapers before a corpse" (104).[9] After a dead man astonishingly undergoes a spontaneous combustion, Jackson refuses to be awed by the death. He "would look toward the fatal spot, and cough, and laugh, and invoke the dead man with incredible scoffs and jeers. He froze my blood, and made my soul stand still" (246). But it is the cultural code that forbids the mourner from focusing on the negative traits of the deceased and directing his anger against him—as Jackson luridly overdramatizes here—which displaces Redburn's early depressive rage onto Jackson.

At the end of the novel, Jackson is on his deathbed. But the "prospect of the speedy and unshunable death now before him, seemed to exasperate his misanthropic soul into madness; and as if he had indeed sold it to Satan, he seemed determined to die with a curse between his teeth" (276). For Redburn, Jackson's deathbed mania is a sure sign of the latter's damnation: "With short breaths panting out his maledictions," Jackson reminds Redburn of "the diabolical Tiberius at Capreae," who suffered "unspeakable mental terrors only known to the damned on earth, yet did not give over his blasphemies, *but endeavored to drag down with him to his own perdition, all who came within the evil spell of his power*" (276, my emphasis). The doubts Babbalanja expresses in *Mardi* warn that Melville is pandering to his audience's prejudices here, but it cannot be ruled out that Melville was of several minds about the possibility of damnation, and that he could not decide on an interpretation of deathbed mania. Redburn pietistically condemns Milton's portrayal of Satan because it "dilutes our abhorrence with admiration": "But in historically canonizing on earth the condemned below and lifting up and lauding the illustrious damned, we do but make ensamples of wickedness; and call upon ambition to do some great inquity, and be sure of fame" (276).

Redburn's critics are not sure of the intent of the narrator's Christian rhetoric. I maintain that Melville was in debate with himself about Redburn's sentiments. Hawthorne said that Melville could never make up his mind on ultimate questions. It is this ambivalence that made the resolution of Melville's unresolved grief difficult, if not impossible. Without a stable and deeply felt frame of reference, both spiritual and social, darker emotions either needed to be diluted with the rhetoric of sensibility or given over to a melodramatic character like Jackson. While the characterization of Jackson can hint at a relation to Allan's deathbed mania—when Jackson gets up from his deathbed to work the ship at the end of the voyage, he looks like "a man raised from the dead"—his name (and claim to be related to General Jackson) link up to Andrew Jackson's presidency during Allan's fall and death (295). Further, Jackson's age, "thirty, or perhaps fifty," evokes Melville's age as he writes (thirty) and his father's age at death (fifty) (57). However, Jackson performs the linking object role: he both keeps these hints under control and holds at a distance Melville's identification with the elements of his characterization which revive fears that the son might follow in the father's footsteps.[10]

THE ST. BURY BLADE

Soon after the foundering of his "filial pilgrimage" to the spots Walter Redburn had visited in Liverpool, Redburn realizes: "It was a sad, a solemn, and a most melancholy thought. . . . Yes, the thing [the guidebook] that had guided the father, could not guide the son" (154, 157). On the heels of this insight, Redburn discovers the prodigal son who has gambled away his inheritance, Harry Bolton, "a native of Bury St. Edmunds" (217).[11] "Even in conversation," the narrator observes, "Harry was a prodigal; squandering his aristocratic narrations with a careless hand; and, perhaps, sometimes spending funds of reminiscences not his own" (221). In his prodigality Harry evokes Allan Melvill's investment and loss of his relatives's funds in his business. Redburn "was all anxiety that Harry should accompany me home" (218). "This incontrovertible son of a gentleman," "my young blade of Bury," revives in Redburn his sense of class (216, 217). Like Allan Melvill, who took great pride in his Scottish ances- try, Harry brags about his aristocratic friends, but he does so to the point where Redburn begins to suspect "the rigid morality of my friend, as a teller of the truth" (223).

Through Harry, Melville gives us a glimpse of what it felt like to lose his father, but he also revenges himself on his father through the St. Bury Blade. In the most unbelievable episode in *Redburn*, Harry tells Redburn that he goes to London with "hopes of recovering a considerable sum, lost in some way he chose to conceal" (224). Their visit to Aladdin's Palace, gambling den and bordello, restages Melville's father's abandonment of or "bolting" from him. It also depicts Allan's conversion into a maniac through his business failure. When he enters Aladdin's Palace, Redburn feels "as if all the Paris catacombs were underneath" its floor (Allan Melvill, as noted above, imported French goods) (228). Redburn hears a "hollow, boding sound, which seemed sighing with a subterraneous despair" or a displaced grief (228). While trying "to assume a careless and lordly air," Redburn felt his "face burning with embarrassment, and for the time, I must have looked very guilty of something" (229).[12]

In what feels to Redburn like "the delirium of the moment," he notices that Harry "laughed strangely" and "looked wildly from his eyes" (229, 231). Harry hands him a letter and makes him promise to take it to "Bury" and leave it there should he not return (232). Redburn then suspects that "Harry was crazy": "I held the purse in my motionless hand, and stared at him, till the tears almost started from my eyes" (232). With a "wild sort of laugh," Harry asks, "'What's the matter, Redburn? . . . you are not afraid of me, are you?— No, no! I believe in you, my boy" (232). Redburn then asks, "'What in heaven's name do you mean? . . . you don't really intend to desert me in this strange place, do you, Harry?' and I snatched him by the hand" (232). Although the melodramatic scenario undercuts the seriousness of this moment, in it Redburn reenacts, if in shrill form, the panic of abandonment that the adolescent Melville would have

felt in the loss of his father and the terror of seeing his father turn into
a maniac. There is also a sadistic edge to Harry's treatment of Redburn in the Aladdin scene. It is as if Melville registers here a source of
rage toward Allan: Harry's sadism evokes Melville's feeling of abandonment by his father.

Left alone Redburn "shuddered at every footfall, and almost
thought it must be some assassin pursuing" him: "the whole place
seemed infected" (Allan Melvill died after a debilitating fever)
(233). Just before Redburn sees the second maniac figure "wildly
darting" past him, he hears "ivory rattling": the sound of dice but also
an allusion to the rattling of bones (Bolton later refers to dice as " 'the
bones' ") (233, 234). Finding Harry's conduct "unaccountable. . . .
he had seemed almost another person from what he had seemed
before," "that ivory rattling" inspires in Redburn "a dreadful feeling"
(233, 234). A "very pale" Harry returns, now himself on the brink of
mania: he tears up the letter "like a madman" and "deliriously laughed" (234). "Now utterly bewildered, and frightened,"—as the young
Melville must have felt as his father shouted on his deathbed—
Redburn finds himself dependent on the destabilized Bolton (234).
Suddenly drawing his knife, Harry hands it over to his friend explain-
ing, " 'They serve suicides scurvily here . . . they don't bury them
decently' " (235). "Assuming a treacherous, tropical calmness," Harry nails his empty purse to the table with his knife: " 'that's my
skeleton' " (235). Still ignorant of what Harry has been up to, Redburn is sworn to secrecy by Bolton never to ask him about his " 'secret' " (235). "He shouted, with the foam at his lips" so that Redburn
becomes "more and more alarmed at his wildness" (235, 236).

In reminiscing about Bolton, Redburn experiences "a feeling of
sadness, never to be comforted" (252). Harry's sea career carried him
to an "ocean grave, which has buried you up with your secrets, and
whither no mourning pilgrimage can be made" (252). "But why this
gloom at the thought of the dead? And why should we not be glad? Is
it, that we ever think of them as departed from all joy? Is it that we
believe that indeed they are dead?" (252). Yet Harry lives "over
again, as I recall your image before me. I see you, plain and palpable

as in life; and can make your existence obvious to others. Is he, then, dead, of whom this may be said?" (252) But it is not an unmediated memory Redburn revives. His image of Harry is "mixed with a thousand strange forms, the centaurs of fancy; half real and human" (252).

The half real side of Redburn's representation of Harry contains an image of Allan Melvill that evokes the anger of his son's conflicted grief. Like the importer of fine goods, Allan Melvill, Harry is himself a "small, silken person," who travels with a "collection of silks, velvets, broadcloths, and satins" (277, 254). Melville, though, revenges himself on his father for abandoning him by throwing Harry to the sailor-wolves. Petrified of ascending the rigging, Harry exposes himself to the scorn of the "merciless crew" (257). As if Melville is obliquely condemning his father, the sailors immediately recognize Harry as a gambler and "a very equivocal character" (254). Once in New York, Redburn soon leaves for a visit to his family and abandons Harry. The novel concludes with Redburn "relating all I know of what overtook Harry Bolton" (311).

We are left with a portrait of Harry's instability—"how liable he was to yield to the most sudden, crazy, and contrary impulses"—that points to the unstable, unresolved grief Melville harbors for his father (311). Redburn's first impulse in searching for Harry is to scan the papers for reports of "suicides" and drowned persons (312). Fearing that while in New York Harry "must have had the most terrible incitements to committing violence upon himself," Redburn has projected his own suicidal urges and feelings of instability onto Harry (311–12).[13] But, through killing off Harry, Redburn vents the anger of his chronic grief, which had earlier recoiled on himself in his suicidal depressive rage. Speculating on Harry's whereabouts, Goodwell, Redburn's friend who fails to find work for Bolton, cannot believe that Harry's "melancholy could bring him to the insanity of throwing himself away in a whaler" (311). However, when Redburn later finds himself the victim of just such an insanity—what, for Melville, can be a pathological identification with his father's last illness—he learns that Harry has been crushed to death between a whale boat and a whale (311).

MERCHANTABLE GRIEF

> There are classes of men in the world, who bear the
> same relation to society at large, that the wheels do
> to a coach: and are just as indispensable.
>   Herman Melville, *Redburn*

That the business of catching whales ultimately victimizes Harry makes sense within the novel's critique of the relation between grief, class interests, and the commercial spirit. Redburn's recollections of his father obliquely condemn his father by drawing attention to the class trappings of his position as a gentleman. Mr. Jones, the family friend who helps Redburn find a job aboard a ship, introduces him to his prospective employer as the son of " 'a gentleman of one of the first families in America' " (16). Before bilking Redburn of a fair wage, Captain Riga sardonically asks, underlining the novel's subtitle, " 'then this fine lad is *the son of a gentleman?'* " (16, my emphasis). Each time Redburn reminisces about his father he drives home the contrast between his own destitute situation and his father's monied position: "my father, whom I so much liked to hear talk French, as he sometimes did to a servant we had"; "my father used to entertain strange gentlemen over their wine after dinner"; and at one point, Redburn offers a sailor some snuff from "an old tortoise-shell snuff-box of my father's" (7, 27). As a youth Redburn "never thought of working for my living" and anticipated going to college (36). Following out Walter's route through Liverpool, Redburn imagines "How differently my father must have appeared [i.e., well-dressed]. . . . And little did he think, that a son of his would ever visit Liverpool as a poor friendless sailor-boy" (154). Redburn keeps harping on his father's "sacred memory," but the contrasts he continually draws between his own poverty and his father's genteel trappings serve to indict Walter Redburn for leaving his son impoverished (150). Redburn thinks of the "trials and troubles" his father endured that led up to his bankruptcy, then looks "at my own sorry garb, and had much ado to keep from tears" (155). In a moment of parody of his own youthful self-pity, Redburn points toward a buried rage at the cause of his sorry condition, as he constructs a sentimentalized version of Maria Melville's bereaved rage.

In Liverpool, Redburn presents a devastating description of the poverty of the city. Two dramatic vignettes point out the spirit of commerce that controls the experience of bereavement. The graveyard around the Church of Saint Nicholas has become "crossed and re-crossed by thorough-fares" (178). Because the tombstones lay flat, "multitudes are constantly walking over the dead" and the dock workers eat their dinners off of the grave stones (178). The basement of the church has been turned into a "Dead House," in which bodies are exposed until they are claimed. Redburn witnesses a sailor "stretched out, stark and stiff, with the sleeve of his frock rolled up, and showing his name and date of birth tattooed upon his arm. It was a sight full of suggestions; he seemed his own head-stone" (178). Commenting that a reward is offered for recovering the bodies of those who have fallen into the docks, Redburn gets to the heart of his critique: "There seems to be no calamity overtaking man, that can not be rendered merchantable. Undertakers, sextons, tomb-makers, and hearse-drivers, get their living from the dead" (179).

Redburn deepens his indictment of the dominant commercial spirit when he comes upon a dying mother and her children in a basement of the "prison-like cotton warehouses" (180). Approaching police, neighbors, and merchants in the area, Redburn meets with a bland indifference to the fate of the dying family. A voice from a nearby building identifies Redburn's real target: " 'You're crazy, boy . . . do you suppose, that Parkins and Wood want their warehouse turned into a hospital?' " (182) Redburn's eloquent jeremiads emerge from his perception of the way commerce has shaped feeling: "Ah! what are our creeds, and how do we hope to be saved? . . .

Surrounded as we are by the wants and woes of our fellow-men, and yet given to follow our own pleasures, regardless of their pains, are we not like people sitting up with a corpse, and making merry in the house of the dead?" (184).

Redburn makes a damning case against commercial values by showing that the fever sweeping through the immigrants on board the *Highlander* is caused by the terrible conditions in which they are forced to live.[14] Just before his ship reaches New York, Captain Riga orders that the steerage be cleaned up (299). The social misrepresentation, however, goes further: the shipping interests contrive "to suppress the detailed circumstances of disasters" such as the fever that ravaged the immigrants (292). "What a world of life and death, what a world of humanity and its woes, lies shrunk into a three-worded sentence" in the newspapers: "you mark not the wringing of hands and torn hair of widows and orphans:—all is a blank. And one of these blanks I have but filled up" (292).

In describing the fever among the immigrants, Melville draws out the class implications on board ship. The cabin passengers are separated by a rope from those who travel in steerage. Earlier in the novel Redburn caustically noted, "Lucky would it be for the pretensions of some parvenus, whose souls are deposited at their banker's, and whose bodies but serve to carry about purses, knit of poor men's heart-strings, if thus easily they could precisely define, ashore, the difference between them and the rest of humanity" (242). At the onset of the fever, several cabin passengers suddenly become religious (288). Of the immigrants Redburn observes,

> But those who had lost fathers, husbands, wives, or children, needed no crape, to reveal to others, who they were. Hard and bitter indeed was their lot; for with the poor and desolate, *grief is no indulgence of mere sentiment, however sincere, but a gnawing reality, that eats into their vital beings;* they have no kind condolers, and bland physicians, and troops of sympathizing friends; and they must toil, though tomorrow be the burial, and their pall-bearers throw down the hammer to lift up the coffin. (290, my emphasis)

Redburn powerfully transforms into cultural critique the shame and rage evoked by his name:

> We talk of the Turks, and abhor the cannibals; but may not some of *them*, go to heaven, before some of *us?* We may have civilized bodies and yet barbarous souls. We are blind to the real sights of this world; deaf to its voice; and dead to its death. And not till we know, that one grief outweighs ten thousand joys, will we become what Christianity is striving to make us. (293)

Melville's unresolved grief for his father undergoes two different transformations in *Redburn.* The anger directed at Allan gets displaced and distanced through Jackson and Bolton, but this anger itself is transmuted into incisive social critique. The attack on commerce and class most effectively emerges in relation to the question of grief. Grief itself cuts through Redburn's mixed tone and exposes his own class biases and the nature of his character as a social construct. Like the cabin passengers, Redburn cannot open his own vital being to the gnawing reality of grief. Even in his attack on the passengers he abjures intense feeling: "Now, whenever we discover a dislike in us, toward any one, we should ever be a little suspicious of ourselves" (261). Reluctantly, Redburn slightly relaxes the social control of feeling: "but nevertheless, I will let nature have her own way for once; and here declare roundly that, however it was, I cherished a feeling toward these cabin-passengers, akin to contempt" (261). Unable to completely deny his rage, Redburn channels it into overly clever imagery. Of one genteel passenger he observes, "When he dies, his skull ought to be turned into a savings' box, with the till-hole between his teeth" (261).

Melville's perception of the limitations of his audience in part constructs Redburn's persona.[15] Several times Redburn excuses his narration from the grisly details of reality with remarks like, "for such is the fastidiousness of some readers, that, many times, they must lose the most striking incidents in a narrative like mine" (286); "Propriety forbids that I should enter into details," he claims at another point (191). There can be no doubt Melville satirizes Redburn's gentility by making him a member of the Juvenile Total Abstinence

Society and of an Anti-Smoking Society organized by the principal of his Sunday school (42, 46). At one point, a prig Redburn admonishes the sailors's "absence of proper views of religion," and at another, he plays up his "superiority" to a sailor "in a moral way" (48, 49). Several chapter titles, as well, poke fun at Redburn's prissiness: "Redburn *Deferentially* Discourses Concerning the Prospects of Sailors" (136, my emphasis). In addition, Redburn both voices the millennialism that *Mardi* condemns and defends the ideology of motherhood as sainthood (169, 40). Melville also portrays Redburn as a naive narrator: "But I don't know exactly how to explain what I mean"; "But I was telling about"; "But no so fast; I did not mean to tell that yet" (41, 42, 143). Yet Redburn is an unstable construct of contradictory social voices. Pietistically discussing "the best death of the Christian," he can abruptly voice the social radicalism of one who believes in "firm, creedless faith, that embraces the spheres" (291).

As a social construct, Redburn himself in part performs the role of the living linking object. His conventionality owes a great deal to the pietistic values—a mixture of genteel and Calvinist admonitions—Melville's mother voices in her letters (see Chap. 1). But he also attempts to break out of his docile role through his radical, albeit Christian, outrage. Like the glass ship—the paternal legacy—with which he identifies, Redburn himself appears to be a figure in need of mending: an unstable assemblage of naivete, piety, and penetrating insight into the dominant social code. He is a composite of the mixed feelings—derived in part from his mother's style of bereavement—Melville seemed to have harbored in his memory of his father. While one could certainly claim that through either a want of craftmanship or through a lack of emotional investment in *Redburn* Melville unsuccessfully sustains his persona, one cannot, on the evidence of similar sentiments expressed in his letters, wholly dissociate Melville from Redburn's gentility and Christian values. Melville also exploits Redburn's conventionality to heighten the tenor of his social critique: if prissy Redburn could be driven to moral outrage, then the abuses must be damning indeed.

The fissures in Redburn's social identity are highlighted in relation to the character of Carlo, who makes the return voyage on the *Highlander*. This adolescent artist's "organ . . . might almost have played the Dead March in Saul, when King Saul himself was buried" (249). His presence bespeaks the experience of adolescent bereavement: "in the twilight pensiveness of his full morning eyes, there seemed to sleep experiences so sad and various, that his days most have seemed to him years" (247). Melville imbues the bereaved male adolescent with womanly traits. Carlo possesses "large and womanly" eyes; his "naked leg was beautiful to behold as any lady's arm" (247). He looks like the pensive woman of early nineteenth-century needle-point mourning pictures: his eye "shone with a soft and spiritual radiance . . . and spoke of humility, deep-seated thoughtfulness, yet a careless endurance of all the ills of life" (247).

Harry Bolton also possesses "large, black, and womanly eyes," as well as the complexion of a "mantling brunette, feminine as a girl's" (216). Harry's "effeminacy of appearance," as well as Carlo's, are related to Melville's conversion into his mother's living linking object to his father (257). When Melville enters back into his adolescent grief through Harry and Carlo, he imagines adolescent selves tinged with womanly traits because of the overlay of Maria's image of Allan onto her son's youthful consciousness.

Through Carlo's music Redburn feels "the artist's repairing hand": "though the notes be broken, here's that within that mends them" (251, 250). "Full of poetry, gushing from every rent," Carlo himself seems in need of repair (247). He enacts Melville's fantasy of a liberating, though genteel, art: "His whole figure was free, fine, and *indolent*" (247, my emphasis). But Carlo—a figment of an upper class projection of art onto the masses—also penetrates through the poses of literary melancholy and sensibility that Redburn has been hiding behind. " 'Most always the rich best fancy the sad,' " Carlo observes, " 'the poor the merry' " (248). "Sadness," Carlo implies, has been "rendered merchantable," in contrast to the "gnawing reality" of grief of the impoverished immigrants denied a consoling outlet in social representations (179).[16]

THE PRODUCTIVE POWER OF LABOR

Prior to Redburn's shipping out, a family friend, Mr. Jones, puts into his hands a dust-covered book for his improvement. Jones advises Redburn that herein he can learn "the true way to retrieve the poverty of my family" (86). Redburn takes a stab at Smith's *Wealth of Nations*, hoping it will serve him as a "secret talisman, which would transmute even pitch and tar to silver and gold" (86). But the first chapter, *"Of the causes of improvement in the productive power of labor,"* proves "dry as cheese and crackers," and Redburn finds that as he reads about the *"wages and profits of labor"* he does not derive "any profits myself from my pains in perusing it" (87). Instead, he finds the "best reading" in the book to be the "half effaced pencil-marks" on the fly leaf: the signature of Jones's father (87).

Although "the very leaves" of Smith's tome "smelt of saw-dust" to Redburn, Melville's novel dramatizes the relation between his protagonist's unresolved grief for his father and the class and commercial codes that dominate the world Redburn portrays (87). To work through chronic grief, *Redburn* suggests, involves countering the influence of these hegemonic cultural codes. The novel charts a progress in which the genteel but impoverished hero finds an outlet in "the productive power of labor" for his depressive rage against the social codes that victimized both father and son. By the end of the novel—when, as we shall see, he joins in solidarity with his fellow oppressed sailors—Redburn's private griefs have become translated into an eloquent jeremiad against the values out of which his own persona has, in large part, been socially constructed.

While using his father's guide-book to Liverpool, Redburn comes upon a monument not in the *"Gentleman's Pocket Companion"* (146). It is a statue of Lord Nelson "expiring in the arms of Victory" (155). Redburn repeatedly returns to view the statue, but in his eyes the real hero of the statue is not Nelson. Although "Victory is dropping a wreath on the dying admiral's brow," Redburn is much more fascinated by the figures at the base of the statue (155). "Four naked figures in chains . . . seated in various attitudes of humiliation and

despair" are "emblematic of Nelson's principal victories" (155). Redburn, however, rewrites this emblem.[17]

For him the abject figures suggest "four African slaves in the marketplace" (155). The slaves, though, are figures of mourning: one's
head is bowed, "as if he had given up all hope of ever feeling better.
Another has his head buried in despondency, and no doubt looks
mournfully out of his eyes, but as his face was averted at the time, I
could not catch the expression" (155). The African slave trade,
Redburn recalls, was once the "principal commerce of Liverpool"
(155). The statue revives a memory of his father discussing abolition
with visitors (155–56). For Redburn, the statue transforms into a
commentary on the dominant social codes that once enforced the
slave trade and that now, in the hegemony of the commercial spirit,
cuts man off from his deeper and darker feelings. Redburn, in short,
identifies not only with the slaves but with the way their bereavement
is set in the marketplace. This is the one moment in the narrative
where Walter Redburn is identified with a positive social virtue, in
contrast to the unbelievable idealization with which his son elsewhere imbues him.[18]

In blaming the dominant commercial code for victimizing his
father, Redburn does not let us forget that Walter Redburn "became
a bankrupt, and died" (36). More complexly, the novel enacts both
at the outset and in the conclusion Redburn's identification—a sign
of pathological mourning—with his father's bankruptcy. This act of
identification suggests Redburn's own imprisonment within the psychic economics of the marketplace that played a significant role in
producing his father's tragedy. Each act of identification nearly triggers a full expression of his depressive rage, but because of Redburn's
partial social construction by genteel codes he swiftly disavows his
own rage.

On his boat trip to New York, Redburn is "horror-struck" when he
learns that due to the unstable market conditions of the river trade
the price of his passage has risen (12). He must "grimly wait" to be
humiliated because he cannot pay his fare, and he feels "that despera-
tion and recklessness of poverty": "My whole soul was soured within

me" (12). Feeling "too wicked" to explain his case "in plain, civil terms," he responds "in a loud angry voice" to the clerk's request for his fare (13). Ordered out into the storm by the clerk, "the devil in me then mounted up from my soul," and he refuses to leave the cabin (13). With his gun pointed at the genteel passengers who now stare at him, Redburn, unable to "account for my demoniac feelings," agrees with a passenger's assessment that he must be "crazy" (13). In a final self-punitive gesture—and an ultimate identification with the exposure that led to Allan Melvill's fatal illness—Redburn marches out into the storm and spends the night there.[19]

When Redburn appears before Captain Riga to collect his wages he learns that because he ran away from the ship in Liverpool and lost several tools overboard, he in fact owes Riga money. He confesses to the captain that "*I was a bankrupt,* and could not pay him" (307, my emphasis). However, this time Melville permits Redburn to act out his rage in solidarity with his fellow oppressed sailors: thus Melville momentarily transforms pathological identification into social critique.[20] The crew, who had "bestowed upon" Riga (a surname already associated with the "rigged" quality of commercial exchange) "a name unmentionably expressive of their contempt," line up before "their late lord and master," turn around and make "a motion, which was a polite salute to every thing before them, but an abominable insult to all who happened to be in their rear" (308). This social performance may also describe Redburn's outwardly pietistic voice and his "subterraneous" indictment of the very social codes that both shape his persona and bury the rage of Melville's chronic grief in the fissures of the novel's complex, culturally constructed tone (308).

CHAPTER FIVE

Buried Griefs: Social Death
in *White-Jacket*

In our man-of-war world, Life comes in at one
gangway and Death goes overboard at the other.
Under the man-of-war scourge, curses mix with
tears; and the sigh and the sob furnish the bass to
the shrill octave of those who laugh to drown buried
griefs of their own. Checkers were played in the
waist at the time of Shenly's burial.

For every one knows what a luxury is grief, when you
can get a private closet to enjoy it in, and no Paul
Prys intrude.
Herman Melville, *White-Jacket*

THIS STATE'S PRISON MAN-OF-WAR WORLD OF OURS

In the metaphor of embattlement *White-Jacket* insists on, "this old-
fashioned world of ours" is not only a "man-of-war" one but is also a
"State Prison," in which "immutable ceremonies and iron etiquette"
rule feeling (375). White-Jacket refers to his fellow sailors as "all
hopeless prisoners like myself; all under martial law" (174). The ex-
convict from Sing-Sing, Shakings, calls the ship "a sort of State
Prison afloat" (175).[1] Throughout his narration, White-Jacket himself sustains this penal imagery. Forbidden to sing while they work,
the sailors seem "like convicts, in profound silence" (58). He refers

to "this State's Prison man-of-war of ours," "a sort of sea-Newgate," and he compares the marines aboard ship with "turnkeys to jails" and observes of sailors' uniforms that they are "aptly manufactured . . . in a State Prison ashore" (175, 176, 374, 378). He compares life in the navy to "living in a market," or "life in a large manufactory" (35). Like the officers on the *Neversink*, whose "feelings belonged to their profession," or like Captain Claret, of whom White-Jacket observes, "What he was, the usages of the Navy had made him," the social order imprisons every American in what seems to Melville's narrator "an oaken prison" (209, 367, 383).

The sequence of six chapters detailing the illness, death, and burial of White-Jacket's mess-mate, Shenly, illustrates Melville's deepening insight into the social codes that shape feeling. Shenly's death brings to a head Melville's perception that the common American is little better off than a convict in a state prison. Debilitated by a pulmonary disorder, Shenly is hospitalized in the close, unventilated ship's hospital.[2] When White-Jacket arrives to stand watch by what proves to be Shenly's deathbed, the latter has been reduced to "the mere foundering hull of a man" (336). White-Jacket becomes intimately involved in Shenly's death and burial. After Shenly dies before his eyes, White-Jacket washes the corpse and helps to carry it on deck for the burial. Although a messmate appears to relieve him, White-Jacket chooses "to remain where I was till daylight came" (337). Observing the bantering naval undertaker and his assistant, White-Jacket intercedes to prevent them from taking the "last stitch" on the corpse, that is, from running stitches through Shenly's face (338).

Chapter 81, "How they Bury a Man-of-war's man at Sea," scathingly indites the values implicit in this naval ritual: "In a man-of-war, every thing, even to a man's funeral and burial, proceeds with the unrelenting promptitude of the martial code" (341). The order for Shenly's burial is given "in the same hoarse tones" as any other command (341). As the chaplain recites the funeral service by rote, a boatswain's mate roars orders to the men who have crowded near to gain a better view. The following chapter details "What remains of a Man-of-war's-man after his Burial at Sea" (343). The purser's only interest in Shenly is to ask "attorney-like questions" of the witnesses in order to ascertain if his will is accurate (343). Finally, Shenly has been reduced to the bookkeeper-like notation in the purser's books, "D. D.": "Dead and Discharged" (344).

As Shenly's body plunges into the ocean, a checker-player sweeps in his winnings and "old jests" are bantered about (345). In his role as chronicler of the state's prison, White-Jacket confesses: "This man-of-war life has not left me unhardened. I can not stop to weep over Shenly now; that would be false to the life I depict; wearing no mourning weeds, I resume the task of portraying our man-of-war world" (345). "When a shipmate dies," White-Jacket observes near the end of his narrative, "straightway we sew him up, and overboard he goes; our world-frigate rushes by, and never more do we behold him again; though, sooner or later, the everlasting under-tow sweeps him toward our own destination" (399). However, White-Jacket himself cannot so simply turn away from death. At one point he becomes fascinated by those parts of the ship "shrouded in mystery": "They looked like the gloomy entrances to family vaults of buried dead" (127). He learns that these vaults literally contain explosive material: the ship's stores of gunpowder (128). "Outwardly re-garded," he admits, "our craft is a lie . . . all its store-rooms of secrets, forever slides along far under the surface" (399). But White-Jacket wears his secrets on his back: the garment that gives him his name becomes a kind of entry to Melville's family vaults of buried dead, in which the explosive material of unresolved grief festers.

Critics often argue that the symbolization of the jacket splits off from, or feels superimposed on, the rest of the narrative. Once one notices that White-Jacket heavily invests his narration with questions of death and grief, the jacket as symbolic of an ever-threatening death—both the social death of the state prison and a more intimate identification with the dead—seems a fitting emblem of the novel's meaning.[3] Death peers out of many images in the novel. One character's voice sounds "like the great bell of St. Paul's, which only sounds when the King or the Devil is dead" (34). Sailors polishing a cannon "reminded one of a swarm of black wasps, buzzing about rows of white head-stones in a church-yard" (45). Drunk, incarcerated sailors seem "stretched out stark and stiff, with their arms folded over their breasts, like so many effigies of the Black Prince on his monument in Canterbury Cathedral" (55).

Unable to sleep in the cramped, hot conditions on board ship, White-Jacket raises his hammock above those of his shipmates, but his "luckless hammock was stiff and straight as a board; and there I was—laid out in it, with my nose against the ceiling, like a dead man's against the lid of his coffin" (80). Sailors catching a doze in the daytime lay together in "the way in which they box up subjects intended to illustrate the winter lectures of a professor of surgery" (83). The summons to witness a flogging "carries a thrill, somewhat akin to what we may impute to the quick and the dead, when they shall hear the Last Trump, that is to bid them all arise in their ranks, and behold the final penalties inflicted upon sinners of our race" (135). The sailors need to fill their idle moments with drink because, as one sailor notes, "anything that smacks of life is better than to feel Davy Jones's chest-lid on your nose" (176–77). The thirteen offenses of the Articles of War punishable by death are read monthly to the sailors and White-Jacket reproduces each of them with their chilling refrain, "Shall suffer death!" (283–84). Shenly's death and burial represent the culmination of the narrative's numerous allusions to death.

The symbolism of the white jacket introduces Melville's own struggle with unresolved grief, which then appears in the context of the state's prison social order. Allan Melvill suffered his fatal exposure while returning from a trip to save the faltering coat and cap factory he had been managing. At the outset of *White-Jacket*, the protagonist describes "manufacturing an outlandish garment of my own devising, to shelter me from the boisterous weather we were so soon to encounter" (3). The white jacket thus performs an identification with the circumstances of Allan Melvill's death; and, in so doing, the jacket announces Melville's unresolved grief for his father. Functioning as a linking object, which through the act of identification serves to control conflicted grief, the jacket fosters the "illusion of being able to keep or 'kill' someone now dead with whom the ego perceives the mourner has unfinished business." "There is a particular day of a particular month of the year," White-Jacket confesses, "which, from my earliest recollections, I have always kept the run of, so that I can even now tell just where I was on that identical day of every year past since I was twelve years old."[4] The day, we are told, "comes in Spring" (173). Allan Melvill died in the winter of Melville's twelfth year, so that Melville's grief would have been intensely present that spring.

The narrative insists on the jacket as an agent of death. It was "white as a shroud," and "my shroud it afterward came very near proving" (3). After Shenly is hospitalized, one of White-Jacket's messmates, Priming the gunner's mate, blasts him for bringing bad luck to the mess by raising its total to thirteen. White-Jacket says, "How I cursed my jacket, that it thus seemed the means of fastening on me the murder of one of my shipmates [the wounded foretopman whom Surgeon Cuticle's surgery succeeds in killing], and the probable murder of two more [Baldy—who falls to his death after an ambitious officer works him too hard—and Shenly]" (333). The three victims are all messmates of White-Jacket.

The manufacture of the white jacket evokes the act of composing a novel at the same time that it conjures up a moral threat. The jacket is made out of a shirt "folded double at the bosom" and cut open, "much as you would cut a leaf in the last new novel"—or would stab someone (3). This image of reading/murder then gives way to that of patching together a text out of multifarious sources—Melville's habitual method of composition. "With many odds and ends of patches," White-Jacket quilts the inside of his garment (4). While ostensibly quilted to protect him from exposure, the jacket evokes the threat of death. It has become as "stiff and padded, as King James' cotton-stuffed and dagger-proof doublet" (4). Yet the jacket remains unfinished. White-Jacket cannot procure a coat of black paint because his fellow sailors had stolen enough of it to cause it to be placed under lock and key; the jacket thus becomes a "universal absorber" in the rain (4). Instead of protecting him from the elements, the jacket serves as a perpetual reminder of his vulnerability. His mess complains of the "disagreeableness of a perpetually damp garment" (62). Twice the jacket "came near being the death of me" (76). Early in the narrative, White-Jacket sits in the rigging at night and "give[s] loose to reflection" (76). The stars seem to be "luring us . . . to die and be glorified with them" (76). "Thinking of things past, and anon of the life to come," White-Jacket suddenly "came to myself with a rush, and felt something like a choking hand at my throat" (77). He then nearly falls from the rigging because the sailors beneath him fear that the white spot in the rigging is a drowned man's ghost. They let loose a yard to "test my corporeality" and this nearly causes his fall (78). Discovering that the jacket has nearly victimized him by making him appear to be a ghost, "In a rage I tore off my jacket, and threw it on the deck" (78). After joking about the jacket needing to be "dyed," once more he approaches the captain of the paint room for a coat of black paint—"when but one dab of paint would make a man of a ghost"—but is refused that request that would turn his life-threatening garment into mourning costume (78). The unfinished jacket thus gestures toward Melville's unresolved grief.

Allan Melvill's import business suffered from the advent of auctions for imported goods.[5] After a sailor dies on the *Neversink* and his clothes are sold at an auction, White-Jacket conceives the idea of getting rid of his jacket at one of these auctions. "Had it not once jeopardized my very existence? And I had a dreadful presentiment that, if I persisted in retaining it, it would do so again" (201). However, the sailors at the auction are quick to recognize the jacket of "Jack Chase's pet" and they wonder "how it came among the bags of deceased mariners" (202). One sailor remarks that it "Gives me the *fever-nagur* to look at it"—one recalls here that Allan Melvill died after a fever (202). After his failure to auction off the jacket, White-Jacket visits the purser, who is in charge of "all the financial affairs" of the ship (204). The purser's desk is "as much littered with papers as any Pearl St. merchant's": Melville's father's business had been at one time located on Pearl Street (205).

White-Jacket later records "how this jacket, for the second and last time, came near proving his shroud" (391). Jack Chase, captain of the foretop and White-Jacket's surrogate father, assigns him to perform a job in the rigging that nearly proves his death. But the "business" he attempts to perform evokes the tailoring metaphor with which the narrative opened (392). He carries a line, two hundred feet long, "far out on the giddest of yards, and after being wormed and twisted about through all sorts of intricacies" it must be dropped down to the deck (391–92). This task is "like threading a fine cambric needle with rather coarse thread" (392). Although he is advised to dispense with his jacket, he finds it too cold to do so. A lurch of the ship throws "the heavy skirts" of his jacket over his head, "completely muffling" him (392). A second lurch topples him "head foremost" into the sea (392). As he falls, his "father, mother, and sisters" revolve through his consciousness; all of his experience "seemed intensified in one fixed idea" in his soul (392). His "braided, blended emotions" give way to "the feeling of death" that encompasses him as he enters the sea (393).

When he bobs to the surface, he feels as though "pinioned in a feather-bed" and his jacket restrains him from swimming (394). "I whipped out my knife . . . and ripped my jacket straight up and down, as if I were ripping open myself" (394). The crew mistakes the jacket for a shark and their harpoons succeed in sinking it. Yet White-Jacket's dramatic moment of symbolic self-transformation— at least this is what this birth-death imagery has suggested to the novel's critics—has little value in the man-of-war world: ten minutes after he has been fished out of the sea, he is sent back up to the rigging to finish his job (394).[6]

The conflicts of unresolved grief that the pathological identification of the white jacket performs and the social death that White-Jacket everywhere delineates come together in three scenes: the protagonist's flirtation with being flogged, the set-piece about Surgeon Cuticle, and "The Great Massacre of the Beards."[7] When White-Jacket first boards the *Neversink* he is given a list of numbers which designate his assignments to various stations and duties; however, the officer who gave him this list neglected to assign him to his

post during "tacking ship" (11, 277). When confronted by the imminent threat of being flogged for not performing the duty he was never
assigned, White-Jacket feels his "man's manhood" well up; he feels
he must assert the "privilege, inborn and inalienable, that every man
has, of dying himself, and inflicting death upon another" (280). He
fantasizes ramming Captain Claret overboard and becoming "a murderer and a suicide" (281).

In looking back on his emotions, he notes, "There are times when
wild thoughts enter a man's heart, when he seems almost irresponsi-
ble for his act and his deed" (280). At one and the same time, White-
Jacket identifies with Melville's father's deathbed mania—wild behavior for which Allan Melvill cannot be held responsible—and
transforms Allan's death into a heroic act of social protest. In dying
Allan had recourse to "the last resources of an insulted and unendurable existence" (280). In fantasizing Claret's murder, White-Jacket
expresses Melville's anger against an unjust social order and vents
Melville's rage against being abandoned by his father. This last point
is driven home by White-Jacket's allusion to "two well-known poetical comparisons between a sea-captain and a father (276).

With his wig, glass eye, and false teeth, in his very person Surgeon
Cuticle seems "a curious patch-work of life and death" (248).[8] A
man whose humanity has been sacrificed to professionalization, Cuticle has been rendered "seemingly impervious to the ordinary emotions of humanity" (251). Because he possesses "the name of being
the foremost Surgeon in the Navy," his fellow physicians do not
prevent Cuticle from performing an unnecessary amputation—another scene of dismemberment—of White-Jacket's wounded mess-
mate (248). Prior to performing the operation, Cuticle divests himself of "all inorganic appurtenances" so that he comes to look like a
"death's-head" (258). While he "seemed enacting the part of a Re-
generator of life," he is "a *memento mori* to behold!" (259) When told
his patient has expired on the operating table, Cuticle betrays not a
trace of feeling: the surgeon personifies the social death of the state's
prison (264).

When Cuticle awakens each morning he opens his eyes to gaze, with "not the slightest touch of concern," on a figure of intense bereavement: the cast of the horned woman he has hung on his wall as a prized specimen of "morbid Anatomy," his "peculiar love" (249). Cuticle unfeelingly stares at

> the head of an elderly woman . . . wonderfully expressive of a gnawing sorrow, never to be relieved. You would almost have thought it the face of some abbess, for some unspeakable crime voluntarily sequestered from human society, and leading a life of agonized penitence without hope; so marvelously sad and tearfully pitiable was this head. But when you first beheld it, no such emotions ever crossed your mind. All your eyes and your horrified soul were fast fascinated and frozen by the sight of a hideous, crumpled horn, like that of a ram, downward growing out from the forehead, and partly shadowing the face; but as you gazed, the freezing fascination of its horribleness gradually waned, and then your whole heart burst with sorrow, as you contemplated those aged features, ashy pale and wan.

Howard P. Vincent has shown that Melville based the horned woman on illustrations in the popular press entitled "The Sunday Widow" or "The Horned Mother." The horned woman bears the traces of Melville's bereavement for his father as influenced by his mother's grief. Maria Melville's Calvinist sense of depravity emerges from the cast: "The horn seemed the mark of a curse for some mysterious sin, conceived and committed before the spirit had entered the flesh. Yet that sin seemed imposed, and not voluntarily sought; some sin growing out of the heartless necessities of the predestination of things; some sin under which the sinner sank in sinless woe" (249). The horned woman combines the intense bereavement Melville's culture had burdened women with socially symbolizing and the distorted sign of manhood, the "crumpled horn," which evokes the imagery of dismemberment that, as we have seen, has been found characteristic of male expressions of loss. The personification of social death, Cuticle, collects this most intimate emblem of bereavement as a professional prize of sorts. The linking object theory enables us to see how Melville has displaced this representation of his own maternally influenced bereavement into a scenario which epitomizes the social death that thwarts the resolution of his blocked grief.[9]

The white jacket itself suggests a feminization. It is "stuffed out about the breasts like a Christmas turkey" and "about the loins . . . shorter than a ballet-dancer's skirts" (100). As he constructs the jacket, he makes a "gash" that also may hint at a gender inversion (3). Recall as well the skirts of his jacket muffling him in his fall. Early on we are told that in a dark night the protagonist is "gleaming white, as the White Lady of Avenel," who appears in Scott's *The Monastery*, also the source of the name of *Pierre*'s Mrs. Glendinning, modeled in part on Maria Melville (5).[10]

White-Jacket's intertwined themes of social death and arrested grief come to a climax in old Ushant's resistance against Claret's order to trim his beard. The narrator makes plain the symbolic import: "the beard is the token of manhood" (368). Ushant, "a sort of sea-Socrates," refuses to relinquish the last vestige of dignity the state's prison has left him: " 'old Ushant's beard is his own!' " (364) While even Jack Chase "mournfully" submits to a trim, with the words, " 'you are about to shear off my manhood,' " Ushant stands up to both a flogging and incarceration to emerge as a "heroic old man" by novel's end (360, 361). However, the absurdity of his resistance, and the reduction of manhood to the length of one's facial hair, indicates the hegemony of the state's prison for Melville.

The pose of sensibility White-Jacket strikes in narrating this episode puts us on notice that authentic feeling has been pushed to the margins of the man-of-war world: "As I now deviously hover and lingeringly skirmish about the frontiers of this melancholy recital, a feeling of sadness comes over me that I can not withstand" (355). Real expression of bereavement in White-Jacket's world can be better glimpsed in his companion Nord, who is marked by an "incommunicable grief" (51).

Himself a figure of conflict—a man-of-war on an intrapsychic level—White-Jacket reveals that his sense of his own masculinity has been divided between identification with the genteel manners his "sea tutor and sire" Jack Chase epitomizes and the radical stances

that fuel the novel's social critique. White-Jacket maintains a genteel
contempt for most of the sailors with whom he serves, viewing their
"subordination" as something "which should by all means be re-
tained" (166). Although, as we have seen, he scathingly indites the
arbitrary laws of the criminal code, his critique is not motivated by a
"romantic belief in that peculiar noble-heartedness and exaggerated
generosity of disposition fictitiously imputed" to man "in novels"
(138, 304).[11]

White-Jacket's views on the question of sin and innate depravity
will not reduce to a stable formulation.[12] "Depravity in the oppressed
is no apology for the oppressor," he argues: "In a large degree,"
depravity is "the effect, and not the cause and justification of oppres-
sion" (142). Although we may be "oppressed by illiberal laws," we
are also "partly oppressed by ourselves": "the worst of our evils we
blindly inflict upon ourselves" (399). White-Jacket also voices Calvinist sentiments: "This old-fashioned world of ours afloat" is "full of
strange contradictions; and though boasting some fine fellows here
and there, yet, upon the whole, charged to the combings of her
hatchways with the spirit of Belial and all unrighteousness" (390).

White-Jacket can at one moment advocate Manifest Destiny and
millennialism—"we Americans are the peculiar, chosen people"—
and then claim that fate "sustains an armed neutrality," and that "in
our own hearts, we mold the whole world's hereafters; and in our own
hearts we fashion our own gods . . . Ourselves are Fate" (151, 320–
21). His final thoughts in the novel are perhaps the most telling:
"whatever befall us, let us never train our murderous guns inboard; let
us not mutiny" (400).[13] Whether he refers here to social revolution
or to the threat of self-destruction, in suicide or madness, he draws
attention to the instability that plays so large a part in the shifting
opinions which split apart his own persona. The social text of his
voice darkly points to the disruptive influence of Maria Melville's
complexly mixed—genteel and Calvinistic—style of bereavement
on the incommunicable grief that lays buried just beneath the surface
of her son's art.

CHAPTER SIX

A Thing Writ in Water:
Allan Melvill's Epitaph

Deep & Secret grief is a cannibal of its own heart.
Bacon

Deep memories yield no epitaphs
Herman Melville, *Moby-Dick*

Two gender-related findings of the Harvard Study of Bereavement illuminate the role of mourning in *Moby-Dick*. As we have seen, the male subjects of this study tend to define their sense of loss in terms of dismemberment, whereas the women studied register a sense of abandonment. The preceding chapters of this book have demonstrated that the imagery of dismemberment pervades Melville's work. Ahab's dismasted state, however, most dramatically performs this social symbolization of male bereavement. The Harvard Study has also found that one-third of the women interviewed displayed "generalized hostility" three weeks after their loss, while none of the men showed this reaction. Nevertheless, the male subjects reported that it took them longer to feel that they had overcome their bereavement; a third of the men reported an inability to cry, claiming that they felt choked up. [1] And it is this finding that takes us deeply into the complexities of grief and gender in *Moby-Dick*.

In his shattered sense of corporeal and psychic wholeness, Ahab is

Melville's most uninhibited male mourner. The rage that surfaces in Ahab's character contrasts starkly with the genteel denial of anger often exhibited by Melville's male characters—the important exception to this being Ahab's prototype, *Redburn's* Jackson. Contemporaries of Melville could simply not accept the extent to which Ahab melodramatically vents his morbidity: this was the object of sharp attacks on the novel. Twentieth-century critics turn Ahab into anything but what Melville portrayed him as: a bereaved monomaniac. Ahab still expresses dark feelings which Melville's readers feel more comfortable translating into less painful abstractions. [2]

Why does Melville allow Ahab a heightened bereavement? Elsewhere in his fiction he largely obeys the cultural codes that burden women with the public symbolization of grief. I contend that Ahab performs the social role ascribed to the female mourner—although he exceeds even that role in the intensity of his public expression of grief—because his character is shaped by Melville's sense of his mother's conflicted grief for his father. Through Ahab's character, Melville portrays the power of his mother's bereaved rage and its crucial influence on his own grief for his father. Although Ahab's identification with Maria Melville's grief is kept on the novel's margins, it momentarily breaches the surface in "The Candles," where Ahab, while attempting to "'read my sire,'" claims for himself a "'queenly personality.'" Ishmael portrays Ahab as both the damned maniac and the embattled hero in quest of an ultimate showdown with all the Evil in the universe, but Ahab's divided delineation has a great deal to do with the contradictory images of Maria's husband, as damned deathbed maniac and as an idealized figure that she communicated to her son through her conflicted grief. [3]

Ahab represents Melville's attempt to exorcise from his inner world the complex image of his father he internalized from his mother's grief. For this reason, Ahab exhibits the symptoms of Allan Melvill's last weeks of life: deathbed mania. Through Crazy Ahab, Melville attempts to transform the mania into both penetrating insight into the tragic dimensions of existence and the heroic resistance to Fixed Fate. Ahab's characterization expresses a doubleness that goes to the heart of the energies of the novel. A morbid figure and one of tragic grandeur, his character opens itself both to Melville's fears of the paternal image of the deathbed maniac that threatened him from within and to Melville's sense of the overwhelming and dangerous rage of his own unresolved grief, compounded by the influence of the rage of a mother's grief on the anger of a child's sense of abandonment by his parent.[4]

Ahab exists as the object of perception and creation of Ishmael, a narrator marked especially by a mordant sense of humor and by occasional insights into the complexity and the fluidity of reality underlying social representations. However, Ishmael's narration also often participates in the Victorian American social codes that militate against the public expression of intense feeling, such as what his culture termed excessive grief.[5] And both Ahab and Ishmael share the stage with a "tremendous apparition," Moby Dick (448). While, on the one hand, Ishmael perceives that the whale "must remain unpainted to the last"—"I have ever found your plain things the knottiest of all," he observes slyly—on the other hand, Ishmael views Ahab's intense bereavement through the cultural codes that cause Ahab to harbor "the mad secret of his unabated rage bolted up and keyed in him" while he endeavors to appear "but naturally grieved" after his return from the voyage on which Moby Dick sheared off his leg (228, 312, 162, 161). By portraying Ahab's unnatural bereavement in terms of his culture's social construction of grief and madness, Ishmael dramatizes how he must view Ahab's excessive grief in terms of monomania.

As Ishmael oscillates between his mixed response to Ahab's grief—he both condemns Ahab for expressing intense bereavement and enviously idealizes him for doing so—and Moby Dick's resistance to representation, the novel generates much of the energy and excitement of its rich language. This narrative shifting, combined with Ishmael's penchant for shiftiness as a narrator, splits Melville's attempt to represent his unresolved grief into confrontation with an incarnation of his living linking object role and his respect for the complexity of feeling that eludes social representations. When Moby

Dick finally appears, Ishmael's imagery intimates his sense of the whale as "a thing writ in water," an inscription of the natural world's fluid writing but also an echo of Keats's gravestone epitaph: "Here lies one whose name was writ in water" (453).[6]

Both grief and the white whale, the novel suggests, cannot finally be possessed in the terms of social representation available to Ishmael. The theme of possession comes to the fore when Ishmael angrily protests against the legal argument that assumes women are property. "Possession," in Ishmael's scathing analysis, has become "the whole of the law" (333). In his representation of Moby Dick, which obliquely critiques his own convention-bound portrayal of Ahab's intense bereavement, Ishmael attempts to subvert patriarchal social codes in his preference for a more fluid state of affairs, one in which his readers are "but a Loose-Fish and a Fast-Fish, too" (334). The "'fluid consciousness'" Sophia Hawthorne perceived in Melville transforms *Moby-Dick's* readers into Fast-Fish, held by a Loose-Fish of complex narrative animation—one that seduces us into the powerful experience of morbid grief, which threatens to subvert from within the melodramatic generic languages in which Ahab comes to life.[7]

THE SOOTHING SAVAGE

The bereaved's continuing sense of "containing" the
person lost gives rise to an elated state of mind.
John Bowlby, *Loss*

In the linking object theory, the surviving parent transfers grief to the child. That process is paralleled in *Moby-Dick* by Ahab's success in wedding the crew to his aggrieved quest.[8] When Ahab crosses the lances of his mates, "it seemed as though, by some nameless, interior volition, he would fain have shocked into them the same fiery emotion accumulated within the Leyden jar of his own magnetic life" (145–46). Ishmael confesses that "because of the dread in my soul" he shouts out Ahab's oath against the whale along with the rest of the crew: "A wild, mystical, sympathetical feeling was in me; Ahab's quenchless feud seemed mine" (155). The transference of emotion works so successfully on the crew that "at times his [Ahab's] hate seemed almost theirs" (162). Ishmael, as well, "gave myself up to the abandonment of the time and the place" and sees Moby Dick through Ahab's eyes: as the embodiment of "the deadliest ill" (163). In the final chase scenes, Ahab's grief has fully taken hold of the crew's emotions. His "purpose now fixedly gleamed down upon the constant midnight of the gloomy crew" (437). "Alike, joy and sorrow, hope and fear, seemed ground to finest dust, and powdered, for the time, in the clamped mortar of Ahab's iron soul. Like machines, they [the crew] dumbly moved about the deck" (438).

Before Ahab effects the transference of his grief, Ishmael, in his relationship with Queequeg, the soothing savage, offers a counter-story to what he presents as the monomaniac obsession and the powerful influence of Ahab's bereavement. From the outset of the narrative, Ishmael reveals his interest in the subject of death and mourning. He presents us with an Etymology supplied by a Late Consumptive Usher, who loved to dust his grammar books because "it somehow mildly reminded him of his mortality" (1). Ishmael next inserts Extracts of passages on the whale gathered from world literature by a Sub-Sub-Librarian, with whom he enjoys sitting and feeling "poor-devilish, too; and grow[s] convivial upon tears . . . and in not altogether unpleasant sadness" (2).

From this evocation of the fashionable melancholy of sentimental literature, Ishmael turns to his narration proper with an expression of morbid feelings that flirts with exceeding the bounds of the sentimental and Byronic poses from behind which he often teases us. He edges his introduction of himself with aggressive and angry instructions: "Call me Ishmael. Some years ago—never mind how long precisely" (12). Momentarily, though, he shifts into an Irvingesque pose of genteel melancholy: "having little or no money in my purse, and nothing particular to interest me on shore, I thought I would sail about a little and see the watery part of the world" (12). He then confesses to feelings that are darker than the melancholy of the

sentimental novel but which are recited in the hyperboles of a joky
tone that immediately undercuts authentic emotion:

> It is a way I have of driving off the spleen, and regulating the circula-
> tion. Whenever I find myself growing grim about the mouth; whenever
> it is a damp, drizzly November in my soul; whenever I find myself
> involuntarily pausing before coffin warehouses, and bringing up the
> rear of every funeral I meet; and especially whenever my hypos get such
> an upper hand of me, that it requires a strong moral principle to prevent
> me from deliberately stepping into the street, and methodically knock-
> ing people's hats off—then, I account it high time to get to sea as soon
> as I can. This is my substitute for pistol and ball. (12)

Ishmael, while confessing to angry and suicidal feelings, also indicates his partial allegiance to genteel codes of feeling: by shipping out
he regulates his morbidity. The introductory paragraph closes with
his argument that "almost all men in their degree, some time or
other, cherish very nearly the same feelings towards the ocean with
me," that is, although he has just revealed socially unacceptable
feelings, most people feel similarly, and they too seek out the ocean
for solace and as an escape from acting out dark impulses. Ishmael's
tone is usually described by critics in terms of expansiveness and
fluidity, but its final emphasis often falls—as it does here—on the
social control of feeling.[9]

Ironically, in signing up on the Pequod, Ishmael will find himself
on a coffin warehouse of sorts and bringing up the rear of a funeral,
especially after the carpenter makes Queequeg a coffin-canoe, Ahab
fulfills the Parsee's riddle with its imagery that finally turns both
Moby Dick and the Pequod into hearses, and Ishmael falls off Ahab's
whaleboat, thus bringing up the rear of the Pequod's funeral. The
opening chapters of the novel take us through a series of scenes in
which death and grief are evoked; however, these morbid themes are
struck by a wonderfully alive, exuberant, and joshing voice that is
careful not to overtly exceed Victorian American codes of feeling.

Upon his entry to Nantucket at night, Ishmael observes that the
candles in the town's windows are "like a candle moving about in a
tomb" (18). After he stumbles into a black church, The Trap, he

thinks he's descended into Tophet (19). A visit to the whaleman's chapel affords Ishmael an opportunity to muse expansively on grief and death: "Each silent worshipper seemed purposely sitting apart from the other, as if each silent grief were insular and incommunicable" (39). He notices that "so plainly did several women wear the countenance if not the trappings of some unceasing grief, that I feel sure that here before me were assembled those, in whose unhealing hearts the sight of those bleak tablets [marble epitaphs] sympathetically caused old wounds to bleed afresh" (40).[10] Ishmael puts the emphasis on the ceaseless side of female grief: the aspect of bereavement Ahab melodramatically and, as Ishmael's genteel side sees it, offensively develops. Ishmael speculates, "How it is we still refuse to be comforted for those who we nevertheless maintain are dwelling in unspeakable bless; why all the living so strive to hush all the dead; wherefore but the rumor of a knocking in a tomb will terrify a whole city. All these things are not without their meanings" (41). With characteristic dark humor, however, Ishmael joshes us about his willingess to face the mortal threat of a sailor's life: "But somehow I grew merry again. Delightful inducements to embark, fine chance for promotion" (41).

Ishmael feels a sense of foreboding when he eyes the gallows-like pots suspended from the topmast on the doorway of the Try-Pots Inn. He then sums up the imagery of the opening of the novel: "It's ominous, thinks I. A Coffin my Inn-keeper upon landing in my first whaling port; tombstones staring at me in the whaleman's chapel; and here a gallows! and a pair of prodigious black pots too! Are these last throwing out oblique hints touching Tophet?" (64). Into this morbid pattern of imagery, Ishmael places his comical conversion experience with Queequeg, the fallen cannibal. Descended from a royal Kokovokoian family, Queequeg desires to visit the West "to learn among the Christians, the arts whereby to make his people still happier than they were" (57). Soon disillusioned by "the practices of whalemen," Queequeg becomes "fearful [that] Christianity, or rather Christians, had unfitted him for ascending the pure and undefiled throne" of his forefathers; "as soon as he felt himself baptized again," he will return to his island (57).

Through Queequeg's characterization, Melville offers a rewriting of his memory of his father that runs counter to his later attempt to exorcise the linking object role through Ahab. [11] Queequeg does not equal Allan Melvill in any simple allegorical equation. Rather there are details in the delineation of Queequeg that bear on Melville's grief work. In Ishmael's relationship with Queequeg, Melville fantasizes a resolution of his conflicted grief. This relationship is framed by two deathbed scenes: the first, in Peter Coffin's marriage bed, slyly hints at the deathbed connotation; the second is an overt deathbed scene, which inverts Allan Melvill's death and provides the stage prop that ultimately saves Ishmael: the coffin life-buoy.

Ishmael first hears about his prospective bedmate from his landlord, Peter Coffin, who "sky-larks" with Ishmael by telling him that the sailor he will be sleeping with is out selling heads. Ishmael concludes the sailor must be "'stark mad, and I've no idea of sleeping with a madman'" (26). But, insofar as Allan Melvill peers through facets of Queequeg's characterization, this is precisely what Ishmael will do: climb into bed with a displaced and inverted version of a deathbed maniac. To place his protagonist in such a situation realizes Melville's deepest fear: the threat of the usurpation of his sense of self by the image of the damned deathbed maniac his mother's grief had deposited into his formative consciousness.

As Ishmael, "at the dead of night," peers out terror-stricken at the monstrous creature—"the devil himself"—in his bedroom, he first describes Queequeg as taking his "new beaver hat" out of his bag (29). The factory Allan left at his death as the only inheritance to his family manufactured beaver hats and bearskin coats. [12] Later, when Queequeg is locked in a trance during his Ramadan observance, Ishmael throws his own "heavy bearskin jacket" over his friend (80). Queequeg's oddest garment is the heavy mat he wears as a kind of poncho. When Queequeg enters the bedroom he tries on what seems to him this "door mat": it was "uncommonly shaggy and thick, and I thought it a little damp"; when he doffed it, he noted that it had "a hole or slit in the middle" (28, 27). This would seem to be sexual innuendo, preparing the scene for Ishmael's comical conversion into

Queequeg's wife and their subsequent marriage. In his initial association with the mat/womb, Queequeg, as a kind of site on which
Melville's grief for Allan is rewritten, evokes what the linking object
theory posits: the maternal encompassment of the father's image. In
name, "Quee/queg" hints at the presence of the queenly personality
that later emerges in the margins of Ahab's characterization.

Like Allan Melvill, who took great pride in his noble Scottish
ancestry, Queequeg, also descended from noble ancestry, possesses
"a certain lofty bearing" (52). But unlike the deathbed maniac and
bankrupt Melvill, Queequeg "looked like a man who had never
cringed and never had a creditor" (52). Queequeg, like Melville's
father, winds up on his deathbed after he "caught a terrible chill
which lapsed into a fever" (395). But the fallen cannibal inverts the
failed businessman's death. Rather than Melvill's deathbed shouts,
Ishmael, applying the codes of the good Christian death, is exposed
to the "higher and holier" thoughts that flit across Queequeg's face
(396).[13] As Pip observes, " 'Queequeg dies game' " (398). Queequeg,
though, suddenly recovers from his illness, and he explains that "at a
critical moment, he had just recalled a little duty ashore, which he
was leaving undone; and therefore had changed his mind about
dying" (398). "In a word, it was Queequeg's conceit, that if a man
made up his mind to live, mere sickness could not kill him" (398).
The calmly dying, then dutiful Queequeg, in control of his mortality,
rewrites Melville's memory of both his father's deathbed mania and
Allan Melvill's seeming abandonment of his duties to his large
family.

Ishmael's marriage night with Queequeg in the Spouter Inn complexly rewrites this memory. Ishmael recalls a childhood experience
after awakening to find Queequeg's arm "thrown over me in the most
loving and affectionate manner. You had almost thought I had been
his wife" (32). In it his cruel stepmother, who was "all the time
whipping me, or sending me to bed supperless," orders him to spend
the day in bed after he tries to climb up the chimney (32). While in
bed, Ishmael suddenly feels a "supernatural hand . . . placed in
mine" (33). The feeling of Queequeg hugging him evokes the memo-

ry of the sensations Ishmael felt while holding the hand of the "un-imaginable, silent form or phantom" (33). In the comparison be-tween the two experiences Ishmael sets up, the details related to Melville's grief work that play through Queequeg's characterization would seem to identify the phantom with a figure equivalent in Ishmael's life to the role Allan Melvill played in Melville's. In Quee-queg the alternately terrifying and loving unimaginable form comes to life. [14]

In a moment parallel to the supernatural hand episode, Ishmael undergoes his conversion experience with Queequeg. A storm howls outside their window and "the evening shades and phantoms [were] gathering around the casements" (53). Ishmael's feelings while in Queequeg's "bridegroom clasp" now resurface: "I began to be sensible of strange feelings" (53). His intimacy with Queequeg acts cathar-tically on his former anger and morbidity:

> I felt a melting in me. No more my splintered heart and maddened hand were turned against the wolfish world. This soothing savage had redeemed it. There he sat, his very indifference speaking a nature in which there lurked no civilized hypocrisies and bland deceits. Wild he was; a very sight to see; yet I began to feel myself mysteriously drawn to him . . . I'll try a pagan friend, thought I, since Christian kindness has proved but hollow courtesy. (53)

After they enjoy a "social smoke" of the tomahawk, Queequeg "pressed his forehead against mine, clasped me round the waist, and said that henceforth we were married; meaning, in his country's phrase, that we were bosom friends; he would gladly die for me, if need should be" (53). Presenting Ishmael with his "embalmed head," dividing his money with him, and sharing his worship of Yojo, the too-good-to-be-true Queequeg lies in bed with Ishmael in their "heart's honeymoon . . . a cosy, loving pair" (54).

In the fantasy of emotional closeness he provides Ishmael, Quee-queg heals his friend's "splintered heart and maddened hand" and reopens him to fraternal feeling. Queequeg offers a momentary reso-lution of the grief work Melville performs in the other dimensions of his text. Nevertheless, Ishmael's affection for Queequeg covertly performs an angry gesture: it must have been intended by Melville to outrage and tweak his more conventional contemporary readers. As one critic has noted, it was sleeping with a man of dark skin, not the honeymoon burlesque, that would have offended some of Melville's contemporaries.[15] While Ishmael is melting in Queequeg's arms, Melville was turning his own maddened hand against the civilized hypocrisies of his more straitlaced readers.

In Queequeg's soothing savage influence on him, Ishmael fantasizes the control of the wildness that must have terrified Melville in his father's deathbed mania. But Queequeg has not extinguished Ishmael's morbidity. After Queequeg remains locked in his room all day and into the evening, Ishmael panics and attempts to break down the door. The landlady, Mrs. Hussey, is convinced Queequeg has killed himself because he has retrieved the harpoon she forbade him to take to his room. Upon gaining entry into the room, Ishmael finds Queequeg "cool and self-collected," with Yojo perched atop his head, deep in his Ramadan meditation (80). Claiming tolerance for any religion that does not cause its practioners to "kill or insult any other person," Ishmael confesses that "when a man's religion becomes really frantic"—as it seems to him it has with Queequeg—"when it is a positive torment to him," then he takes that individual aside and remonstrates with him (81). This incident persuades practical-minded Mrs. Hussey to order a sign announcing: " 'no suicides permitted here, and no smoking in the parlor' " (79).[16]

Queequeg's dark side scarily emerges from behind Ishmael's fantasies only once. After making himself comfortable on a sleeping sailor's behind, Queequeg flourishes his tomahawk above the sailor's head: " 'Perry easy, kill-e; oh! perry easy' " (92). Aside from this revelation of cultural difference (his cannibalism), Queequeg appears before us very much as Ishmael wishes us to see him. He is the noble savage, saving the impertinent sailor knocked overboard on the trip out to New Bedford, displaying his skill in obstetrics by rescuing Tashtego from the whale's "tun," and finally saving Ishmael through his mystically inscribed coffin life-buoy.

It is Queequeg who suggests transforming his coffin into a life-buoy (430). While fashioning the life-buoy, the carpenter observes, " 'It's like turning an old coat; going to bring the flesh on the other side now' "—another evocation of Allan's coat factory (430). If Queequeg's characterization in part seems to rewrite and attempts to resolve Melville's conflicted grief, then his legacy to Ishmael, the coffin life-buoy, suggests that through Queequeg, Ishmael transforms his own morbidity into something life-giving. Queequeg's coffin refigures Allan Melvill's death and is the image of the durability of grief, now providing a source of sustenance and creativity (the coffin surfaces from a "vital centre") to which Ishmael clings in the "closing vortex" (470). [17]

THE PARLOR-THEATER OF MOURNING

But ere we start, we must dig a deep hole, and bury
all Blue Devils, there to abide til the Last Day.
Melville to Hawthorne, July 22, 1851, *Melville's
Letters*

Neither hearse nor coffin can be thine.
Parsee to Ahab in Melville's *Moby-Dick*

In her discussion of antebellum mourning practices, social historian Karen Halttunen notes that in the 1850s "the genteel performance enacted by . . . middle-class men and women was becoming more openly and self-consciously theatrical."[18] Halttunen also discusses a social practice popular in the 1850s: the parlor-theater. In this middle-class entertainment, a stage was created in genteel parlors, and productions were mounted in which the line between audience and player was often blurred, as members of the audience were drawn into the performance. Within his narrative, Ishmael sets before us a version of the parlor theatrical in the chapters, prefaced by stage directions, in which Ahab seems to take over the novel. As audience to Ahab's "self-consciously theatrical" grief, Ishmael also finds himself swept across the narrative proscenium and, alternately, drawn into an identification with, resistance to, and an attempt to transform Ahab's "deep helpless sadness" (203).

When Ishmael first queries one of the owners of the *Pequod* about Ahab, Peleg responds: " 'I don't know exactly what's the matter with him; but he keeps close inside the house; a sort of sick, and yet he don't look so. In fact, he ain't sick; but no, he isn't well either' " (76). After losing his leg to Moby Dick on his last voyage, Ahab has been " 'a kind of moody—desperate moody, and savage sometimes' " (77). While on the homeward voyage, Ahab " 'was a little out of his mind for a spell; but it was the sharp shooting pains in his bleeding stump that brought that about' " (77). Instinctively empathizing with him, Ishmael feels "a certain wild vagueness of painfulness concerning Ahab": "a sympathy and a sorrow for him, but for I don't know what, unless it was the cruel loss of his leg" (77). But he also feels something he cannot put into words: "a strange awe of him," but "not exactly awe; I do not know what it was. But I felt it" (77). In his narrative of Ahab's mad quest, Ishmael never does quite decide how he feels about the sometimes Satanic, sometimes nobly grand, bereaved whale hunter.

Ishmael's equivocal response to Ahab echoes Melville's unresolved grief for the father who had also been "a little out of his mind for a spell." But in Ahab, Melville also displaces the rage of his own grief. Ahab's doubleness thus inheres in his reenactment of Allan's death-bed mania and his expression of the anger of Melville's conflicted grief, which has blurred its conflicts with those of his mother's grief. " 'They think me mad,' " Ahab muses, " 'but I'm demoniac, I am madness maddened!' " (147). Ahab, however, plays a larger role: "in his frantic morbidness he at last came to identify with him [Moby Dick] . . . all his intellectual and spiritual exasperations" (160). To Crazy Ahab, Moby Dick personifies all evil. Ahab "piled upon the whale's white hump the sum of all the general rage and hate felt by his whole race from Adam down" (160).

"The truest of all men was the Man of Sorrows," Ishmael speculates, "and Ecclesiastes is the fine hammered steel of woe": "But even Solomon, he says, 'the man that wandereth out of the way of understanding shall remain' (i.e. even while living) 'in the congregation of the dead'" (355). "There is a wisdom that is woe," Ishmael sermonizes, "but there is a woe that is madness" (355). And from this pietistic perspective, Ahab, in his woe, has simply gone too far: he has exceeded the bounds of genteel bereavement.

But in his heightened, transgressive sense of bereavement, Ahab provides deep insight into the experience of mourning. After his ivory leg "all but pierced his groin" in a fall, Ahab connects the pain of his wound to Moby Dick. "All miserable events do naturally beget their like," he muses, "since both the ancestry and posterity of Grief go further than the ancestry and posterity of Joy"; "some guilty mortal miseries shall still fertilely beget to themselves an eternally progressive progeny of griefs beyond the grave" (385). To the degree he represents his biblical namesake, Ahab brings with him into Melville's fictive world the Old Testament's sense of the wisdom in woe, undiluted by the Victorian American fear of intense feeling Ishmael at times adopts. In the Elizabethan rhetoric he inhabits, Ahab finds that "all heart-woes [have] a mystic significance, and, in some men, an arch-angelic grandeur" (386). As Richard Brodhead points out, Melville imagines each of his characters in the fictional mode or genre most appropriate to them. Ahab himself admits as much: "'Cursed be that mortal inter-debtedness which will not do away with ledgers. I would be as free as air; and I'm down in the whole world's books [in a double sense]'" (392).[19]

Ahab would seem himself the offspring of a bereavement that has led to madness: he is the son of a "'crazy, widowed mother, who died when he was only a twelvemonth'" (77).[20] Voicing the conventional view of Melville's culture toward excessive grief, Ishmael identifies Ahab as a monomaniac. According to the ideological codes that forbid a public expression of intense bereavement, Ahab must be defined as crazy. Ahab endeavors to appear "but naturally grieved" after he returns from the voyage on which Moby Dick dismembered him, but to do so means that he must conceal "the mad secret of his unabated rage bolted up and keyed in him" (161, 162). Ashore, Ahab must pose as the genteel mourner.

Through Ishmael's characterization of Ahab, Melville puts into question his culture's definitions of madness and natural grief. In his notes on the flyleaf of a volume of Shakespeare, Melville jotted down, "madness is undefinable."[21] Ahab's madness could be the required cultural labeling for the mourner who attempts to express the full depth of his bereavement, especially the anger, which Victorian Americans attempted both to regulate and to deny healthful public symbolization. Ahab is subversive in that he would openly and fully grieve. Melville angrily attacks his culture's rules for feeling by staging within literary stereotypes, and so deliberately distorting into melodramatic expression, Ahab's attempt at unabashed grief. These range from the biblical Ahab to the Elizabethan, romantic, and gothic heroes and villains Ahab plays off of. Popular culture genres as well give shape to his presentation. "With slouched hat," like a figure out of a dime novel or a Brockden Brown romance, "Ahab lurchingly paced the planks" (114). Ahab is so gloomy, melancholy, and dark that he could only be a composite—assembled from the cultural forms whose implicit ideological encodings relegate intense expression of negative feelings to unbelievably melodramatic figures.

Melville distorts Ahab's expression of bereavement to implicitly critique the cultural codes that prohibit cathartic expression of conflicted grief. In "The Candles," Ahab voices his grief in Elizabethan and gothic rhetoric that turns it into something ornately unreal. Standing before the corpusants that flame in the yardarms "like gigantic wax tapers before an altar"—a kind of Gothic stage prop—Ahab seems to be speaking in front of the tapers that sometimes surrounded a corpse in Melville's time. The tapers, though, are the corpse in this case, as Ahab takes as his own the Parsee's worship of fire. Speaking as a tragic Elizabethan on the stage, Ahab claims, " 'In the midst of the personified impersonal [i.e., the fire], a personality stands here. Though but a point at best; . . . yet while I earthly live, the queenly personality lives in me, and feels her royal rights. . . . Oh, thou foundling fire . . . thou too hast thy incommunicable riddle, thy unparticipated grief. Here again with haughty agony, I read my sire' " (417). The importation of an alien diction not only threatens to empty his speech of feeling. but it nearly parodies the palpable unparticipated grief that underlies his mad quest. On the margins of this inauthentic language, Melville hints at the queenly personality of his mother that speaks through the social text of Ahab's enraged bereavement.[22]

Queen Nature, " 'thou dark Hindoo half of nature . . . thou art an infidel, thou queen,' " Ahab elsewhere says of her, appears in more homely guise as the "the step-mother world" that seems to "joyously sob" over Ahab in "The Symphony" (409, 426–27, 443).[23] With violins at full pitch, Melville stages Ahab's grief here in the genre of the sentimental novel. This chapter opens with the air and the sea playing conventional gender roles in a performance that parodies sentimental diction. "The pensive air was transparently pure and soft, with a woman's look" and the sea appears "robust and man-like" (442). The "feminine air" has "gentle thoughts," while the "masculine sea" possesses "strong, troubled, murderous thinkings" (442). With "the sun . . . giving this gentle air to this bold and rolling sea; even as bride to groom," "the poor bride gave her bosom away" with "fond, throbbing trust" and "loving alarms" (442).

Into this saccharine scene, Melville inserts Ahab, who "dropped a tear into the sea" (443). Observing Ahab's betrayal of emotion, the son-like chief mate, Starbuck, "seemed to hear in his own true heart the measureless sobbing that stole out of the centre of the serenity around" (443). Overcome by his own narration of his melancholy history to Starbuck, Ahab pauses to ask him to " 'brush this old hair aside; it blinds me, that I seem to weep' " (444). In his appeal to Ahab's domestic side to turn him away from his quest, Starbuck delivers a speech straight out of sentimental fiction: " ' 'Tis my Mary, my Mary herself! She promised that my boy, every morning, should be carried to the hill to catch the first glimpse of his father's sail . . . See! see! the boy's face from the window! the boy's hand on the hill!' " (444). Like the representations of mourners in the popular culture, Ahab's glance was "averted" (444).[24] Ahab concludes this chapter by retreating into the diction of melodrama. In the voice of the Byronic hero he muses: " 'Is it I, God, or who, that lifts this arm? . . . Where do murderers go, man! Who's to doom, when the judge himself is dragged to the bar?'" (445). Like a lurid gothic character, Ahab finally "blanched to a corpse's hue with despair" (445).

Ultimately, Ishmael fails in his efforts to control Ahab's excessive grief by keeping it within the bounds of the melodramatic generic languages through which he imagines Ahab. Ahab's terrifying impact on Ishmael and on the other principals of the narrative disrupts and unsettles the novel and overrides Ishmael's gamesome manipulation of literary genres. Ishmael feels "foreboding shivers" when he catches his first glimpse of Ahab's "overbearing grimness" (109, 110). The pugnacious mate Stubb flees from the "overbearing terrors" in Ahab's "aspect" (113). When Starbuck fantasizes making Ahab his prisoner, he cannot act against him because " 'he would be more hideous than a caged tiger, then. I could not endure the sight; could not possibly fly his howlings' " (422).

In his first speech Ahab observes that going to his cabin " 'feels like going down into one's tomb' ": " 'my grave-dug berth' " (112). Ahab terrifies, on the one hand, because he brings out into the open Melville's fear of his internalization of the image of his father as deathbed maniac and as possibly damned according to his mother's Calvinism. But just as frightening is the uninhibited rage Ahab vents—an overwhelming anger that evokes a child's distorted perception of the rage and conflicts of Maria Melville's grief, as it influenced Melville's own adolescent grieving. What makes this all the more difficult for Melville to come to terms with is the other side of his mother's image of his father: that of the beloved, idealized figure. Ahab first stands before the crew as a "moody stricken" figure "with a crucifixion in his face; in all the nameless regal overbearing dignity of some mighty woe" (111). To her grandchildren Melville's mother seemed "stern" and of a "dignified stateliness." It would seem that Ahab's portrayal blurs Melville's recollection of the regal overbearing dignity of his moody stricken mother's grief with his fears of his father's deathbed mania and his need to keep alive the noble image of his father.[25]

The fears Ahab elicits seem directly related to Melville's disturbing memory of his father's deathbed mania. "Of all mortals," Ishmael says of Queequeg on his deathbed, "some dying men are the most tyrannical" (397). Starbuck directly and intimately interacts with Ahab. Of the impact Ahab makes on Starbuck, Ishmael observes: "That immaculate manliness we feel within ourselves . . . bleeds with keenest anguish at the undraped spectacle of a valor-ruined man" (104). Starbuck's bravery "cannot withstand those more terrific, because more spiritual terrors, which sometimes menace you from the concentrating brow of an enraged and mighty man" (104). By the end of the quest, "there lurked a something in the old man's eyes, which it was hardly sufferable for feeble souls to see" (437).26

THE ENDLESS END: A FLUID EPITAPH

Death is only a launching into the region of the
strange Untried; it is but the first salutation to the
possibilities of the immense Remote, the Wild, the
Watery, the Unshored.
Herman Melville, *Moby-Dick*

The final chapters of the novel present several perspectives on bereavement. In the "shameful story" of the blacksmith Perth's "wretched fate," Ishmael offers a little moral tale—the kind that might have been found in a pietistic antebellum magazine—about the "fifth act of the grief" of an alcoholic's "life's drama" (401).27 Our first image of Perth evokes Melville's memory of his father's fatal winter exposure. On "one bitter winter's midnight," Perth, fearing that he may lose his feet to frostbite, seeks shelter in a barn (401). Once a prosperous blacksmith with a wife and children, Perth drinks his way into the loss of his home and family and becomes "a vagabond in crape; his every woe unreverenced" (402). Had Perth died immediately after his ruin, Ishmael points out, his wife might have had a fashionable "delicious grief" (401). Instead, the sea beckons "alluringly" to Perth's "death-longing eyes": " 'Here is another life without the guilt of intermediate death . . . Come hither! put up *thy* gravestone, too, within the churchyard'" (402).

Ahab measures his own condition against Perth's: "'I am impatient of all misery in others that is not mad . . . How cans't thou endure without being mad?'" (403) More to Ahab's liking is Pip's bereaved lunacy, with its evocation of "heaven's sense" (347). Pip falls out of Stubb's whaleboat during the hunt and the latter by abandoning Pip "indirectly hinted, that though man loves his fellow, yet man is a money-making animal" (346). Seeing in Pip's madness a kind of "'holiness,'" Ahab adopts him and takes him to live in his cabin (427). Railing at the "'frozen heavens'"—"'Ye did beget this luckless child, and have abandoned him'"—Ahab sentimentally confesses the impact of Pip's suffering on him, "'Thou touchest my inmost centre, boy; thou art tied to me by cords woven of heartstrings'" (428). With his hand in Ahab's, Pip observes, "'had poor Pip but felt so kind a thing as this, perhaps he had ne'er been lost!'" (428)

In Ahab's relationship with Pip, Melville toys with the anger of his own memory of being abandoned by his father. Finally, Ahab also abandons Pip because he finds him "'too curing to my malady'" (436). Pip, though, offers himself to Ahab as a surrogate limb: "'do ye but use poor me for your one lost leg, . . . I ask no more, so I remain a part of ye'" (436). Insofar as Ahab's dismemberment symbolizes his bereavement, Pip, evoking here Melville's childhood self abandoned by his father, attempts to undo the loss by making Ahab whole again. But Pip merged with Ahab would too explosively reconnect Melville's unresolved feeling of abandonment (Pip) to his displaced bereaved rage (Ahab).[28]

Moby Dick himself provides another version of bereavement. As "a long sleek on the sea," the whale seems to "shed off enticings" (445, 447). "Soft metallic-like marks as of some swift tide-rip, at the mouth of a deep and rapid stream" cover him (445). When Moby Dick breaches the surface, Ishmael notices his "scrolled jaw" (448). Ishmael explains that a whale's submerged course can be discerned by the canny whale hunter who can decipher "the proverbial evanescence of a thing writ in water, a wake" (453). Moby Dick thus seems characterized as a kind of fluid writing, but the imagery of the novel's conclusion also associates him with bereavement—the play on wake of the preceding quote. The whale's pyramidical white hump alludes to the Egyptian burial site, and, as noted earlier, a thing writ in water alludes to Keats's gravestone epitaph (159). When "this tremendous apparition" menaces a whale boat his "glittering mouth yawned beneath the boat like an open-doored marble tomb" (448). After the Parsee becomes entangled in his whale line and pinned to Moby Dick, the whale becomes the first hearse of the Parsee's prophecy (464).

For Ishmael, Moby Dick's whiteness conjures up elusive ambiguity: "the most meaning symbol of spiritual things" but also "the intensifying agent in things the most appalling to mankind" (169). And the whale, as an object of perception, resists our attempts at representation. Confessing his inability to read the whale's brow, Ishmael exclaims, "I put that brow before you. Read it if you can" (293). However, our attempts to do so are undercut by Ishmael's claim that "in gazing at such scenes, it is all and all what mood you are in" (317). The whale, according to Ishmael, "must remain unpainted to the last" (228).

Moby Dick's association with bereavement, then, can only be a result of Ahab's obvious projections onto him, of the covert need to grieve Melville expresses through Ishmael—or, in a larger sense, of the work of mourning Melville performs in the novel. When the *Rachel*, searching for Captain Gardiner's lost twelve-year-old son, enters the novel's last chapters, Melville's grief for the father he lost at twelve rises closer to the surface (435). Earlier, the *Pequod's* crew had heard in the night "a cry so plaintively wild and unearthly—like half-articulated wailings of the ghosts of all Herod's murdered Innocents" (428). Ahab, perhaps realizing these were men lost at sea, claimed they were the cries of bereaved seals; the old Manx sailor later says it was indeed the men on Gardiner's lost boat whose cries were heard (429). Gardiner pleads with Ahab, a fellow Nantucketeer, to help in the search for the boy, but the *Rachel* has also brought news of having done combat with Moby Dick only " 'yester-day,' " and Ahab obsessively flies off after his prey (434).[29]

As if in contrast to a father's bereaved search for his lost twelve-year-old—an inverted version of twelve-year-old Melville's grief—Ishmael portrays Ahab as acting out his bereaved rage destructively. After Moby Dick wrecks the *Pequod*, Ahab exclaims as he flings his harpoon, " 'Oh, now I feel my topmost greatness lies in my topmost grief' " (468). In his very attempt to fully possess and feel his grief, Ahab strangles himself on the whale-line that "ran foul" (468). And as researchers of mourning have observed, the separation pain of grief is often experienced as a choking sensation. In what looks like a fatal expression of grief, the conventional side of Ishmael symbolizes the consequences—in terms of the dominant social codes of Melville's culture—of allowing one's bereavement a full expression.[30]

The alternative to cathartic grief can be glimpsed in Ishmael's rescue by that stock biblical figure of bereavement, Rachel, genteelly "weeping for her children" (436).[31] The "devious cruising" *Rachel* discovers Ishmael—now viewed as a standard character in the senti-mental novel, "another orphan"—in "her retracing search after her missing children" (470). The novel's conclusion thus displaces the marginalized appearance of Maria Melville's powerful grief in Ahab's monomania with a conventional figure used by Melville's culture to burden women with the public, but restrained, symbolization of grief. However, the bereaved rage that Ishmael refuses to allow Ahab to authenticate in public discourse does not remain buried beneath "the great shroud of the sea" for long (469). In *Pierre,* the ambiguities of Melville's unresolved grief more powerfully and disruptively breach the surface of his imagination.

CHAPTER SEVEN

Cunning Purpleness: *Pierre*'s
Subversive Mourning Art

Now I know this, that in the commonest memorials,
the twilight fact of death first discloses in some secret
way, all the ambiguities of that departed thing or
person; obliquely it casts hints, and insinuates
surmises base, and eternally incapable of being
cleared.
Pierre, in Melville's *Pierre, or The Ambiguities*

At a crucial juncture in his abortive development into a serious writer, Pierre learns of his mother's death.[1] "No smallest ring or memorial had been sent him . . . and yet it was reported that an inconsolable grief had induced his mother's mortal malady, and driven her at length into insanity, which suddenly terminated in death" (285). In struggling to come to terms with his grief— "this delirium of his soul"—Pierre "could not define where that line was, which separated the natural grief for the loss of a parent from that other one which was born of compunction" (286). He "cursed himself . . . as the murderer of his mother" (289).

Some days after the news of his mother's death reaches him, "somewhat mastering his emotions, Pierre again sits down in his chamber; for grieve how he will, yet he work he must" (295). But when he sits, "suspended, motionless, blank," before his writing desk, "a general and nameless torpor—some horrible foretaste of death itself—seemed stealing upon him" (341, 342). In the "death-fiend" of his trance, Pierre allegorizes his writerly paralysis in the figure of the "doubly incestuous" Enceladus, impotently revolting against his imprisonment on the slope of the Delectable Mountain on Mrs. Glendinning's estate (347). After glimpsing his "own duplicate face" on the Titan's "armless trunk," Pierre awakens from his excursion through the landscape of his thwarted creativity and confronts the full force of "all his actual grief" (346).

Pierre's relationship with his mother dominates the novel. He feigns marriage to his putative sister, Isabel, to protect his mother from learning of Mr. Glendinning's sexual misconduct. After his mother disowns him for taking up with the "plebian" Isabel, Pierre slowly self-destructs, as if he has internalized her reprobation (194). The news of her fatal grief damns Pierre to a self-punitive, final crack-up. "Dabbling in the vomit of his loathed identity," Pierre renounces his writerly self; his cousin lashes him across the face; and Pierre murders his cousin (171)—thus delivering himself to the city dungeon—the Tombs—and literalizing his earlier sense of himself as "this most unwilling states-prisoner of letters" (340).

Although he can shield his mother from the legacy of the real Mr. Glendinning, Pierre himself must confront the conflicts—or the ambiguities with which Isabel pollutes the novel—of his own revived grief for his father. But Pierre finally falls precisely because he cannot relinquish the idealized version of his father that his mother inculcated in him.[2] Midway through the novel, Pierre feels "strung in all his sinews and nerves to the holding of his father's memory intact" (178).

Several critics have noticed that Isabel becomes Mrs. Glendinning's sexual double. However, the mournful Isabel also functions as a displaced version of the powerful influence on Pierre of Mrs. Glendinning's grief, which is initially only potentially explosive and then, after Pierre champions Isabel, fatally so. Subversively, Isabel threatens to transform Mrs. Glendinning's idealized image of Pierre's father into one of a sexual profligate. Isabel darkly represents the conflicts of mourning that both mother and son ultimately, and self-destructively, deny.[3]

Isabel also plays the role of Pierre's muse, albeit a disenabling one. Isabel embodies Pierre's involvements as he struggles to become a serious writer. She represents "not the book, but the primitive elementalizing of the strange stuff, which in the act of attempting that book, has upheaved and upgushed in his soul" (304). However, as a displaced version of the conflicted grief that Pierre and his mother deny, Isabel plays the role of a mediatory zone in which the ambiguities of mourning are controlled. Her tumultuous and unstable figure is one of the disruptive forces lying behind *Pierre's* strange stylistic contortions.

Stylistically, *Pierre* is a parody—and a relatively weak one—of popular fiction. There is a deeply serious substratum to the cunning purpleness of the novel's style. Recent biographical discoveries suggest that *Pierre* is to be read as the "blasphemous rhapsody" the publishers Steel, Flint, and Asbestos accuse Pierre of writing (356). New evidence indicates the strong likelihood that Melville's father sired an illegitimate daughter, and *Pierre*, then, should be read from the perspective of those members of Melville's family who were aware of this misconduct: as a potentially blasphemous swinging open of Allan Melvill's skeleton closet. This act would have been most painful to Melville's mother, Maria.[4]

Henry Murray established the biographical parallels in *Pierre*, which include the similarities between the forceful personalities of Pierre's mother and Maria Melville, between Mr. Glendinning and Melville's father, and between Lucy and Melville's wife, Elizabeth. The new evidence linking Melville's father to Mr. Glendinning, dispels the notion that *Pierre* is a mostly failed attempt to tease Melville's family by thrusting them into the world of popular fiction. Melville had a greater emotional investment in the novel. At stake in *Pierre* are Melville's own conflicts about his chronic grief for his father.[5]

As we have seen, for Melville to work through his conflicts toward his father involved coming to terms with the images of his father he had inherited from his mother's bereavement. And this is nowhere more evident than in *Pierre*. In the novel, the protagonist cannot finally renounce his mother's images of his father, nor can he escape the influence of her powerful grief. Melville's creativity was powerfully bound up with forging an image of his father with which he could live and from which he could gain sustenance through positive identification, as *Pierre* dramatizes. Object-relations mourning theory posits that conflicted grief cannot be resolved until the mourner separates the negative from the positive traits of the dead. Coming to terms with the negative characteristics of the deceased means the mourner can psychically reinvest himself or herself in the admired attributes of the dead. With the inner representation of the dead made whole, the mourner can finally "bury" the dead.[6]

To gain access to his richest creative powers, Melville needed to reconcile contradictory images of his father. In *Moby-Dick*, he did precisely this through Ahab's explosively unstable conflation of the split images of Melville's father. *Pierre's* distorted style shows that Melville could not bury his inner dead and that the results imbued his art with a compelling strangeness and complexity. The novel possesses an undeniable fascination, for the reader is seduced by the emotional urgencies behind the bizarre style and absurd plot conventions. I argue that *Pierre's* self-tormenting, almost self-loathing, style performs a complex grief work, one which opens the novel to subversive insight into the social codes that thwart the resolution of the ambiguities in Melville's mourning art.[7]

THE MOURNING FIGURE

Melville appropriates Isabel, his darkly subversive siren, from the most conventional of sources: the needlepoint mourning art created by upper-class women and in vogue from the early 1800s to the 1840s. Anita Schorsch describes the mourning picture as "an imaginary garden planted with symbolic foliage," which included an urn, a tree, and, most significantly for *Pierre*, a "classically restrained [female] mourning figure." In his own home Melville could have seen a mourning picture of a lady grieving over a tomb by a weeping willow: his mother sewed needlepoint mourning art. In *Pierre*, Melville appropriates his mother's mourning art, as he partially models his attempt to authenticate his grief on her cultural style of bereavement. However, in his hands mourning art conventions are transformed, and its ideological texture exposed. The classically restrained mourning figure becomes the gothic heroine Isabel, whose "wild plaints" and melodramatic performances on her mother's guitar project from Pierre's disordered mourning (149).[8]

Pierre first meets Isabel on a visit to the Miss Pennies's sewing circle. As if to draw attention to her "sewn" social origin, Isabel pierces her side with a sewing needle upon catching her first glimpse of Pierre, provoking the supernatural shriek that reopens him to grief for his father. The pastoral opening of *Pierre* comes straight out of the mourning picture. Lucy asks Pierre to recite once more "the story of the face,—the dark-eyed, lustrous, imploring, mournful face," and the "eyes of steady, flaming mournfulness" reappear to him in a setting that closely resembles the needlepoint mourning picture (37).

While his mother is absent from home, Pierre walks to a riverbank and sits by the "half-bared roots of sadness" of a "primeval pine tree"—a standard icon of the mourning picture (40). The "gentle pine tree drops melodious mournfulness" on Pierre, who has displaced the female figure in the needlepoint mourning art scenario (40). Gazing up into the tree's branches, though, he sees " 'the face' " of Isabel, which seems to implore him, " 'Come to me' " (40). " 'Is grief a self-willed guest that *will* come in,' " Pierre asks, as he clearly establishes Isabel as a personification of revived grief (41).[9]

Pierre's speech beneath the pine creates a revealing backdrop for the role Isabel will play in his life: " 'Yet I have never known thee, Grief. . . . I have known . . . pensiveness . . . sadness . . . but thou, Grief! art still a ghost-story to me. . . . Not that I would be without my too little cherished fits of sadness now and then; but God keep me from thee. . . . I shudder at thee! The face!—the face!' " (41). The novel's inauthentic sentimental voice undercuts the seriousness with which we take this scene. However, the import is inescapable: as the mourning figure, Isabel brings to life the ghost story of Pierre's grief for his father. Although he senses that something powerful lurks behind the face that may "'suddenly seize me, and possess me, wholly,'" for Pierre it remains a "'concealing screen . . . a muffledness'" (41).

Isabel eventually takes over Pierre's life, to cataclysmic ends, but she never wholly seizes and possesses him. By the end of the novel, he has come to repudiate her sisterhood and to suspect that both she and he have been duped by her "imaginative delirium" (354). The novel allows Isabel to play the role of the mourning figure, but she remains a split-off representation of a grief that for Pierre remains dangerous and which he ultimately disavows.

Isabel's role in the novel, however, cannot be dissociated from Pierre's. Isabel symbolizes the creativity to which Pierre cannot gain access in his attempted conversion into a serious author. As she narrates her life story, "the sweet, wild power of the musicalness" of the "far interior voice" attracts Pierre; later in the novel, the "deep voice of the being of Isabel" bewitches him (113, 118, 173). Isabel comes to be Pierre's very creative stuff. She claims to be "'all plastic in thy hand'"; he answers, "'I most carefully and most tenderly egg thee'" (189). "'Thy hand is the caster's ladle, Pierre,'" Isabel confesses, "'which holds me entirely fluid. Into thy forms and slightest moods of thought, thou pourest me; and I there solidify to that form, and take it on'" (324). Isabel serves not only as Pierre's muse but also as his copyist. When she "played her mystic guitar . . . Pierre felt chapter after chapter born of its wondrous suggestiveness; but, alas! eternally incapable of being translated into words" (282). The grist for Pierre's creative mill, Isabel personifies The Ambiguities of the novel's subtitle: he "strove to condense her mysterious haze into some definite and comprehensible shape" (136). She embodies what the narrator calls "the wide fluidness and ethereal airiness of spontaneous creative thought" (283).[10]

In her dual role as mourning figure and as Pierre's creativity, Isabel links Pierre's unfinished work of mourning to his writing. The first words Pierre's protagonist, Vivia, speaks are, "'A deep-down, unut-

terable mournfulness is in me'" (302). Isabel confesses about her
memory that "'little could I recall, but the bewilderingness;—and
the stupor, and the torpor'" (122). As he sits before his writing desk
prior to the Enceladus dream, Pierre's creative energies are overwhelmed by an Isabelian experience: he lapses into "a general and
nameless torpor" (342).[11]

Isabel's performances on her mother's guitar exemplify the intertwined experiences of mourning and creativity which captivate
Pierre. "'I never knew a mortal mother,'" Isabel begins her history
(114). Initially her tale seems a counterstory to the dominating influence Pierre's mother exerts on him, but her communion with her
mother through the mystic guitar soon identifies Isabel with an over-
powering maternal presence. Isabel herself becomes a commanding
figure—a "dark, regal being"—to Pierre when she imperiously orders
him to "'Bring me the guitar!'" and then forbids him to speak (152,
126). The maternal guitar emits "sounds of melodiousness, and
mournfulness" as it is "vailed" under Isabel's hair (126). Before her
second performance on the guitar, Isabel claims, "'There is no sex in
our immaculateness,'" but the guitar's music is "wonderfully and
abandonedly free and bold"; when she first played for him, she
"swayed to and fro with a like abandonment, and suddenness, and
wantonness" (149, 126).

Her mother's "'secret name'" inscribed inside the guitar "'thrills
me through and through,'" Isabel confesses: "'So secret, wholly
hidden, yet constantly carried about in it . . . always vibrating to the
hidden heart-strings—broken heart-strings; oh, my mother, my
mother, my mother!'" (149). Placing the guitar on the "casement-
bench" Isabel kneels before it and claims, "'thou shalt hear my
mother's spirit'" (149). After this displaced maternal performance of
creativity/mourning, Pierre "now first became vaguely sensible of a
certain still more marvelous power in the girl over himself and his
most interior thoughts and motions;—a power so hovering upon the
confines of the invisible world, that it seemed more inclined that way
than this" (151). For Pierre, the maternal music evokes "an ever-
creeping and condensing haze of ambiguities" (151). Looking back,

Pierre realizes that it was at this moment that Isabel "bound him to her by an extraordinary atmospheric spell" (151). At the end of the novel, when Isabel's hair "arbored" Pierre in "ebon vines," he displaces the maternal guitar as the symbol of an intertwined experience of creativity and mourning. (362).[12]

Isabel's influence over Pierre, then, is derived from her ability to link creativity and mourning to a sexualized maternal presence. Isabel not only invokes her mother in the moment that she bewitched Pierre, but she also seems to have displaced Pierre's mother's dominating influence in his life (128). The thought of Isabel "brought his mother with blazing prominence before" Pierre (104). Isabel's "immense mournful stateliness" displaces the "haughty widow," who is also described as a "stately beauty" (332, 4, 20). In a revealing narrative sequence, after Pierre "imprinted repeated burning kisses" on Isabel and "would not let go her sweet and awful passiveness," the narrative breaks and the next section begins with the line, "Mrs. Glendinning walked her chamber; her dress loosened" (192, 193).[13]

However, Isabel attempts to subvert the influence Mrs. Glendinning has had over Pierre's grief for his father. Unlike Isabel, Mrs. Glendinning has been "uncankered by any inconsolable grief" (4). She has imbued in her son "the profoundest filial respect" (14). " 'Never rave, Pierre, and never rant,' " she instructs her son, " 'Your father never did either. . . . He was always exceedingly gentlemanly: and gentlemen never rant' " (19). Under his mother's influence, his father has become a "perfect marble form" in Pierre's inner shrine: " 'always think of him and you can never err; yes, always think of your dear perfect father' " (68, 19). She assumes an imperiously controlling attitude in her dealings with her "docile" son (19). At one point she imagines she will have Pierre " 'handcuffed to the table' " in order to " 'manage' " him " 'one way or another' " (60). When she abruptly announces to Pierre that she has changed her mind about delaying his marriage to Lucy and that they will marry within a month, Pierre responds, " 'I suppose, then, I have next to nothing to say in the matter?' " " 'Next to nothing, Pierre!' she responds "what at all have you to do with it, I should like to know?' " (55).[14]

It is Mrs. Glendinning's idealized image of her husband that her son has "buried" in his "filial breast" (68). Under his mother's tutelage, Mr. Glendinning has become "Pierre's fond personification of perfect human goodness and virtue" (68). His mother has "stamped in Pierre's soul the cherished conceit, that his virtuous father, so beautiful on earth, was now uncorruptibly sainted in heaven" (69). Yet even before Isabel's appearance, Pierre has been confronted by another representation of his father in the "chair-portrait."[15]

In this portrait, Mr. Glendinning appears as a "brisk, unentangled, young bachelor . . . light-hearted, and a very little bladish perhaps," who appears to his son to be smiling "a little ambiguously and mockingly" (73, 80). Mrs. Glendinning, though, possesses a "remarkable distaste" for this version of her husband (82). To account for her dislike of the portrait, Pierre imagines the chair-portrait's voice:

> Faithful wives are ever over-fond to a certain imaginary image of their husbands; and faithful widows are ever over-reverential to a certain imagined ghost of that same imagined image. . . . Look again, I am thy father as he more truly was. . . . Behold, what is this too ardent and, as it were, unchastened light in these eyes, Pierre? I am thy father, boy. There was a certain, oh, but too lovely young Frenchwoman. Youth is hot, and temptation strong. . . . Look again. Doth thy mother dislike me for naught? . . . Do not all her spontaneous, loving impressions, ever strive to magnify, and spiritualize, and deify, her husband's memory, Pierre? . . . Consider; for a smile is the chosen vehicle for all ambiguities, Pierre. When we would deceive, we smile; when we are hatching any nice little artifice. (83–84)

Pierre imagines this version of his father's voice while in "reveries and trances" (84). When he regains mastery of himself, we witness him "upbraiding himself for his self-indulgent infatuation"; "the streams of these reveries" do not "seem to leave any conscious sediment in his mind" (84, 85). After reading Isabel's letter announcing her illegitimate status, he "saw all preceding ambiguities . . . ripped open," leaving an "interior gash" of revived grief (85, 70). "Now his remotest infantile reminiscences—the wandering mind of his fa-

ther—the empty hand, and the ashen—the strange story of Aunt
Dorothea [who told young Pierre the story behind the chair-por-
trait]—the mystical midnight suggestions of the portrait itself; and
above all, his mother's intuitive aversion, all, all overwhelmed him
with reciprocal testimonies" (85). What had been "inexplicably
mysterious" about the portrait and "inexplicably familiar" about Isabel's face "now coincided" and "by some ineffable correlativeness,
they reciprocally identified each other, and, as it were, *melted into
each other, and thus interpenetratingly uniting*, presented lineaments of
an added supernaturalness" (85, my emphasis).

The chair-portrait and Isabel's face can be likened to the "two
mutually absorbing shapes" the narrator alludes to in Dante, but the
novel carefully stages this identification within the context of Mrs.
Glendinning's influence on Pierre (85).[16] Structurally, the novel
delineates both Mrs. Glendinning's and Isabel's influence over Pierre
before it turns to characterize his memory of his father. And Pierre
cannot renounce—from the beginning to the end of the novel—his
identification with his mother's idealized image of his father. The
"strange relativeness, reciprocalness, and transmittedness, between
the long-dead father's portrait, and the living daughter's face" ultimately seem to Pierre a delusion produced by his own "intense procreative enthusiasm" (197, 353). Even in his initial linkage between
the two faces, Pierre "in his own memory of his father . . . could not
recall any distinct lineament transmitted to Isabel," but he "vaguely
saw such in the portrait" (197).

His insistence that it is not his father but "the portrait's painted
self" which "seemed the real father of Isabel" denies what the novel
otherwise insists on (197). The image of Mr. Glendinning that Isabel
thrusts before Pierre derives from the dark side of Pierre's memory of
him. Her "imploring face" and "wandering" consciousness revive
Pierre's "covered . . . up" image of his father on his deathbed (198,
71). Pierre's father had "died of a fever and, as is not uncommon in
such maladies," the novel takes pains to tell us, "toward his end, he
at intervals, lowly wandered in his mind" (70). Significantly, Mrs.
Glendinning was not present to witness her husband's "delirious"

end (70). But "one evening, when the shadows intermingled with the curtains; and all the chamber was hushed . . . Pierre but dimly saw his father's face" and heard his "strange, plaintive, infinitely pitiable, low voice" call "'My daughter! my daughter'" (70). The sentimental sugarcoating of the scene momentarily drops away when Mr. Glendinning's "low voice" becomes "a sudden, pealing wail," and his son "snatched the dying man's hand" and watched his other hand, "ashy white as a leper's," clutch for his absent daughter's hand (70, 71).[17] The nurse in attendance wonders aloud to Pierre, "how it was, that so excellent a gentleman, and so thoroughly good a man, should wander so ambiguously in his mind" (71).

Pierre has been able to banish this scene from his mind—it "seemed to survive to no real life" in him—until "the first glimpse of Isabel's letter caused it to spring forth. . . . Then, again, the long-hushed, plaintive, and infinitely pitiable voice was heard,—'My daughter! my daughter!' followed by the compunctious 'God! God!'" (71). When Isabel pierces her side with her sewing needle, her "sudden, long-drawn, unearthly, girlish shriek, from the further corner of the long, double room" seems the "double" of the "sudden, pealing wail" of Pierre's father on his deathbed (45). Isabel's "sudden shriek seemed to split its way clean through" Pierre's heart and "leave a yawning gap there" because she personifies his revived grief for his father (45). Dressed in black, Isabel sits by the casement and her chest palpitates "as though some choked, violent thing were risen up there within the teeming region of her heart" (46). To Pierre she presents an "immemorial face" (47).

The immediacy with which Isabel comes to embody Pierre's revived grief can be glimpsed in the conversation he and his mother have on the way home from the Miss Pennies's. Sensing that her son has been powerfully affected by his experience there, Mrs. Glendinning asks him, "'were you really wandering, Pierre?'" To which he answers, voicing an identification with the deathbed wandering of his father that Isabel has brought back to life, "'never before in my whole existence, have I so completely gone wandering in my soul'" (48).

In her letter to Pierre, Isabel comments on her own writing, " 'and so, behold again how I rave' " (64). Of herself she observes, " 'silence becomes this grave' " (64). After he reads her letter Pierre exclaims, " 'am I now truly led in this night of my grief?—I will be a raver, and none shall stay me' " (65). In his first encounter with her, Pierre finds himself enveloped in her "mournful hair," which probably connoted to Melville and his contemporary readers the locks of hair used as mourning mementoes (112). She seems arisen from a "grave," as "the death-like beauty of the face" confronts him (112). "She seemed as dead;—as suffocated" (112). She sits on a "bench within the double casement," as though situated within a coffin (112). For Isabel, her " 'utmost blessing now, were to lie down and die' "; her " 'present feeling,—more death-like to me then all my grief gone by' " (113). When she pauses in her story she seems "still as death" (121). Further, her earliest name was Bell which connotes the funeral bell (148). "With her head averted from him, and mutely resting on her hand," Isabel resembles the bereaved female figure in the needlepoint mourning picture (145).[18]

Isabel's style of narration mimics the wandering of Pierre's father on his deathbed: " 'I can not but talk wildly upon so wild a theme' " (115). She begins one speech, " 'if mad myself sometimes' " (189). During her childhood, she claims to have spent five to seven years in an asylum.[19] She remembers of this experience seeing coffins being taken from the asylum (119). She confesses that " 'I must always continue to be a child' " because of her traumatic upbringing; Pierre later thinks of her as "the glorious child of Pride and Grief" (148, 173).

In responding to the shadow Isabel casts over his father, Pierre ponders "the eternal impossibility of logically exonerating his dead father, in his own mind, from the liability to this, and many other of the blackest self-insinuated suppositions" (138).[20] However, "all this came over Pierre with a power so infernal and intense, that it could only have proceeded from the unretarded malice of the Evil One himself. But subtilly and wantonly as these conceits stole into him, Pierre as subtilly opposed them" (138). Pierre assumes the "magnanimous purpose to screen thy father's honorable memory from reproach," but instead he turns his anger toward his father against himself, as "he dashed himself in blind fury and swift madness against the wall" (171).

With a willed blindness to the contradictions implicit in his actions, Pierre is "determined at all hazards to hold his father's fair fame inviolate from anything he should be in reference to protecting Isabel" (172). He feels an "absolutely inflexible . . . determination" to assume "the enthusiastic, and apparently wholly supererogatory resolution to hold his father's memory untouched" (177). Unable to relinquish his mother's "pure, exalted idea of his father," he rationalizes that "of whatsover unknown shade his father's guilt might be, yet in the final hour of death it had been most dismally repented of" (82, 178). But he wonders, "Mince the matter how his family would, had not his father died a raver? Whence that raving, following so prosperous a life? Whence, but from the cruellest compunctions?" (178)

The conflicts Pierre feels in his revived grief for his father—whether to condemn or exonerate him—are embodied in the merging of Mr. Glendinning and Isabel: "And as his father was now sought to be banished from his mind, as a most bitter presence there, but Isabel was become a thing of intense and fearful love for him; therefore, it was loathsome to him, that in the smiling and ambiguous portrait, her sweet mournful image should be so sinisterly becrooked, bemixed, and mutilated to him" (197). Although he is able to burn his collection of "mementoes and monuments of the past," including the chair-portrait, Isabel in fact magnifies his deepest conflicts toward his father (197).[21] As the chair-portrait burns, its Isabelian "imploring face" prompts Pierre to burn his hand in an attempt to rescue it (198).

THE ENCELADUS DREAM

But, as sometimes men are coffined in a trance,
being thereby mistaken for dead; so it is possible to

bury a tranced grief in the soul, erroneously
supposing that it hath no more vitality of suffering.
Herman Melville, *Pierre, or, The Ambiguities*

After he burns his family letters Pierre exclaims, "'Henceforth,
cast-out Pierre hath no paternity, and no past,'" reversing the narrator's earlier sense that Pierre's "very horizon was to him as a memorial ring" (199, 8). But Pierre's identification of his creativity with
Isabelian consciousness belies his earlier conviction that "'I will no
more have a father'" (87). Instead, Pierre identifies with his father's
deathbed madness by becoming a raving author. After a day's work at
his writing desk, Pierre resembles "'some imprudent sick man,
willfully burst from his bed'" (305). Pierre's Enceladus vision at his
writing desk reveals that his creativity has assumed the form of disordered mourning.[22]

When Pierre imagines revealing Isabel's identity to his mother, he
realizes that "the idea of at all divulging his secret to his mother . . . was made repelling by its hopelessness, as *an infirm attack upon
her citadel of pride*" (91, my emphasis). In his Enceladus dream, Pierre
imagines the impotent Titan's assault on the "terrific towering palisade" that has blocked his ascent up Mrs. Glendinning's Delectable
Mountain (344).[23] The dream recreates Pierre's fear of his mother's
dangerously explosive, potential grief. Soon after learning of Isabel's
identity, Pierre "vaguely felt, that upon the concealment, or the
disclosure of this thing, with reference to his mother, hinged his
whole future course of conduct, his whole earthly weal" (91). In the
dream, his fear of violating her image of his father's "perfect marble
form" surfaces in the armless trunk of the alternately paralyzed and
then rebellious Titan. In Enceladus's plight, Pierre critiques the control his mother's bereavement has over his own response to his father's death. The scenario not only arrests Pierre's work of mourning
but it also implicates his chronic grief in his creative impasse. At the
center of his creative landscape, "high up, and towering, all-forbid-
ding . . . grew the before unthought of wonderful edifice of his
mother's immense pride," which keeps in place the idealized image of
her husband in Pierre's arrested mourning (89).

On one level, Pierre's Enceladus vision records the failure of the creative spirit to attain the heights of a lofty vision, an unscalable inner romantic mountain.[24] Of Pierre's creative struggles, we are earlier told, "He would climb Parnassus with a pile of folios on his back" (283). His inner landscape is called "the Switzerland of his soul" (284). The narrator foreshadows Pierre's failure to gain this summit: "Only by judicious degrees, appointed of God, does man come at last to gain his Mont Blanc" (284). But Pierre "hath ringed himself in with the grief of Eternity. Pierre is a peak inflexible in the heart of Time" (304).

The old church tower on which he gazes as he writes is an "emblem to Pierre of an unshakable fortitude, which deep-rooted in the heart of the earth, defied all the howls of the air," but the feelings Pierre's writing evokes in him derive from Isabelian instability (271). He has internalized her death wish and her version of creativity. "He is learning how to live, by rehearsing the part of death" (305). Initially, "against all the dismal lassitude, and *deathful* faintness and sleeplessness, and whirlingness, and craziness . . . he like a demigod bore up" (339, my emphasis). Nevertheless, he writes "with the feeling of misery and *death* in him" (339, my emphasis). As his writing carries him deeply into himself, "the *deadly* feeling of faintness" more often overwhelms him (340, my emphasis). Immediately prior to the Enceladus vision, he feels "some horrible foretaste of *death* itself" (342, my emphasis). Ultimately, Pierre seems to write from within the maternal bereavement/creativity of Isabel's mother's guitar. "Through the lashes [of his eyes] he peered upon the paper, which so seemed fretted with woes" (345). As noted earlier, by novel's end, he will have displaced the guitar as the creative vehicle under Isabel's hair.

In his "dream or vision," Pierre imagines an excursion to the Mount of Titans, located "not far" from the hills around "his ancestral manor" (342). A "moody, disappointed bard" gave the mountain its name, changing it from the Delectable Mountain, a title given to it by an "old Baptist farmer" enamored of Bunyan (342). From a distance the mountain seems a "sweet imposing purple promise" (343). However, on closer view, this "so chameleon a height" possesses "long and frequent rents among the mass of leaves [which] revealed horrible glimpses of dark-dripping rocks, and mysterious mouths of wolfish caves" (343). "Piercing within" the "lowermost fringe" of mountain-forest, "suddenly you stood transfixed, as a marching soldier confounded at the sight of an impregnable redoubt" (344). The "purple promise" has "cunningly masked . . . a terrific towering palisade of dark mossy massiness" (344). The water dripping from it "distilled upon you from its beetling brow . . . chill as the last dews of death" (344). The strong connotation of female sexuality is reinforced by the phallic imagery of the surrounding "grim scarred rocks [which] rallied and re-rallied themselves; shot-up, protruded, stretched, swelled, and eagerly reached forth; on every side bristling with a hideous repellingness" (344).

But imagery of mourning overlays this scene of deathlike sexuality. " 'Mid this spectacle of wide and wanton spoil," falling rocks sound like "wailing women and children" (344). The feelings the scene evokes in the narrator—"Stark desolation; ruin, merciless and ceaseless; chills and gloom . . . curtain by that cunning purpleness"—closely resemble Pierre's feelings in the early stages of his revived grief (344). This scene also recalls the feelings of Tommo as he spent a night in the ravine where his leg ailment began, but now the scene is linked more closely to the forces blocking Melville's arrested grief. Soon after learning of Isabel's identity, Pierre gazes "upon the charred landscape within him" with a "heart now changing from iciness to a strange sort of indifference" (86). He feels the "numbing sensation" recent mourning theory identifies as the first stage of grief, and he "began to struggle against this inertness as the most treacherous and deadliest of symptoms" (86, 87). However, he feels "without power to shake the grim tranquillity which possessed him" (86).[25]

In Pierre's revived grief, "the long-cherished image of his father now transfigured before him from a green foliaged tree into a blasted trunk" (88). The "sense of horrible forlornness, feebleness, impotence, and infinite, eternal desolation," which overwhelms Pierre in the early stages of his retriggered bereavement, sends him to bed, "often Grief's first refuge" (93). The image of his father as a blasted trunk transforms into the "armless trunk" of the "shamelessly recumbent" impotent Titan, Enceladus (93, 346). The grief-stricken Pierre, who took to bed "almost without bodily consciousness . . . careful not to break the spell by the least movement of a limb" and "steadfastly faced his grief," transforms into the "petrified" Titan (93, 346).

Enceladus appears as the dreamer descends the mountain. "Beaten off by such undreamed of glooms and steeps," the defeated visionary is "fixed by a form defiant, a form of awfulness," who attempts what the dreamer could not: an assault on the palisade to gain the mystic heights (344, 345). However, "Enceladus the Titan, the most potent of all giants, [is] writhing from out the imprisoning earth;—turbaned with upborne moss he writhed" (345). Earlier, in the "hostile necessity and distaste" with which he wrote, Pierre was called "this most unwilling states-prisoner of letters" (340). Because he felt himself to be "gifted with loftiness, merely that it might be dragged down to the mud," Pierre "began to feel that in him, the thews of a Titan were forestallingly cut by the scissors of Fate" (339). Yet again, just prior to the onset of his dream, in revulsion against the act of writing "the very blood" in Pierre's "body had in vain rebelled against his Titanic soul" (341).

In the Titan "turbaned with upborne moss," then, Pierre imagines the still-birth of his writerly self. But the setting in which this abortion occurs provides evidence that Pierre's creativity has been thwarted by the influence of maternal bereavement on his chronic grief. The soil which imprisons Enceladus, "that deathless son of Terra," belongs to Pierre's mother (345). Mrs. Glendinning herself can be as overawing to Pierre as the Mount of Titans. In one scene, "she slowly rose to her feet, and her full stature of womanly beauty and majesty stood imposingly over him." "'Beware of me, Pierre,'" she threatens, "'There lives not that being in the world of whom thou hast more reason to beware" (130).26

It is female sexuality—the "palisade of dark mossy massiness"—

which blocks the dreamer's progress toward a mystic vision. But what this female presence evokes are the sounds of "wailing women and children," in addition to emotions that, as we have seen, resemble the terrifying numbness of the first stage of grief. By turning "his vast trunk into a battering-ram," Enceladus assaults the palisade; however, in the above context, the resistance of the "doubly incestuous" Titan—the son and grandson of incest—seems an attempt to either incestuously "possess" or to angrily break through maternal bereavement (346, 347).[27]

The Titan condenses the images of both the disempowered writer and the blasted trunk of the father. At the climax of the dream, Pierre sees his own face on Enceladus's armless trunk: "With trembling frame he started from his chair, and woke from that ideal horror to all his actual grief" (346). It is as if Pierre, in an act of identification characteristic of disordered mourning, has stepped into the trembling frame of his father's chair-portrait. Perhaps, even more forcefully than Ahab, Enceladus draws attention to the imagery of dismemberment which characterizes male expressions of loss.[28]

"AN UNSUMMED WORLD OF GRIEF"

I remember now those first wise words, wherewith
our Savior Christ first spoke in his first speech to
men:—"Blessed are the poor in spirit, and blessed
they that mourn."
Herman Melville, *Pierre, or the Ambiguities*

Corporations have no souls . . .
Vivia, in Melville's *Pierre, or, The Ambiguities*

The Enceladus dream transforms the scene Pierre often viewed from his closet in Saddle Meadows. From his window, he could see the "purple hills" that were "storied with the great deeds of the Glendinnings" (92). The view from his room in the Church of the Apostles modifies this scene: as he writes, he gazes out on "a wilderness of tiles, slate, shingles, and tin" or the "old gray tower" of the church (271).

Pierre, however, writes from within a new tower, "a fearful pile of Titanic bricks," erected by the church's congregation of merchants and accountants "to be promiscuously rented to the legal crowd" (266). The church has been "divided into stores; cut into offices; and given for a roost to the gregarious lawyers" (266). But because the upper floors render the lawyers inaccessible to their clients, the congregation rents them out to artists, "fugitive French politicians, or German philosophers," who, as artist Apostles, are "secretly suspected to have some mysterious ulterior object, vaguely connected with the absolute overturning of Church and State, and the hasty and premature advance of some unknown great political and religious Millennium" (267, 269). The narrator imagines the building in economic terms: "full purses [the lower floors of lawyers] and empty heads [the freethinkers]" (267).[29]

From within this carefully drawn social setting, Melville situates Pierre's artistic activity so as to anticipate Marxist analysis: the artistic activity of the superstructure resting on an economic base. The location of the church within the city links this scene of writerly debacle to the setting in which Melville's father's import business went bankrupt. The church is located in lower Manhattan, an area filled with "immense lofty warehouses of foreign importers" (265). The displacement of the church by commerce extends as well to the "old church's burial inclosure," which has been "usurped" by iron fencing (266).

Pierre insists on the hegemony of the dominant cultural codes, especially a genteel and commercial ethos, and the way they shape feeling. The "flashing revelations of grief's wonderful fire" instruct Pierre in the social construction of his mother: "She was a noble creature, but formed chiefly for the gilded prosperities of life . . . bred and expanded, in all developments, under the sole influence of hereditary forms and world-usages" (88–89); "He too plainly saw, that not his mother had made his mother; but the Infinite Haughtiness had first fashioned her; and then the haughty world had further molded her; nor had a haughty Ritual omitted to finish her" (90). As she cracks up, she condemns the "dreary heart-vacancies of the conventional life" which have domineered over her: "'Accursed be those four syllables of sound which make up that vile word Propriety'" (90, 195).

Pierre's projections onto the Memnon Stone highlight the relationship between conventional cultural codes and the influence of maternal bereavement on his grief.[30] The "beetlings and the menacings" of the Mute Massiveness of the Memnon or Terror Stone anticipate the dreamer's petrification before the "beetling brow" of the palisade's "mossy massiness" (134, 344). While growing up, Pierre had often climbed the Memnon rock, but after learning of Isabel's identity he uses the stone to morbidly symbolize his identification with the revived grief and paternal traits she represents: he "slid himself into the horrible interspace" formed between the stone and the earth "and lay there as dead": "'If the miseries of the undisclosable things in me, shall ever unhorse me from my manhood's seat; . . . then do thou, Mute Massiveness, fall on me!'" (134). The Memnon stone is also described as "shaped something like a 'lengthened egg'" (132). The still-birth of his manhood that Pierre intimates beneath this egg foreshadows his creative impasse in the Enceladus dream.

As if to reinforce the symbolic self-immolation, the reader is told that as a child Pierre fantasized "that he would like nothing better for a headstone than this same imposing pile; in which, at times, during the soft swayings of the surrounding foliage, there seemed to lurk some mournful and lamenting plaint, as for some sweet boy long since departed in the antediluvian time" (133–34).[31] The myth with which Pierre associates the rock involves the Egyptian monument built by the "wailing subjects" of Memnon, who with "enthusiastic rashness" fought on another's account and died (135). The Isabel-like "lamenting plaint" Pierre projects onto the stone derives from the legend that "Touched by the breath of the bereaved Aurora [Memnon's mother], every sunrise that statue gave forth a mournful broken sound. . . . Herein lies an unsummed world of grief" (135).

Pierre's association of the Terror Stone with maternal bereavement is situated in the context of dominant cultural codes: "But Memnon's sculptured woes did once melodiously resound; now all is mute. Fit emblem that of old, poetry was a consecration and an obsequy to all hapless modes of human life; but in a bantering, barren, and prosaic, heartless age, Aurora's music-moan is lost among our drifting sands, which whelm alike the monument and the dirge" (136). The narrator's own economic image of an "*unsummed world of grief*" hints at the incorporation of mourning into a commercial ethos.

While grieving over his mother's death, Pierre takes a walk "to wear off his sharper grief" during which he passes the "very plain, composed, manly figure" of Plinlimmon, the preeminent Apostle philosopher (289).[32] In Pierre's bereaved "moods of peculiar depression and despair," Plinlimmon's "mystic-mild face in the upper window of the old gray tower began to domineer in a very remarkable manner upon Pierre" (292). Like Isabel and Pierre's father, the philosopher initially seems a mysterious face to Pierre. After Pierre "procured some muslin for his closet-window; and the face [Plinlimmon] became curtained like any portrait," the philosopher seems a displaced version of the chair-portrait (293). Plinlimmon's face heightens the ambiguous smile of the chair-portrait: Pierre imagines that the philosopher "at last wore a sort of malicious leer to him" (293). This new face seems to comment on Pierre's writerly struggles: "Vain!, Fool!, Quit!" (293).

Plinlimmon represents both the crippling paternal image—"the tower face"—that Pierre has inherited from his mother's haughty bereavement and the plinth-thin version of genteel manhood that Mrs. Glendinning would have her "docile" boy play (290). The "hat-lifting, gracefully bowing, gently smiling" philosopher, who exudes "something passive," performs the "manly" role of a "face" that "did not respond to anything" (290, 293). While "that remarkable face of repose . . . seemed to have no family or blood ties of any sort," the bereaved Pierre initially is attracted to him as an alternative to the upsurging conflicts of grief his mother's death has intensified (290). Plinlimmon's repose comes to be the social death men are forced into by an emotionally hollow gender role: the "acquiescence" and the "something latently visible in him which repelled"

(290). Repose, as well, connotated to Melville's contemporaries the sleep of death prior to the reawakening into the millennium.[33]

At first Plinlimmon's insight into the " 'provisional' " nature of " 'our so-called wisdom' " might seem to exonerate Pierre's father by its argument that "in things terrestrial (horological) a man must not be governed by ideas celestial (chronometrical)" (211, 214). Finally even Plinlimmon's evasive relativism damns Mr. Glendinning. The philosopher's doctrine of " 'practicable virtue' " concludes by arguing that we must " 'interfere not with the eternal truth, that, sooner or later, in all cases, downright vice is downright woe' " (215).

Plinlimmon bears on Melville's own grief work in several revealing ways. The cap and coat factory Allan Melvill left behind him figures into the characterization of the philosopher, whose very "clothes seemed to disguise this man" (290). When Pierre and his "mournful party" set off from the tavern to New York City, the innkeeper comments, " 'it's as sad as funerals' " (205). As Pierre rests his hand on the coach seat "to steady his way," he finds a torn copy of Plinlimmon's tract, EI (205). Pierre cannot grasp the doctrine of " 'virtuous expediency' " EI preaches (214). Later Pierre will search in vain for EI, not realizing that it has "helped pad the padding" of his coat by falling into its lining (294). As if to parallel the fate of EI, in the last sentence of the chapter introducing Plinlimmon, we are told that there are some things that men think they imperfectly understand which they actually understand and yet, so to speak, though contained in themselves, are kept a secret from themselves. . . . The idea of Death seems such a thing" (294).

In the very writing which he imagines that Plinlimmon condemns him for attempting, Pierre identifies with the circumstances of Allan Melvill's fall. Pierre is forced to admit about his " 'bunglingly written' " youthful writing that " 'like protested notes at the Bankers, all those written things of mine, are jaggingly cut through and through with the protesting hammer of Truth!—Oh, I am sick, sick, sick!' " (273). Allan Melvill's bankruptcy, which led to his fatal illness, was caused when a creditor called in his note. Pierre performs another version of the secret partnership that victimized Melville's father.

While Allan imported French goods, Pierre takes up with a French import, Isabel. *Glendinning*, as well, hints at Allan's "ending" and the "lending" of funds, borrowed from relatives, that produced his bankruptcy.[34]

On a larger level, both in his choice of the novel's plot and in his decision to write in in such a bizarre way, Melville mimicked his father's demise: "Not the gibbering of ghosts in any old haunted house . . . will so make the hair to stand, as when a proud and honorable man is revolving in his soul the possibilities of some gross public and corporeal disgrace" (336). The narrator recognizes that "it is a pride-horror, which is more terrible than any fear" (336). This is the backdrop against which Melville must have read the etiology of his father's deathbed mania. However, by writing *Pierre* in a strangely mixed style, Melville seems to willfully bring on himself a "gross public and corporeal disgrace" at the hands of his reviewers.[35]

Pierre's parody of literary versions of melancholy and mourning subtly reenacts Melville's powerful, unresolved grief work. "For the deeper that some men feel a secret and poignant feeling," the narrator self-reflexively observes, "the higher they pile the belying surfaces" (224). "In the hour of unusual affliction, minds of a certain temperament find a strange, hysterical relief, in a wild, perverse humorousness. . . . nothing short of temporary madness," which, in Melville's case, suggests an identification with his father's deathbed mania (186). While Melville's narrator can "wax harmlessly sad and sentimental," by identifying writing with Isabel's version of creativity, he admits what the novel bears out: "It is impossible . . . to write without apparently throwing oneself helplessly open" (259).

Finally, *Pierre's* stylistic cunning purpleness seems a deliberate attempt to subvert or to perversely scramble the popular generic languages Melville's audience valued. By devaluing these forms of discourse, Melville seems to revenge their sentimental diminution of the experience of mourning. *Purple* connoted to Melville's contemporaries not only overly lavish writing but also profanity and the color that symbolized the bereavement of the royalty. By profaning while working from within the popular languages in which his culture debased mourning, *Pierre* performs a version of that "dialect of sin and death" known as the Flash, which "the night-occupants of a notorious stew" spew forth during their riot in the police house, as the stock figures of gothic and sentimental fiction, Isabel and the seduced and abandoned Delly Ulver, shrink back in terror (240). On a more intimate level, the novel's self-loathing style and the disgust it registers for the literary conventions it exploits seem a retaliation against the cultural system of meaning that produced his father's fall and held in place Melville's chronic grief.[36]

At the outset of the novel, the narrator had theorized that the "marked anomalousness of America" consisted in "how wonderfully to her, Death itself becomes transmuted into Life": "For indeed the democratic element operates as a subtile acid among us; forever producing new things by corroding the old" (9). As *Pierre's* style corrosively transforms the conventions of domestic fiction, the novel's profane dialect of sin and death revives Melville's delayed grief.[37] "The flashing revelations of grief's wonderful fire" become a version of the Flash as they illuminate a profane image of the idealized father, while Pierre, unable to escape the influence of his mother's image of his father, struggles with "the ambiguities which hemmed him in[to]" her genteel mourning picture (337).

Afterword: The Ritual of
American Renaissance

It is said that mourning, by its gradual labor, slowly
erases pain; I could not, I cannot believe this;
because for me, Time eliminates the emotion of loss
(I do not weep), that is all. For the rest, everything
has remained motionless.
Roland Barthes, *Camera Lucida*

MELVILLE'S MOURNING POEM

Melville began *Billy Budd* in 1886 shortly after his eldest son, Stanwix, died. This last loss revived the issues of Melville's lifelong,
unresolved grief for his father. Melville's novel plays off of his
culture's mourning conventions. Billy is the rose nipped in the bud—
the most common image found in the standard mourning poem; Billy
as the "young mute" in an early draft of the novel probably refers to
the mutes hired to stand outside the house of mourning and look sad;
and Billy's origin—he was found in a silk-lined basket on a door-
knocker—gestures toward the black crape badge on the mourner's
door-knocker, which in America was replaced by a basket of flowers
(144 n. 51).[1]

These customs symbolize the double bind in Victorian America's
desire both to prolong mourning and to control and limit the ex-

pression of grief's conflicts, but Melville exposes these ideological currents by wedding them to Billy's "vocal infirmity" (82). The contradictions of Melville's culture emerge as Billy splits apart into an innocent but violent figure.[2] Melville's art partially transforms the conflicts of his grief into a radical intelligence which probes the ideologies that condition cultural textuality. Billy, Vere, and Claggart become bits of cultural currency, but Melville arrests the attempts within the novel to reductively value them. To the crew, the story of Claggart's indictment on a charge of "mysterious swindle" has a "secret currency" (65). Vere is nicknamed "Starry Vere" and "This got currency" (61). To Vere, Billy is "a 'King's Bargain' . . . 'a capital investment at small outlay or none at all'" (95). In the foretopman's poem, Billy comments, "A jewel-block they'll make of me tomorrow, / Pendant pearl from the yardarm" (132).

Yet there is another side to the influence of Melville's chronic grief on *Billy Budd*—a side that reveals the extent to which Melville's mourning falls victim to his culture's fear of the conflicts of grief. In this dimension of the novel, Melville can be seen as reflecting on the psychosocial forces that killed his creative élan in the early 1850s. *Billy Budd*, then, also mourns for Melville's creativity. His inside narrative opens onto an inner primal ground, on which the major characters of the novel—Billy, Vere, and Claggart—perform the obstructed process of Melville's mourning.

In the genesis of the novel, Melville initially imagined Billy as an older, guilty mutineer. Neither Claggart nor Vere appeared in the original ballad out of which the narrative evolved. In the prose headnote to the poem, Billy's conception began to change: he became the innocent Handsome Sailor. Claggart was the next character to emerge, as if Melville had split the Ur-Billy into good and bad sides. The final addition of Vere to the novel suggests that he reunited and reincorporated Billy and Claggart into a defective version of the naturally good man, who suffers perhaps from not only a monomania of obsessed duty, but also from mental instability.[3]

The novel associates Billy with instinctive, natural life, with roses, gold finches, horses, dogs, and with an infant in the cradle (45, 52,

44). Billy is also associated with creativity, as he sings and makes up his own songs (52). In one of his dimensions, Billy is linked to a principle of growth; he seems to personify the creative élan from which Melville was cut off soon after he completed *Moby-Dick*.

Claggart, on the other hand, in part personifies the forces that obstructed Melville's creativity. One of the forces that silenced Melville as a novelist was his family's suspicion that his writing was impairing and might permanently damage his mental health (see Chap. 1). At the crucial moment of his fatal accusation of Billy, Claggart nears him, "With the measured step and calm collected air of an asylum physician approaching in the public hall some patient beginning to show indications of a coming paroxysm" (98).

The family suspicion of Melville's emotional stability intensified because Melville's mother turned him into a living linking object to her husband. In a sentence deleted from his manuscript, Melville observed of Claggart, "Behind these frescoed walls of flesh, it is the closeted skeleton" (165 n.). The crew's suspicion of Claggart as a "chevalier," who has found his way into the navy "by way of compounding for some mysterious swindle," evokes Melville's memory of the bankruptcy into which his father's underhanded business dealings plunged his family (65).

Claggart "looked like a man of high quality, social and moral, who for reasons of his own was keeping incog" (64). Further, Claggart reminds Vere of a "perjurious witness in a capital case before a court-martial ashore": as such he seems the tarnished image of Melville's father brought to the bar of his son's conscience (94). The lingering trace of an accent in Claggart's speech links to Allan Melvill's French import trade, as does Claggart's "peculiar ferreting genius" (64, 65). Claggart's "self-possessed and somewhat ostentatious manner" mirrors Allan's pretentious upper-class manner (94). When Claggart looks at Vere like Jacob's "envious children . . . deceptively imposing upon the troubled patriarch the blood-dyed coat of young Joseph," Melville evokes both the memory of the faltering coat-factory Allan left as a legacy to his family and perhaps as well his own sense of abandonment—the fate of Joseph—after his father died (96).

The *Oxford English Dictionary* gives as one of the connotations of *clag:* a stain or flaw in character. *Clag* can also connote a sticky substance on one's clothing and an encumbrance on one's property.[4] *Clagg/art* thus signifies the way Allan's death stained, flawed, and clung to Melville's sense of his creative powers.

Melville, in effect, uses his mother's Calvinist lexicon to explain Claggart's hatred of Billy. Because "that lexicon which is based on Holy Writ" is no longer popular, the narrator applies to Claggart Plato's notion of "Natural Depravity: a depravity according to nature" (75). This is a definition "which, though savoring of Calvinism, by no means involves Calvin's dogma as to total mankind" (75). Claggart possesses "the mania of an evil nature . . . born with him and innate" (76). Claggart as damned from a thinly veiled Calvinist perspective implies, as T. Walter Herbert observes, that Melville had to contend with the possibility that his mother's Calvinism damned his father because he died after a deathbed mania.[5] If we take one aspect of Billy to signify Melville's creative élan, then that side of Claggart which represents the damned image of Allan Melvill becomes Melville's experience of victimized creativity.

Melville added Vere to the novel late in the composing process to reincorporate Billy's split sides into a far more complex portrait. Figuratively speaking, Claggart—Vere's monomaniac side—induces Vere to murder his naturally good, creative side—Billy. Vere executes Billy because of his fear of mutiny, as Melville, one can argue, sacrificed his novelistic career because he internalized his family's fear that his creativity threatened him with an inner mutiny. It is significant for this reading that the narrator compares the Nore Mutiny to "the distempering irruption of contagious fever in a frame constitutionally sound"—an allusion that recalls the feverish Allan Melvill on his deathbed (55).

Maria Melville's role in this process is suggested by the derivation of Vere's name: Marvell's "starry Vere" refers to the mother of the girl Marvell tutored (152 n.). Maria's Calvinism influences the way in which Vere is described as announcing Billy's execution to the crew, who react "in a dumbness like that of a seated congregation of believers in hell listening to the clergyman's announcement of his

Calvinist text" (117). Vere's attitude to the crew—"'You know what sailors are'"—suggests that he views them as naturally degraded (112). Further, Vere's allegiance to a martial code links to Maria's role as a daughter of General Gansevoort.

Melville identifies with Vere—they both are independent-minded, bookish, and esoterically allusive. Vere represents Melville's self-image as it had been fashioned out of his internalization of his mother's image of his father. As one version of her living linking object, Vere is also liable to the charge of mental instability. After Billy kills Claggart, Vere summons the surgeon to verify that Claggart is dead. Because Vere is unusually excited the surgeon wonders if Vere is "unhinged" (102). The surgeon evasively concludes that he is serving "under a captain whom he suspects to be not mad, indeed, but yet not quite unaffected in his intellects" (102). Judging from the biographical record, this could easily be the Melville family's attitude to his behavior (see Chap. 1).

The relationship between Billy, Claggart, and Vere reproduces Melville's obstructed grief. When accused of mutiny by Claggart, the violence of Billy's feelings obstructs his speech. It is Vere's "fatherly" tone that triggers the fatal blow with which Billy hits Claggart (99). Caught between Melville's threatening image of the fallen father (Claggart) and his fear of an inner mutiny as a result of his internalized image of his father (Vere), Melville's creativity (Billy) can only lash out violently and, ultimately, self-destructively.[6] Melville's narrator says "uncompromisingly told" truth has "ragged edges," which reveals the ideologies shaping cultural textuality, but his chronic grief holds him hostage to the cultural codes forbidding an open confrontation with intense conflict (128).

THE RADICAL INTELLIGENCE OF MELVILLE'S
WORK OF MOURNING

Throughout this book I have described the ways in which Melville's chronic grief for his father influences his art. However, when the conflicts of this grief break through the surface of his fiction, Melville radically critiques social codes. Does grief, then, transform art into social critique?

Sacvan Bercovitch has argued that a rhetoric of consensus in the ideology of America undercuts the supposed subversiveness of radical American writers. Because it prescribes the rhetoric in which dissent can be inscripted, the American Jeremiad implicates the dissenting author in a culturally determined ritual process: "In antebellum America, the summons to dissent, because it was grounded in prescribed ritual forms, ruled out the threat of radical alternatives." Furthermore, Bercovitch attempts to show "how American radicalism could become a force against basic social change." For Bercovitch the process applies equally well to ethnic, feminist, and politically subversive voices in the American wilderness of rhetorical consensus. 7

Bercovitch grounds his argument on anthropologist Victor Turner's theory of ritual as a social process. Turner argues that ritual is a triparite social process, consisting of separation, liminality, and reintegration. However, Bercovitch fails to emphasize Turner's theory that in liminality *irreparable* conflicts emerge. According to Turner, these conflicts are not resolved once the initiate is reintegrated into the social structure.

Turner derived his notion of liminality, or the condition of being "betwixt and between" social structures," from Arnold Van Gennep's work on funeral rites. We gain a rich social perspective on the conflicts of mourning by viewing them in terms of the irreparable conflicts that emerge in the liminal phase of Turner's model of ritual. If we apply Turner's theory of ritual to the process of mourning, his first stage, separation, can be linked to the early phases of grief—numbness, bewilderment, anger, and yearning. His second stage, liminality, applies to what John Bowlby describes as the phase of grief dominated by disorganization. Out of this phase, Bowlby argues, a healthy process of grief generates a renewed sense of reorganization, which, I suggest, approximates Turner's final stage of reintegration into the social structure. By viewing mourning from the perspective of Turner's model of ritual as a social process, we are able to theorize that the irreparable conflicts of Melville's grief keep him in a liminal posture in relation to social codes, thus making possible the deep social insight of his art but also exposing him to the continuing influence of these codes.[8]

If we translate the last stage of Turner's model of ritual, reorganization, as regeneration, we are in a position to situate mourning at the center of the American imagination, with its profound interest in spiritual regeneration and in literature as a species of renaissance. The cost of a regenerate style—whether in life or art—exposes the social dimension in the American writer's vulnerability to depression. The fluid liminality of American life destabilizes our psychosocial primal ground. Our culturally shaped, evolving identities undo, even as they elicit, attempts both to bury griefs and to sustain the work of regeneration. This ritual perspective on identity delivers us to Sophia Hawthorne's image of Melville: "his fresh, sincere, glowing mind . . . is in a state of 'fluid consciousness.'" By transforming his unresolved mourning into a radically liminal perspective on culture, Melville dramatizes the dangers of the margin, even as these forces both empower and ultimately victimize his creativity.[9]

Notes

INTRODUCTION

1 Richard Chase both finds the father-son theme central to Melville and comments on Melville's need to separate out a viable image of his father from the
image of the deathbed maniac (*Herman Melville: A Critical Study*, 148–49).
Newton Arvin observes that Melville "was to spend much of life divided
between the attempt to retaliate upon his father for this abandonment [his
death] and the attempt, a still more passionate one, to recover the closeness
and the confidence of a happy sonhood" (*Herman Melville*, 23). E. H. Miller
argues that Melville's subject matter involves a reestablishment of the son's
relationship with his father (*Herman Melville: A Biography*, 117). Carolyn
Karcher writes insightfully about Melville's ambivalent attitude to authority
(*Shadow Over the Promised Land*, 7). Also see Robert Carothers, "Herman
Melville and the Search for the Father: An Interpretation of the Novels."

2 Martha Pike, "In Memory Of: Artifacts Relating to Mourning in Nineteenth-Century America," 310.

3 Raymond Weaver gives the earliest biographical account of the relationship
between Melville and his mother—one presumably based on family legend:
"Between Maria and her son there existed a striking personal resemblance.
From his mother . . . Melville seems to have inherited a constitution of very
remarkable vigor, and all the white intensity of the Gansevoort aptitude for
anger." Maria "must have been baffled by this mirror image of herself—
fascinated, and at the same time contemptuously revolted." Further,
Melville was said to have commented on his relationship with Maria that
"'She hated me'" (*Herman Melville: Mariner and Mystic*, 61, 62). For more
recent discussions of Maria's relationship with Herman, see E. H. Miller,
Herman Melville: A Biography, and T. Walter Herbert, *Moby-Dick and
Calvinism*.

4 Nina Baym, "Melville's Quarrel With Fiction," 909–23.

5 Dominick LaCapra, "Rethinking Intellectual History and Reading Texts," 35, 42. Barbara Johnson, "Teaching Deconstructively," 148 n. 1.

6 Richard Huntington and Peter Metcalf, *Celebrations of Death*, 12; Arnold Van Gennep, *Rites of Passage.*

7 Ira Glick et al., *First Year of Bereavement*, chap. 13, 261–82, esp. 263, 265.

8 See Anita Schorsch, *Mourning Becomes America*, n. p. Martha V. Pike and Janice Gray Armstrong "In Memorium," 67; C. R. Jones, *Memento Mori*.

9 See Victor Turner, *Ritual Process*. And for his important qualifications to the application of liminality to modern cultures, see "Liminal to Liminoid in Play," 53–92.

CHAPTER 1: THE HOUSE OF MOURNING

1 Allan Melville's journal of July 16, 1843, BA. All transcriptions from unpublished archival letters are my own; unreadable words are indicated by a line. All archival sources used by permission.

2 In the preface to a mourning anthology, John Keese notes, "In times of bereavement, the mind often becomes utterly depressed, and bewildered at its inability of expression" (*Mourner's Chaplet* iii). Two ground-breaking articles on delayed grief liken one of the feelings of grief to a tightness in the throat and to choking (Helene Deutsch, "Absence of Grief," 12–23; and Erich Lindemann, "Symptomatology and Management of Acute Grief," 186–200).

3 For Melville's early years, see esp. William H. Gilman, *Melville's Early Life and Redburn*; Leon Howard, *Herman Melville: A Biography*; Eleanor Melville Metcalf, *Herman Melville: Cycle and Epicycle*; Herbert, *Moby-Dick and Calvinism*; and Jay Leyda, *Melville Log*. Howard, *Herman Melville: A Biography*, 7. Peter Gansevoort to Thomas Melville, Jan. 10, 1832, GLC. Howard, *Herman Melville: A Biography*, 7.

4 For Melville on buried griefs see *WJ*, 345. See James J. Farrell, *Inventing the American Way of Death*, 221; Paul C. Rosenblatt, *Bitter, Bitter Tears*, chap. 11, 152–74; Robert Habenstein and William M. Lamers develop the difference between rural and urban mourning customs, and they argue that Victorian America lacked "a uniform and enduring set of conventions" for mourning (*History of American Funeral Directing*, 259).

Keese turns the poet into a grief specialist: "a being preeminent for his sorrows" (*Mourner's Chaplet*, iii). Ann Douglas finds that the dead are "altogether accessible to the living" in Victorian America. *Feminization of American Culture*, 251. Charles Jackson agrees: "The dead would be drawn into the lives of the living as never before in the American past" (*Passing: The Vision of Death in America*, 61–62). For a good illustration of this point, see

"Deceased People Whom We Meet Every Day," in *Littel's Living Age*, 222–24; and the illustration from Cornelius Mathews' *Puffer Hopkins* in which figures in coffins converse with a shop's patrons, in *Arcturus* 2 (1841): 145. Melville owned both of these volumes. Merton Sealts, Jr., *Melville's Reading* 327, no. 14.

For an explication of the psychological process by which memories of the dead are revived, see John Bowlby, *Loss*, 65, 200. Joost Merloo writes that the greatest complaint of Holocaust survivors "was that they had not been permitted to mourn over their dead" ("Delayed Mourning in Victims of Extermination Camps," 74).

5 For Freud on splitting see "Splitting of the Ego in the Defensive Process." See Hershel Parker, "Evidence for 'Late Insertions' in Melville's Works," 407–24.

6 Charles Feidelson, *Symbolism and American Literature*, 319, n. to 163; *Young Man's Own Book*, 220.

7 See Mikhail Bakhtin, "Discourse in the Novel," 259–422; and Katerina Clark and Michael Holquist, *Mikhail Bakhtin*, 275–94. Daniel Walker Howe argues that "Rebellion against Victorian society did not make one a rebel against Victorian culture: many who protested rigorously against Victorian society . . . did so in the name of Victorian cultural values" ("Victorian Culture in America," 13).

8 Bowlby, *Loss, passim*. It is more accurate to say that Bowlby revises received Freudian definitions of mourning as decathexis. For an excellent discussion of the shifts in Freud's view toward decathexis, especially his revisionary *Ego and the Id* and "Fetishism," see George Pollock, "Mourning and Adaptation," 344–45. Pollock credits the later Freud with the view that when a significant person dies the mourner's grief may never end.

9 Herbert, *Moby-Dick and Calvinism*, 53. Bolby, *Loss*, 101. Henry Murray observes that grief deserves a separate category in our effort to write the autopsy of Melville's emotional life ("Dead to the World: The Passions of Herman Melville," 505). Schneidman tabulates 1,800 death thoughts in Melville's 4,000 pages of writing (*Deaths of Man*, chap. 14, 165, 171, 177). Lewis Saum finds that Melville was often on "the track of death" ("Death in Pre-Civil War America," 43). Also see Saum's expanded version of this essay in *Popular Mood of Pre-Civil War America*, chap. 4, 78–106.

10 Anthropologists divide on the universality of emotion associated with grief. On the negative side, see Huntington and Metcalf, *Celebrations of Death*, 24, 28; and Edmund Volkart and Stanley Michael, "Bereavement and Mental Health," 278–79. The latter give a fine analysis of how cultural assumptions construct both grief and bereavement. In the same article, see their discussion of gender and grief, 288. For an opposing view, see Paul C. Rosenblatt et

al., *Grief and Mourning*, passim. More recently, Rosenblatt reminds us that the stages of grief are constructs which are not really "abruptly delineable sets of events" (*Bitter, Bitter Tears*, 38). For a provocative discussion of this debate, see Renato Rosaldo, who argues that anthropology's recent over-emphasis on ritual has blinded theorists to the more intimate, universal grief reaction in primitive cultures ("Grief and a Headhunter's Rage," 178–95).

11 For the most comprehensive overview of mourning theory, see Raphael, *Anatomy of Bereavement*, passim.

12 Bowlby, *Loss*, 15. The idea derives from Freud's seminal essay on grief, "Mourning and Melancholia."

13 In a study of over 2,000 nineteenth-century diaries, Rosenblatt finds that the diarists' grief revived throughout their life-cycle (*Bitter, Bitter Tears*, passim). Dewey, "Voices of the Dead," *Discourses on Human Nature*, 131; and "Hereditary Evil," *The Problem of Human Destiny*, 618.

14 Mathews in *Dollar Magazine*, Sealts, *Melville's Reading*, no. 189. Mathews was viewed as a leader of literary Young America and as the coiner of the name of the movement. See John Stafford, *Literary Criticism of "Young America"*, 1; and Perry Miller, *Raven and the Whale*. Mathews in *Arcturus*, 36–38, 133, 315. Duyckinck, "Authorship," *Arcturus*, 23. Alice Kenney points out that Mathews and Duyckinck were also of Dutch extraction and that Melville's association with them seems to have had much to do with shared Dutch values (*Stubborn for Liberty*, 202–03). This becomes of great importance, for instance, when Melville writes Duyckinck, "I love all men who dive." In Dutch, *Duycking* meant "diving." See Sealts, "Melville and Emerson's Rainbow" in *Pursuing Melville*, 380. n. 25.

15 In *Littel's Living Age 2* (Apr. to Aug. 1844): 435–36. Richard Davey, *History of Mourning*, 96.

16 Poe, "Premature Burial," in *The Other Poe*, 161. On Victorian America's anxiety about premature burial, see Lawrence Taylor, "Symbolic Death," 39–48. For the fears produced by a shadowy demarcation between the living and the dead, see Michael Ragon, *Space of Death*.

17 *Poetical Works of William Cullen Bryant*, 20. Melville acquired an earlier edition of this volume shortly after Malcolm's death (Sealts, *Melville's Reading*, no. 94). Kübler-Ross, *On Death and Dying*. Robert Ferguson argues against Bryant's romanticism, instead suggesting that Bryant sought to control conflicted feelings through the use of Archibald Alison's Scottish commonsense philosophy. (*Law and Letters in American Culture*, 187, 193). My discussion of Bryant and Beecher below follows Farrell, *Inventing the American Way of Death*, 32, 79–94, 131 n. 56. On Bryant, also see Charles H. Brown, *William Cullen Bryant*, 58–59, 86–87.

18 Washington Irving, "Strewing Flowers Upon Graves," 190–92. This piece

was taken from the *Sketch Book*'s "Rural Funerals." Details on Irving's life derive from Perry Miller, "Afterword," *Sketch Book*, 371–78.

19 Gloria C. Ehrlich, *Family Themes and Hawthorne's Fiction*, 20–34, esp. 20–21; Gay Wilson Allen, *Waldo Emerson*, see early chapters on impact of death of Emerson's brothers, on Ellen's death, 164–71, and later chapters on Waldo's death; Richard Lebeaux, *Young Man Thoreau*, chap. 6, 167–204; Paul Zwieg characterizes Whitman as "a guilty son who discovers, in a terrifying economy of mental symbols, that he can take revenge and punish himself in the same act": Whitman's father was dying as his son wrote the first edition of *Leaves of Grass* (*Walt Whitman*, 39, 36). Biographies of Poe, Emily Dickinson, and Henry James, among others, also reveal the importance of mourning to their art. See esp. Marie Bonaparte, *Edgar Allan Poe*. Also see Elisabeth Griffith for the important influence on the young Elizabeth Cady Stanton of her father's grief for her mother (*In Her Own Right*). And on Lincoln's possible unresolved mourning for his father, see George B. Forgie, *Patricide in the House Divided*, 80.

On Horace Mann, see Jonathan Messerli, *Horace Mann*, chap. 7; James R. Mellow vividly dramatizes Mann's "anniversary reaction" in *Hawthorne In His Times*, 129–31; Kathryn Kish Sklar, *Catharine Beecher*, 38. I follow Messerli in my remarks on the influence of Mann's conflicted grief on his life's work. Sklar presents the evidence for conflicted grief but does not place the emphasis on it that I do here.

For Edward Everett's anniversary reaction see Forgie, *Patricide in the House Divided*, 161. Melville's wife, Lizzie, describes her step-mother's anniversary reaction: "Monday will be the anniversary of father's death and mother seems to feel so sad at its approach" (letter of Mar. 27, 1863, GLA). Lizzie's granddaughter reports that Lizzie "never tolerated black hair ribbons on her grandchildren. She had been in mourning so often for members of her family that whenever her grandchildren appeared in black she changed them to bright colors." J. E. A. Smith notes that after the Melvilles moved back to New York City "there was scarcely a year when the family could be said to be out of mourning . . . although custom did not in all cases require the wearing of its outward symbols" (Frances Cuthbert Thomas Osborne, "Recollections," in Sealts, *Early Lives of Melville*, 180, 253 n. 1). See Bowlby, *Loss*, 86–93, on searching as a phase of normal grief.

20 My discussion here is based on Elizabeth Longford, *Victoria R. I.*, 307, 308, 310–11, 312, 313, 314.

21 Joel Kovel, *The Age of Desire*, n. 104. See his discussion of Melville on 130–32. Raymond Williams, "Culture," in *Marx*, 46. Recent labor histories exemplify the approach Williams urges. For instance, see Sean Wilentz, *Chants Democratic*, 10.

22 Letter of July 24, 1832, in Gilman, *Melville's Early Life*, 309 n. 69. Alice Kenney, *The Gansevoorts*, 185. Writing on Mar. 4, 1854 to Sam Shaw (GLA), Maria approvingly reports a sermon in which the minister chastised the influence of "a pleasant novel" and "showed the necessity of Teachers to give direction to the minds of most hearers." The Melville family library contained the mourning manual *Fellowship, Letters Addressed to My Sister Mourners* (see catalog of holdings in GLC). The *Mourner's Book: By a Lady*, 71, anthologizes the Rev. Leigh Richmond's "Letters on the Death of His Mother and Father," in which Richmond writes of his grief, "My heart was ready to burst; but I concealed my feelings as much as possible." However, he faints on his return from the funeral.

23 Karen Halttunen, *Confidence Men and Painted Women*, chap. 5, 124, 128, 151, 129, 134, 132. For a graphic example of Victorian self-consciousness about death, see the frontispiece illustration of Wellington's funeral procession in *Illustrated Magazine of Art* 1 (1853). Melville owned this volume (see Sealts, *Melville's Reading*, no. 291). On the ideology of the Heavenly Home, see Ann Douglas, *Feminization of American Culture*, chap. 6, 240–72.

24 Letter of Jan. 17, 1866 to Kate Gansevoort, in Kenney, *The Gansevoorts*, 187. Ann Douglas suggests that women and ministers appropriated the authority of the dead to bolster their disenfranchised position. Further, consolation literature was implicitly a "hostile protest against the competitive, aggressive, non-familial society (see Douglas, *Feminization of American Culture*, 247–49; I cite 243). *Mourner's Book*, "Preface," iv. Halttunen, *Confidence Men and Painted Women*, 134.

25 Francis Parkman, *Offering of Sympathy*, 110. Melville Family Bible, *Holy Bible*, 434. Annotation dated Jan. 5, 1832 (GLC).

26 The anthologists who compiled the mourning manuals were commonly themselves bereaved.

27 Raymond Weaver gives the family legend of Maria taking a nap with her children quietly seated on stools around her bed (*Herman Melville: Mariner and Mystic*, 60). On Maria's difficulties with nervousness, see Howard, *Herman Melville: A Biography*, 3. Aaron, "Etiquette of Grief," 197–213. I am grateful to Lee Mitchell for alerting me to this article and to Professor Aaron for sending me a copy of it. On violating grief's conventions, see Halttunen, *Confidence Men and Painted Women*, 139. Parkman, "The Occasions and Remedy of Excessive Grief," *Offering of Sympathy*, 109. One mourning manualist was willing to tepidly challenge the dominant social code: "I cannot help questioning the common practice . . . of telling the afflicted, 'that they must be submissive—that they must not murmur' " (*On the Duties of Consolation*, 5). Social control of excessive grief may have been required by the greater closeness of the Victorian American to death. Charles O. Jackson

notes that life expectancy at the end of the nineteenth century was forty-seven (in mid-century it was forty) and infant mortality was 162.4 per 1,000 compared to 9 per 1,000 in 1970 ("Death Shall Have No Dominion," 198). Emerson cited in Joyce W. Warren, *American Narcissus*, 36. See Emerson's essay, "Experience"; and Sharon Cameron, "Representing Grief," 15–41.

28 Letter of Oct. 17, 1838, GLA. Letter of Sept. 18[?], 1841, GLA. In a postscript to this letter, daughter Helen writes that she had written Augusta a letter but because Maria disapproved of her "chirography" she asked her to recopy it. When Helen refused, an enraged Maria tore up the letter. On Maria's activities in youth, see Kenney, *The Gansevoorts*, 173.

29 Letter of June 27, 1850, GLA. Farrell, in *Inventing the American Way of Death*, cites Maria's opening quote as part of the Episcopal "Order of the Burial of the Dead" (41).

30 Herbert, *Moby-Dick and Calvinism*, chap. 3, 57–68. Herbert needs to be supplemented by Farrell's argument on the mix of "various cosmologies" in American attitudes to death (*Inventing the American Way of Death*, 43). Also see Farrell, *Inventing the American Way of Death*, 37, for a Presbyterian Albany minister, William B. Sprague's *Letters on Practical Subjects to a Daughter* (1834).

31 *Mourner's Book*, 278–79. Parkman, *Offering of Sympathy* 113–14. Halttunen, *Confidence Men and Painted Women*, 124. See Thomas Lacquer, "Bodies, Death, and Pauper Funerals," 125. "By the nineteenth century, death and the funeral were occasions far more for the contemplation of the biography of the deceased than the future of his soul." I am indebted to Michael Rogin for calling my attention to this article.

32 Parkman, *Offering of Sympathy*, 113, 115, 117.

33 We do not know how much Maria learned after Allan's death of the circumstances that led to his bankruptcy, but given her strong personality it seems possible that she satisfied her curiosity. See Kenney, *The Gansevoorts*, 197; Gilman, *Melville's Early Life*, 41; and Herbert, *Moby-Dick and Calvinism*, 47–50.

34 Amy Puett Emmers, "Melville's Closet Skeleton," 238. For a fuller discussion see Amy Puett, "Melville's Wife." Emmers suggests that *Pierre* so outraged the Melville family that Maria Melville in particular sought to deflect him from fiction. Mrs. B. and Mrs. A. M. A. have recently been identified. See Henry Murray et al., "Allan Melvill's By-Blow," 1–6.

35 Vamik Volkan, *Linking Objects*, xii, 285, 211, 368. While Volkan works from an oedipal orientation, I am arguing from a revisionary psychoanalytic model, one which brackets the veracity of the oedipus complex and that allows for the greater influence of social codes on self-development. Volkan argues that adolescence, with its loosening of ties to childhood internalized

images, itself provides an intrapsychic model for adult mourning. From this perspective, if Melville's grief for his father prevented him from achieving the rite of passage through adolescent maturation, this would further contribute to his unresolved grief. Bowlby, *Loss*, 294, also see 99; and Edna Furman, *A Child's Parent Dies*. Beverly Raphael notes that boys in middle childhood usually defend against sadness and helplessness with Ahabian "grandiose bravado." See *Anatomy of Bereavement*, 90, 92; I cite 102.

For critical issues raised by taking an object-relations psychoanalytical approach to literature, see Meredith Anne Skura, *Literary Use of the Psychoanalytic Process*, 172, 185–90; and Richard Kuhns, *Psychoanalytic Theory of Art*. He discusses Melville on 115–22.

36 Leyda, *Melville Log*, vol. 1, 228, 469. On the link between intense creative effort and insanity for Victorian Americans, see G. J. Baker-Benfield, *Horrors of the Half-Known Life*; and Vieda Skultans, *Madness and Morals*. For Melville's attitude to insanity, see Henry Nash Smith, *Democracy and the Novel*, chap. 3, 35–55; and Paul McCarthy, "Melville's Treatment of Insanity Through *White-Jacket*," 167–79. Melville's wife writes in a letter of Nov. 19, 1899 (GLA) to console a bereaved relative: "occupation of mind & body is the surest safeguard from brooding grief." Dewey, *The Problem of Human Destiny*, 613. Bowlby, *Loss*, 100. On a mother converting her son into a surrogate husband, see Josephine Hilgard et al., *"Strength of Adult Ego,"* 267.

37 Allan Melville's journal of July 16, 1843, BA.

38 Letter of Sept. 25, 1839, BA.

39 Letter of Nov. 19, 1842, BA.

40 Letter of May 1, 1841, BA, emphasis added.

41 Letter of Aug. 12, 1839, BA.

42 Letter of May 1, 1841, BA. See Hilgard, "Strength of Adult Ego," 263, on the need for the the mother to appear strong to her children if healthy mourning is to ensue.

43 Letter of May 1, 1841, BA.

44 Letters of May 5, 1842 and May 3, 1843, GLA.

45 Letter of Aug. 7, 1842, BA.

46 When a child assumes the parental role toward their siblings, this signifies what they themselves desire (see Raphael, *Anatomy of Bereavement* 102). Maria to Allan, Mar. 5, 1839, BA. This letter is written on the back of one written by Gansevoort to his brother and it is addressed to Allan in care of General P. Gansevoort.

47 See Ira Glick et al. *First Year of Bereavement*, 263–64. For a discussion of the perspectivist issues raised by reading nineteenth-century culture in terms of twentieth-century grief theory, see Rosenblatt, *Bitter, Bitter Tears*. On separate spheres, see Nancy F. Cott, *Bonds of Womanhood*. For discussion see

Robert J. Kastenbaum, *Death, Society, and Human Experience*, 247. Volkart and Michael argue that the bereaved self-mutilation practiced in some tribal cultures disperses guilt and hostility to the deceased ("Bereavement and Mental Health, 90). Rosaldo confirms this claim ("Grief and a Headhunter's Rage," 178–95).

48 See Kenney, *The Gansevoorts*, 172–5.

49 Lindemann discusses how grief for one death may in fact be a revived reaction to an earlier loss, "Symptomatology and Management of Acute Grief" 193.

50 Gilman, *Melville's Early Life*, 83. Maria to Peter Gansevoort, Dec. 14, 1839, GLC. See Bowlby, *Loss*, 172–201; Rosenblatt, *Bitter, Bitter Tears*, 38; Raphael, *Anatomy of Bereavement*, 110; Kastenbaum, *Death, Society, and Human Experience*, 260.

51 Letter of Jan. 21, 1840, BA.

52 Letter to Augusta, Sept. 25, 1839, GLA. Letter to Augusta, Feb. 6, 1847, GLA. Letter to Augusta, Dec. 8, 1841, GLA.

53 In Kenney, *The Gansevoorts*, 177; Puett "Melville's Wife," 101. Maria accuses Herman of "dumping" her "unceremoniously" at the depot one hour before her train was to arrive: "a more ungallant man———it would be difficult to find. I hope to hear from Herman" (letter to Augusta, Mar. 10, 1851, GLA).

54 For the etiquette manuals owned by Melville's parents, see Sealts, *Melville's Reading*, nos. 7, 8, 57, 132, 142; Kenney, *The Gansevoorts* 220; Letter to Allan, Aug. 7, 1842, BA. See Nancy Chodorow for the argument that exclusive female responsibility for children "exacerbates conflicts about masculinity in men" (*Reproduction of Mothering*, 213). David Pugh argues that in Jacksonian America "Mother" became "both a necessary moral force and a source of contempt" and "the anxieties men felt in a culture suddenly set loose and beset with turmoil were indirectly projected onto women." But Jacksonian men came to possess more of their mothers' values than their fathers' (*Sons of Liberty*, 27, 7–8). Also see Rogin, *Fathers and Children*, esp. chap. 4, 113–25. In a discussion of Jackson's relationship with his mother, Rogin points out that it was not permissible to express anger towards the idealized mother of the antebellum era. Yet Jacksonians were also fearful of domination by women: see *Fathers and Children*, 46, 49.

Rather than "blaming Mommie" for Melville's depressions, my argument draws attention to the cultural construction of mother and to the way this social role victimized both mother and son. Or as *Pierre's* narrator says of Mrs. Glendinning, "the infinite Haughtiness had first fashioned her; and then the haughty world had further molded her; nor had a haughty Ritual omitted to finish her." *P*, 90.

55. Message to Herman in letter to Augusta, Feb. 10, 1854, GLA. Maria notes

that Herman confided to her that he was "very angry at the opinion the serious part of the community here have loudly spoken of the book [*MD*] saying it is more than Blasphemous" (letter to Augusta, Dec. 29, 1851, GLA).

56 Augusta writes that Herman's physicians "have warned him" he could "possibly become a confirmed invalid" if he returned to writing (letter to Peter Gansevoort, Apr. 7, 1857, in Leyda, *Melville Log*, vol. 2, 567). Letter to Allan Melville, Feb. 20, 1861, BA. For a recently discovered letter which suggests that Lizzie suspected her husband's sanity in this period, see *Endless Winding Way in Melville*, eds. Hershel Parker and Donald Yannella. Joyce and Frederick Kennedy question whether Lizzie would have stayed with Herman, and so subjected her children to his influence, if she really doubted his sanity ("Elizabeth and Herman (Part Two)," 7 n. 7).

57 On Maria's influence on the end of Melville's career as a novelist, see Puett, "Melville's Wife, 91, 107; Kenney, *The Gansevoorts*, 161; letter to Augusta, June 7, 1855, GLA.

58 On Maria's matchmaking, see Metcalf, *Cycle and Epicycle*, 42. For marriage in Dutch culture, see Kenney, *The Gansevoorts*, 163. Letter to Augusta, May 30[?], 1847, GLA. In a letter to her cousin a month after her wedding, Lizzie confesses that "my marriage was very unexpected, and scarcely thought of until about two months before it took place." Cited in Joyce and Frederick Kennedy, "Elizabeth Melville and Samuel Hay Savage, 1847–1853," 6 n. 10.

59 For a positive feminist appraisal of Melville, see Kristin Herzog, *Women, Ethnics, and Exotics*, chap. 2, 55–93; for a negative assessment that verges on caricature, see Warren, *American Narcissus*, 115–48.
    Letter to Evert Duyckinck, Feb. 2, 1850 (*L*, 102).

60 "Fragments," in Gilman, *Melville's Early Life*, appendix B, 271. For the "Sunday Window," see Howard P. Vincent, *Tailoring of Melville's White-Jacket*, 138–40; Harrison Hayford, "Significance of Melville's 'Agatha Letters,'" 299–310.

61 Stephen Bernstein et al., "Gender-Identity Problems after Parental Death," 41–45. Also see Bowlby, *Loss*, 103–06.

62 See Martha V. Pike, "In Memory Of," 296–315. Also see Pike and Armstrong, *A Time to Mourn;* Douglas, *Feminization of American Culture;* Halttunen, *Confidence Men and Painted Women.*

CHAPTER 2: THE LIMINALITY OF GRIEF

1 Maria Melville to Augusta Melville, GLA. For overviews of *Typee* criticism see Milton Stern, "Introduction," *Critical Essays on Typee*, 1–16; and Leon

Howard, "Historical Note," *T,* 277–302, esp. 300–01. Maria Melville to Peter Gansevoort, BA. Maria may also have recalled her eldest daughter Helen's congenital lameness, which had been cured by an operation shortly after Allan's death (William H. Gilman, *Melville's Early Life,* 77).

2 Alan Lebowitz sees Toby as one in a series of dark portraits that culminates in Ahab (*Progress into Silence,* 24). E. H. Miller links Toby as leader to Gansevoort (*Herman Melville: A Biography,* 96). Rowland Sherrill finds Toby Byronic (*Prophetic Melville,* 12). A contemporary reviewer, John Sullivan Dwight, views Toby as "a cut-and-dried hero of romance" ("Review of *Typee,*" in Stern, *Critical Essays on Typee,* 29).

Letter of Dec. 24, 1822, Maria Melvill to Peter Gansevoort, on being "much amused . . . in seeing the grave and serious Mr. Melvill altogether unable to control his risibility," cited in Gilman, *Melville's Early Life,* 15.

3 Richard Blau notes the presence in *Typee* of "a symbolic landscape which is a schematic image of the body" (*Body Impolitic,* 8). Sharon Cameron observes, "what makes characters in American novels especially difficult to discuss . . . is their desire to merge with and so become the land, at the same time that the equation of self and landscape is . . . tantamount to death," and "the land is the body the self hopes to become" (*Corporeal Self,* 55). T. Walter Herbert argues that Melville learned from one of his sources, the Rev. Charles Stewart, to turn landscape into ethical commentary (*Marquesan Encounters,* 154).

4 For Richard Chase the fear of cannibalism covers up castration anxiety (*Herman Melville: A Critical Study* 12). Martin Pops links the leg wound directly to Allan's deathbed mania by arguing that madness is a wound to the mind, so that maiming, madness, and castration are interlinked (*Melville Archetype,* 5). Larzer Ziff reads the leg as symbolizing the "alienating force of history" in Typee's mythic time (*Literary Democracy,* 9). For similar views, see Herbert, *Marquesan Encounters,* 163–4; Paul Witherington, "Art of Melville's Typee," 143; Thomas Scorza, "Tragedy in the State of Nature," in Stern, *Critical Essays on Typee,* 240. On the role of dependency anxiety, E. H. Miller comments, "*Typee's* drama is unfolded in terms of food and oral imagery" (*Herman Melville: A Biography,* 124). The later Melville disclaims the reality of the threat of cannibalism: "Anyone who treats the natives fairly is just as safe as if he were on the Nile or the Danube" ("South Seas," in Sealts, *Melville as Lecturer,* 167).

Michael Rogin argues that the swollen leg "signifies the stimulation of Tommo's desire, and prevents him from satisfying it. He pays for his pleasure with his leg's incapacity. . . . To get pleasure, Tommo gives up power" (*Subversive Genealogy,* 44; also see 47–48).

For Freud the psychological introjection or incorporation of the parents to form the superego was "at least analogous to an oral process of physical incorporation" (R. E. Money-Kryle, "Introduction," in *New Directions in Psychoanalysis*, eds. Melanie Klein et al., xi n. 1).

5 Frederick Rosenheim argues that the flight which took Melville "to the cannibal Typees must surely have been motivated by his own cannibalistic phantasies" ("Flight From Home," 18, 29, 30). Harrison Hayford notes that the "mercurial shifts" of Tommo's tone are "vital" to the book's effect ("Afterword," *Typee*, 310).

6 For a psychoanalytically oriented anthropological discussion of the link between cannibalism and dependency anxiety in Marquesan life, see Abram Kardiner, *Individual and His Society*, 224–27.

7 On the influence of travel writing's generic constraints on Tommo's contradictions, see Jane Mushabac, *Melville's Humor*, 7; and Janet Giltrow, "Travel and Structure in Herman Melville's Early Narratives," 18–32. Mitchell Breitweiser argues that Tommo registers "a social contradiction within the meaning of America" ("False Sympathy in Melville's *Typee*," 401). Several critics argue that Melville preserves an ironic distance from Tommo. See Herbert on the influence of Porter and Stewart, *Marquesan Encounters*, 158–59, also 176, 207, 223 n. 13; Samson revises Herbert by claiming that when placed in historical context Tommo's contradictions vanish ("Dynamics of History and Fictism in *Typee*," 278–79); Richard Ruland argues that Tommo is Melville's publisher's narrator and that Melville satirizes him ("Melville and The Fortunate Fall," 318); Russell Thomas points out that Melville follows the same sequence of scenes as Stewart, thus he must have composed with his source open before him ("Yarn for Melville's *Typee*," 27). Robert Abrams believes *Typee* dramatizes the flimsiness of social identity and that it stages the cannibalization of identity ("*Typee* and *Omoo*," 39). Lebowitz takes another tack by arguing that there are two narrative voices, one "immediate" and one "far removed" (*Progress into Silence*, 38). Edward Gredja finds the contradictions necessitated by romance form (*Common Continent of Man*, 21).

8 Linton reports that "the people of the valley lived in a constant state of jitters" due to fear of headhunting and raiding for sacrifice. His informants could recollect back to the 1860s, and they report that the continual war on the island had lasted for generations ("Marquesan Culture," 179).

9 Sagan, *Cannibalism*, 53–54.

10 Kardiner generalizes about Marquesan psychology: "In place of the usual 'castration complex' of the male there is the fantasy of being devoured by the woman" (*Individual and His Society*, 22). Without reference to Kardiner, Rogin arrives at a similar finding about Tommo's psychology (*Subversive Genealogy*, 47–48). Miller also reads Fayaway as a mother figure (*Herman Melville: A Biography*, 128).

11 Hutton Webster notes that the canoe taboo relates to the canoe's use as a vehicle for disposing of male skeletal remains (*Taboo*, 116). Melville alludes to the *Young Man's Own Book;* the caption of its frontispiece illustration runs, "Make it an object to spend some portion of your leisure time in the company of intelligent and virtuous ladies." Mushabac observes that Tommo is "rewriting the *Young Men's Own Book,*" (*Melville's Humor*, 46). On Tommo's tone here also see Joseph Firebaugh, "Humorist as Rebel: The Melville of *Typee*, 115, 119; and Abrams, "*Typee* and *Omoo*," 41, 44.

12 See James Babin, "Melville and the Deformation of Being," 101; and David P. Williams, "Peeping Tommo: *Typee* as Satire," 34, 41.

13 Charles Olson observes of Melville, "From passive places his imagination sprang a harpoon" (*Call Me Ishmael*, 15). Edwin Eigner finds in Melville the nineteenth-century fantasy of a female principle as "generative or motive energy" which it feared it had lost (*Metaphysical Novel in England and America*, 126). Kristin Herzog locates a "terrifying potential" in Melville's women and savages (*Women, Ethnics, and Exotics*, 57). Also see Nina Auerbach on the Victorian imagination's "explosively mobile, magic woman," the mermaid (*Woman and the Demon*, 1, 7).

Helen Petrullo believes that the taboo separates male and female "rites and functions," but that it is administered by men ("Neurotic Hero of *Typee*," 321). Kardiner reports that Marquesan women were treated with "aloofness and disdain" and that the cultural suppression of male jealousy led to a displacement of aggression onto women, who were viewed with a "disparaging attitude." Further, in folklore women were depicted as cannibalistic beasts. (*Individual and His Society*, 203–04.) However, Linton believes that due to the polyandrical nature of Marquesan life the "effective power" lay in female hands; further, he notes that a woman could be a chief, (Kardiner, *Individual and His Society*, 158, 160).

14. For discussion of the chief's effigy, see Milton Stern, *The Fine Hammered Steel of Herman Melville*, 140; and Faith Pullen, "Melville's Typee: The Failure of Eden," 23.

15 See Arnold Van Gennep, *Rites of Passage*, chap. 8, on Polynesian belief in Isles of the Dead. See Herbert's discussion of Melville's parody of "symbolic constructions" of death (*Marquesan Encounters*, 168). For the ideological shift between eighteenth- and nineteenth-century attitudes to death, see Farrell, *Inventing the American Way of Death*, chap. 1, 16–43. The funerary sculpture Tommo describes obliquely pokes fun at the Victorian need to control the fate of the dead: the eighteenth-century skull-and-crossbones mocks the antebellum "impatient attitude" with which the dead chief paddles off to a beneficent heaven. On Melville's use of the memento mori image, see Robert Waite, "Melville's Memento Mori," 187–98.

16 Herbert points out that Porter referred to Marquesan gods as "dolls"; Porter also reports a Marquesan woman protesting the missionary put-down of native gods as "rags" (119, 86). E. H. Miller reads this scene as Kolory's birth of Moa, an example of "'womb envy,'" (*Herman Melville: A Biography*, 128). Also see Bruno Bettelheim, *Symbolic Wounds*.

17 Jean-Jacques Mayoux comments on Melville's "neurotic need for support and sympathy" (*Melville*, 33). Charles Anderson argues that Moa is not an authentic ritual (*Melville in the South Seas*, 171).

18 William Charvat notes that the second American edition deleted this paragraph, presumably because it was found to be offensive (*Profession of Authorship in America*). Miller finds Tommo's voice akin to the "crude assault of a child at bay" (*Herman Melville: A Biography*, 129). Also see Herbert, *Marquesan Encounters*, 156.

19 On Pedro's import see Babin for the view that he relates to the medieval bestiary's cock, whose sacrifice was symbolic of acceptance of death, ("Melville and the Deformation of Being," 92).

20 Charles Haberstroh argues that Typee is a society "without fathers" (*Melville and Male Identity*, 36). Rogin bases his argument on a similar assumption (47). However, Geza Roheim, while acknowledging that anthropological handbooks maintain that there is no real oedipus complex in the Marquesas because the son outranks the father at birth, goes on to claim that Marquesan culture denies the oedipus complex, rather than registers its absence ("Marquesan Culture," 314–15).

21 See Stern for how Marquesan family roles may influence what Marheyo means here (*Fine Hammered Steel*, 132).

22 Richard Fletcher observes that a "considerable portion of his 'Marquesan' is pidgin English in tenuous disguise" ("Melville's Use of Marquesan," 136). This may not be consistently the case, however. John Samson finds that "tomo" is indeed a Marquesan word, which means "to enter into, to adapt to well" ("The Dynamics of History," 281).

23 For a discussion of the problems with *Typee's* conclusion, see Donald Houghton, "Incredible Ending of Melville's *Typee*," 28–31. Anderson tells us that the etymology of "taipi" is unknown even to the Marquesans (*Melville in the South Seas*, 101).

In two chapters appended after the novel's conclusion, Tommo presents first Lord Paulet, the benevolent Englishman who ruled Hawaii briefly, resorted justice there, and then was vilified in the American press as a tyrant. Next, in "The Story of Toby," Tommo describes the duplicitous island vagabond, Jimmy, who initially poses as a benevolent figure, rescues Toby, while in fact he intends to sell Toby to a whaler. As Paulet's paternal benevolence and Jimmy's chicanery offset and invert each other, Melville punctuates his narrative by intensifying the issue of confidence in authority figures.

24 Sagan, *Cannibalism*, 8. Linton offers the harshest view of Marquesan cannibalism. He found evidence of hunger cannibalism after prolonged drought, and of cannibalism simply because the natives liked the taste of human flesh. He also observes that it is not restricted to the enemy dead (Kardiner, *Individual and His Society*, 139, 142).

25 Kardiner argues that because of the threat of famine "food anxiety" plays a major role in Marquesan culture. "The feeling of euphoria or power are induced in this culture by food" (*Individual and His Society*, 199, 221). The importance of the Feast may have been lost on many critics because, as Bruce Rosen notes, the additional material his publisher asked Melville to add to the novel broke the unity of the Feast sequence. Rosen also notes that Porter was the source for the Feast ("*Typee* and *Omoo*," 182, 1).

26 Anderson cites Handy, who believes the Feast is associated with "a memorial or funerary festival" (*Melville in the South Seas*, 164).

27 Herbert cites a missionary's account of a bereaved dance in which the women exposed their genitals as a sign of respect to the dead (*Marquesan Encounters*, 42).

28 For positive readings of Marnoo, see Chase, *Herman Melville: A Critical Study*, 279; Thomas Joswick, "*Typee*: The Quest for Origin," 353; Charles Feidelson, *Symbolism and American Literature*, 165; and Michael Clark, "Melville's *Typee*," 366.

29 On the rigidly controlled Marquesan manners, see Lee Mitchell, "Melville's Cannibals and Christians," chap. 7, 203. In the "South Seas" lecture, Melville remarks that the Typees are "eminently conservative"; he also comically observes that they look to the West as their Utopia (Sealts, *Melville as Lecturer*, 171). Linton comments on the Marquesan fear of nonconformity, noting they hate to be laughed at; they are "essentially a polite people" (Kardiner, *Individual and His Society*, 177).

30 Joswick comes closest to my position. Tommo is a "middle-ground" between the two cultures; he is a "process of mediation" centered on his wounded leg, which is a "metonym of his identity" ("*Typee*: The Quest for Origin," 344–45). While characterizing Tommo's voice in terms of "subtle ambivalent balancing," Herbert sees Melville as locked within the "conceptual framework whose validity he is implicitly challenging" (*Marquesan Encounters*, 173). James Duban points out the racist strains in Tommo's voice (*Melville's Major Fiction*, 9 n. 14). Samson also notes the way Tommo preserves "the terms of his culture" which cause him to represent Typee in "partial and confused images" ("Dynamics of History," 280). Warwick Wadlington notes the "pleasurable irresolution" in Tommo's voice (*Confidence Game*, 66). Also see Richard Brodhead on Melville's use of composite voice (*Hawthorne, Melville, and the Novel*, 22–23).

31 Turner, *Drama, Fields, Metaphors*, 37. All subsequent references in the text.

Herbert uses Turner to study the "social dynamic of meaning" in *Typee's* "dramas of self-definition" as they pertain to "civilization" (*Marquesan Encounters*, 20, 21). Wadlington applies Turner to the American Trickster figure, or what I am calling the Marnoovian voice, marooned between cultural codes (*Confidence Game*, ix–x). Turner, *Drama, Fields, Metaphors*, 13.

32 Turner, *Drama, Fields, Metaphors*, 51. Huntington and Metcalf, *Celebrations of Death*, 24. A conversation C. G. Jung reports illustrates the difficulty of reading another culture's emotional life: "The Pueblo Indians told me that all Americans are crazy, and of course I was somewhat astonished and asked them why. They said, 'Well, they say they think in their heads. No man thinks in the head. We think in the heart'" (*Analytical Psychology*, 9). Handy observes, "The intellect unaided is incapable of comprehending the natives' sense of the immanence of power and of invisible presences in nature" (*Polynesian Religion*, 5). Linton: "The Marquesans gave the appearance of being friendly and open with whites, but were actually very much on guard. It was impossible to tell what was going on in their minds" (*Individual and His Society*, 177).

33 Turner, *Drama, Fields, Metaphors*, 25, 13. On Nukuheva bay as female anatomy, see Petrullo, "Neurotic Hero," 319. Also see Chase, *Herman Melville: A Critical Study*, 126. In her analysis of the male American writer's need to feminize the landscape, Annette Kolodny argues that "the mother's body, as the first ambience experienced by the infant, becomes a kind of archetypal primary landscape to which subsequent perceptual configurations of space are related" (*The Lay of the Land*, 156). Also see Nina Baym, "Melodramas of Beset Manhood," 123–39.

34 Lawrence, in Stern ed., *Critical Essays on Typee* 71. See Bettleheim on initiation rites as "reenactment of child-birth (*Symbolic Wounds*, 22); and Joswick, on the leg wound as a sign of "autochtonous birth" ("*Typee*: The Quest for Origin," 351).

35 Roheim claims Marquesans "represent incest with mother as regression into the mother" ("Marquesan Culture," 314). See Edmund Bergler, "Note on Herman Melville," 388; Edinger on "symbolic incest" making Tommo lame like Oedipus (*Melville's Moby-Dick*, 61 n. 2). Freud argues that all taboo manages inherent ambivalence related to either incest or death of a loved one (*Totem and Taboo*). See Sagan for discussion of Freud (*Cannibalism*, 14). See Handy on Marquesan names as "identical with [a] person or thing" (*Native Culture*, 86). A. N. Kaul describes the ravine scene as "a process of dying, or a process of being born anew" (Stern ed., *Critical Essays on Typee*, 161).

36 *Purity and Danger*, 115, 128, 98. Subsequent references in text. Limb's connotations include "boundary" and "devil's limb"; its root stems from "limen," or threshold, also the root of "liminal" (*OED*, vol. 6, 293–94).

Carroll Smith-Rosenberg applies Turner and Douglas to Jacksonian America ("Sex and Symbol in Victorian America," 59–66). See Turner's response in the same volume, for his own speculations on Jacksonian America as a liminal period ("Commentary on the Essays," 75–78). John Carlos Rowe discusses Derrida's notion of the margin as "another text," which Derrida uses "to open the text" (*Through the Custom-House*, 197 n. 8).

CHAPTER 3: ISLES OF THE DEAD

1 Merrell Davis suggests that "Maramma" derives from Dante's "Maremma." Whether or not this is the case, the issue remains how Melville transforms his sources. Davis' study remains the best place to begin in the criticism of *Mardi*, especially for tracing sources (*Melville's* Mardi, 150).

   Richard Chase argues that "it was the madness his [Melville's] mind, in order to remain a continuing economy, had repeatedly to shed into his fictions" (*Herman Melville: A Critical Study*, 149). Charles Olson comments, "Melville was agonized over paternity" (*Call Me Ishmael*, 82).

   The standard view of *Mardi's* talk remains that articulated in 1849 by Henry Cood Watson: it is "an undigested mass of rambling metaphysics" (review in *N. Y. Saroni's Musical Times*, in *Melville: The Critical Heritage*, ed. Watson G. Branch, 184). However, another contemporary reviewer noticed that it was also "a world of extravagant phantoms and allegorical shades" (M. Philarete Chasles, "Actual and Fantastic Voyages" in Branch ed., 172). Braswell discusses in passing *Mardi's* rejection of a Calvinistic view of immortality; however, he also notes that Melville "makes it appear that he believes in the resurrection of the body" (*Melville's Religious Thought*, 28–30, 46). More recently, Patricia Ann Chaffee concedes that death provides "a considerable amount of grist for Babbalanja's philosophical mill," but she views the death theme as only intermittent in *Mardi*. She also usefully discusses the theme of "life-in-death and death-in-life" ("Lee Shore" 107, 119, 107).

2 William Charvat argues that in *Pierre* Melville dramatizes his "experience with himself and with the literary world between 1846 and 1849": the abortive book Pierre works on is *Mardi* (*Profession of Authorship*, 253).

3 James Duban links the romantic quest for Yillah, one that moves ever westward, to manifest destiny (*Melville's Major Fiction*, 11, 19, 21). Michael Rogin takes an opposing view: "Failing to integrate sexual romance and political allegory, Melville/Taji is the victim at once of intractable political material and of the evil, maternal Hautia" (*Subversive Genealogy*, 63). Michael D. Bell argues that Melville discovered "a rich area of relation between romance and the 'real world.'" Bell finds that "the sacrifice of relation," "the dissociation of symbol or language from meaning," in ro-

mance "was the condition of life itself" in the 1840s (*Development of American Romance*, 124, 155).

Olson: "Melville became unsure of the center" (*Call Me Ishmael*, 99). From the perspective of social change, George Forgie discusses why "actual fathers ceased to provide more or less economic models of roles their sons would grow up to play" (*Patricide in the House Divided*, 28). Also see Joseph Kett, *Rites of Passage*, 30–31.

4 Other instances of theft motif include Yillah's parents killing natives for stealing; Babbalanja accused of being a " 'filcher from old Bardianna' "; and an intriguing image of tree boughs as "arms of night-burglars" invading "old specter houses," which are "haunted by some marvelous story" (308, 281, 100). Of related interest to the stealing motif, see Chase on Melville's "primitive fear" of robbery (*Herman Melville: A Critical Study*, 294).

5 Hanna Segal, 127, 125.

6 In the native priest's sermon at the funeral of a diver, Melville parodies the conventional mourning rhetoric: " 'Mourn not, I say . . . the dead whom ye deplore is happier than the living. . . . Rave not, I say.' But she [the mother] only raved the more" (301).

7 Of Bardianna's death, Babbalanja says he died " 'With a firm lip' " and that his last words were " 'Calmer and better' " (585). Of the Parki's sinking, Taji comments, "It was meet that she should die decently and bravely" (120).

8 Linking Taji and the deathlike Jarl in their boat to the canoe scenes in *Typee*, one might say that now in the canoe-coffin a fantasy of the good father appears.

9 James Jubak also notices the transformation of the pilot fish into Hautia's messengers ("Influence of Travel Narrative," 132). The trees on the way to Hivohetee's, a confidence-man holy seer, look like "files of mutes at a funeral" (358).

10 Davis believes Melville modeled the *Parki* anecdote on material in Frederick D. Bennett's *Narrative of a Whaling Voyage*, (London: Bentley, 1840), (*Melville's* Mardi, 58).

11 Just prior to his descent into Annatoo's hiding place Taji comments that ascending the rigging "was like climbing about in some mighty old oak, and nesting in the crotches" (101).

12 During the Mardian quest, the poet Yoomy's "distrust of my powers" touches upon this sense of diffident masculinity (314). Gene Patterson-Black says, on a more conventional tack, that Annatoo represents "Melville's displacement of some of his own hostility toward the wife and family he felt were tying him down" ("On Herman Melville, 126).

13 Davis speculates that Melville used Charles Anthon's *Classical Dictionary* (New York: Harper and Brothers, 1845), in which *Mardi* signifies "a people

of Asia" (*Melville's* Mardi, 77 n. 2). Chase discusses the "Maimed Man in the glen" motif in Melville (*Herman Melville: A Critical Study*, 12). Adler notes that *Mardi* is French for Tuesday and by derivation the day of Mars, or war (*War in Melville's Imagination*, 15). In the terms of my argument, *Mardi* would thus signify the warlike conflicted grief Melville cannot confront in himself.

Ann Douglas argues that Melville experienced masculinity as a crime because "genuine sexual identity" was illicit in the context of nineteenth-century gender stereotypes (*Feminization of American Culture*, 355).

14 Pops links Aleema to "Lemuel" (*Melville Archetype* 43).

15 It will seem as though this grief reaction pursues Taji with menacing force when Aleema's sons hunt Taji throughout the quest.

16 The image of the sacrificial victim also crops up in "The Piazza," where Marianna, the narrator's depressed female double, is compared to a Tahitian maiden secreted for sacrifice; and in *Billy Budd*, where tongue-tied Billy is likened to a vestal priestess in the moment of immolation.

17 Nathalia Wright contends that *Mardi's* quest has as its true object "an undiscovered, ideal man" ("Head and the Heart," 351). More recently, John Wenke examines Melville's use of "behavioral opposites" in *Mardi* ("Melville's *Mardi* and the Isles of Man," 27). Forgie argues for the 1820 to 1861 era as a "post-heroic age," in which a political anxiety of influence causes post-Revolutionary sons to feel overshadowed by Revolutionary fathers. Due to their democratic zeal, Jacksonians "could find no place for 'heroic virtues'" (*Patricide in the House Divided*, 8, 69. Russell B. Nye claims "Melville's theme was the failure of Self" (*Society and Culture in America*, 24).

18 The other kings are the power-mad but depressed Uhia, jolly but gout-stricken Borabolla and the cynical tyrants Hello and Piko. Hello and Piko are ultimately chased by the grief stricken victim of their war games, "The Despairer," who has lost five sons (448).

19 I find it suggestive that Melville was also twenty-five when he returned from the Pacific and began his creative inner unfolding. Davis links Donjalolo's history to the treatment of the Hawaiian chieftain Tamehameha in Melville's chief source for Polynesian lore, William Ellis's *Polynesian Researches* (London, 1833), (*Melville's* Mardi, 147 n. 6). On "spermatic economy" see G. J. Barker-Benfield, *Horrors of the Half-Known Life*.

20 Rogin argues that Donjalolo is a "parable in political guise" of Melville's family history. Majora represents the recently deceased older brother, Gansevoort, while Melville portrays himself in Donjalolo, who lives, as Melville did, in a household of many women (*Subversive Genealogy*, 51).

21 It is significant for the link to Allan Melvill's fatal walk across the Hudson that the description of these cripples focuses on leg deformities (570).

22 Davis notes that prior to writing *Mardi* Melville had read Darwin's *Voyage of*

the HMS Beagle (*Melville's* Mardi, 49). See Kenney on the "monkey spoon" (*Stubborn for Liberty,* 84).

23 See Davis for evidence of late inserts (*Melville's* Mardi, 81–82). Adler suggests the political allegory may not have been a late insert (*War in Melville's Imagination,* 18). John Higham argues that the failure of European revolutions in 1848 made it "apparent that the political millennium had not arrived" (*Boundlessness to Consolidation,* 16–20). Also see Rogin, *Subversive Genealogy,* 102–54. The phrase "Manifest Destiny" was coined in the 1840s by John O'Sullivan, editor of the *U.S. Magazine and Democratic Review.* Nye observes that "the development of an American sense of mission helped to compensate for the American lack of a past" (*Society and Culture in America,* 26, 11). Rogin argues that Melville used "the Anglophile Federalist perspective of Allan Melville and Lemuel Shaw" to attack his brother Gansevoort's expansionist ethos (*Subversive Genealogy,* 58, 62). But Melville may well have been attacking the ideology that victimized his brother.

24 *Mardi's* satire is much influenced by Melville's work for his friend Evert Duyckinck's satirical journal, *Yankee Doodle.* See also Luther S. Mansfield, "Melville's Comic Articles on Zachary Taylor," 411–18.

25 See Davis on Senator Allen and on Scroll more generally (*Melville's* Mardi, 157, 89–90). Adler points out that Allen was a spokesman for Polk during the war against Mexico (*War in Melville's Imagination,* 22).

26 Allan Melvill believed he was destined for business success; his letters voice his belief that God guided and protected him in his financial ventures. Braswell observes that Allan "saw the hand of God in everything," but Braswell also misidentifies Allan as Calvinistic (*Melville's Religious Thought,* 24). See Herbert for a more accurate portrayal of Allan (chap. 2, 45–56). Given Gansevoort Melville's role as a surrogate father to Herman, it is also significant that Gansevoort protested about the Oregon question shortly before his fatal breakdown while an official at the Court of St. James. Forgie: "So successfully were sentimental conventions settled upon American speech, and beyond speech to internalized belief, that antagonistic feelings toward the fathers seldom reached consciousness, let alone expression" (*Patricide in the House Divided,* 93).

27 Barbara Meldrum comments that "The self-destruction of the artist is in one respect a life-through-death process of rebirth" ("Artist in Melville's *Mardi,*" 464).

28 Daniel Walker Howe comments on how "the Victorian preoccupation with order probably reflected a need for psychological stability amidst the rapid changes occurring during the nineteenth century" ("Victorian Culture in America," 19). Peter N. Carroll and David W. Noble discuss how Manifest Destiny illuminates "a gnawing fear of disorder and an abiding hostility toward the irrational" (*Free and the UnFree,* 168). Peter Gay points out that

the "forms of delay and control" celebrated by the Victorian were themselves "unstable" (*Bourgeois Experience*, 58). Rogin argues that Jackson constructed "a familial politics purified of the temptations to conflict, dependence, and vice, purified of the power of women" (*Fathers and Children*, 15). Forgie discusses the "deceptive stability" of the age, in which an "evanescent" sense of the Union served to destabilize consciousness (*Patricide in the House Divided*, 70, 13). Marvin Meyers argues that Jackson exploited the instability of class and social differences, while at the same time attacking "'the perpetual fluctuation of society'" caused by the Bank (*Jacksonian Persuasion*, 8-9, 18, 26). Charvat argues that in *Mardi* Melville "began to generate ideas out of contradictions in himself" (*Profession of Authorship*, 268). Chase discusses Taji's "flight to reality, to that part of the human-emotional reality alienated by liberal democracy" (*Herman Melville: A Critical Study*, 21). Chase elsewhere stresses the contradictions at the heart of the American novel (*American Novel and Its Tradition*, 16, 8).

29 Davis cites Shelley's "'Oh, weep for Adonais—he is dead!'" (*Melville's Mardi*, 185 n. 2).

30 Davis suggests that Oh-Oh's museum parodies P. T. Barnum and his American Museum (*Melville's Mardi*, 154). For the influence of Chesterfield on early American culture see Arthur Schlesinger, Sr., *Learning How to Behave* 11-12. Braswell identifies the source of "A Happy Life" as Seneca ("Melville's Use of Seneca," 98).

31 Weaver characterizes Allan as "a model of rigid decorum." Weaver also cites Allan's inscriptions in the etiquette manuals he gave to his wife, Maria (*Herman Melville: Mariner and Mystic*, 57-59).

32 By invoking Taji's last crime, the ending may imply what the novel's philosophizing has been denying: the possibility of damnation. On Taji as damned at the end, see H. Bruce Franklin, *Wake of the Gods*, 50.

33 On Dutch dialect folk tales and *Mardi*, see Kinney, *Stubborn for Liberty*, 203. In the source from which Melville took the name *Hautia*, her namesake is the deputy-governor of a Polynesian island, who punishes young chiefs after they break a new law forbidding tattooing. Although Davis recognizes William Ellis as Melville's chief source, he misses this allusion. Instead, Davis cites Bennett's *Whaling Voyage*, in which *hautia* signifies the hibiscus in the society islands (*Melville's Mardi*, 139 n. 2). For Hautia in Ellis, see his *Polynesian Researches* Vol. II, 468-69, 476. If Melville associated tattooing with accession to manhood, then the figure of Hautia stands in his imagination for a force that denies manhood. In *Mardi*, Hautia also plays the role in Polynesian lore of the *vehine hae*, beautiful women who lured men to their caves and devoured them (E. S. C. Handy, *Native Culture*, 257). Kardiner, *Individual and His Society*, 213.

Frederick Rosenheim finds that Allan's death preoccupied Maria and robbed her from Melville ("Flight from Home," 11–12). Davis reads *Yillah* as an anagram for "lily of the valley." In flower books, this flower stood for "'purity and modesty'" and, significantly for my argument, "'the return of happiness'" (*Melville's Mardi*, 137). Davis also discusses the Romantic sources of Yillah and Hautia (*Melville's Mardi*, 75–76, 140–41).

34 On funeral symbolism, see Huntington and Metcalf, *Celebrations of Death*, 12; on the symbolism of the mourning picture, see Schorsch, *Mourning Becomes America*, n. p.

CHAPTER 4: REDBURN'S MOURNING PILGRIMAGE

1 On the history of critical response to *Redburn's* mixed tone, see Hershel Parker, "Historical Note," *R*, 347–49. Parker also suggests that it is "extremely hazardous to infer the author's youthful emotions from Redburn's" (326). Melville's contemporaries were sensitive to this issue. See the Reviews in the *Spectator* and the *London Daily News* in *Melville: The Critical Heritage*, ed. Watson G. Branch, 192, 195. Also see Gilman, *Melville's Early Life*, 227, 240; Lawrance Thompson, *Melville's Quarrel with God*, 78. Elmer Pry claims that the novel's tonal shifts are not flaws, but "sensitive artistic probings of Wellingborough Redburn's difficulties in sorting expectations from realities." ("*Redburn* and the 'Confessions,'" 187). While confessing to Evert Duyckinck that he took little pride in *Redburn*, Melville observes, "an author can never—under no conceivable circumstances—be at all frank with his readers" (Letter of Dec., 14, 1849, *L*, 96). On Melville's negative attitude to *Redburn*, see Parker, 321–23.

2 Weaver calls *Redburn* "malicious self-satire" (*Herman Melville: Mariner and Mystic*, 79). Rogin argues that Melville may have denigrated his performance in *Redburn*—he called it trash—because he felt disturbed by the painful family material it unearthed. Redburn's bitterness may have less to do with Melville's adolescent state of mind than with the critical failure of *Mardi*. Rogin incisively discusses how Redburn has "internalized his dead father" and notes that Redburn's idealization of his father blocks the expression of "intensified feelings of rage, betrayal and abandonment" (*Subversive Genealogy*, 63, 65).

3 Arguing that Melville's attitude to *Redburn* shifted as he wrote, Parker observes that after the arrival in Liverpool the narrator, for the most part, drops his comical tone ("Historical Note," *R*, 318, 323–24). Gilman remarks on *Redburn's* "morbid intensity" and on Melville's "addiction to melancholy," learned esp. from Lamb and Ossian. Melville annotated a passage from Ossian's Fingal: "What can be finer than this? It is the soul of melancholy" (*Melville's Early Life*, 233). Also see Thompson, *Melville's Quarrel with God*, 73; and E. H. Miller, *Herman Melville: A Biography*, 154.

4 E. H. Miller observes that Melville's imagery of dismemberment reflects "his own hurt inner landscape," and that his "fictional world is a wounded world crying out to be reconstituted or made whole" (*Herman Melville: A Biography*, 167, 168).

5 Rogin: "Redburn gets inside the Queen only as her destroyed captain," who signifies the "doom" Redburn will inherit from his father (*Subversive Genealogy*, 64).

6 On searching as a normal phase of grief, see Bowlby, *Loss*, 86–93.

7 For the other appearances of "maniacs," see R, 201, 233, 235. On "subterraneous" imagery, see 228, 180, 243.

8 Rogin argues that "Redburn's internalized anger enters the world, through Jackson's provocation, and is directed, by way of the jacket, against Redburn's inherited identity" (*Subversive Genealogy*, 66–68). Jackson's linking object role would explain the ambivalence Charles N. Watson, Jr. notes in Redburn's attitude to Jackson ("Melville's Jackson," 8–10).

9 This is the germ for Ahab's confrontation with the flames that burn in the yardarms like "gigantic wax tapers before an altar" (*MD*, 415).

10 Gilman calls Melville a "Christian rebel," who cannot completely escape his early religious training. He notes that Melville usually attended church during his travels (*Melville's Early Life*, 242, 125, 141). Herbert revises Gilman by arguing for the influence of Allan Melvill's Unitarianism, thus setting up a conflict between Melville's parents' religious influences on him. We have recently learned that in later years Melville became a communicant in the Unitarian church. See Hershel Parker and Donald Yannella, eds., *Endless, Winding Way in Melville*. Thompson argues that Melville set up a "covertly skeptical and satirical attitude toward his inherited Calvinistic belief" (*Melville's Quarrel with God*, 75). Braswell stresses the complexity of Melville's religious thought. In his school textbook, *English Reader*, Melville annotated Matt. 26:45: "This is ironical." In adulthood he annotated St. Paul's counsel, "Hast thou faith? Have it thyself before God": "The only kind of faith—one's own." Melville's Pittsfield neighbor, Sarah Morewood, noted of his dinner-table comportment in 1850–1851 that her husband "dislikes many of Mr. Herman's opinions and religious views—It is a pity that Mr. Melville so often in conversation uses irreverent language" (*Melville's Religious Thought*, 71, 11, 19, 52). On Melville's loss of frame of reference, see Herbert, *Moby-Dick and Calvinism*, passim.

Bell observes of Jackson's link to Andrew Jackson: "his demonism represents the peril of democratic revolution, of the unleashing of the primary depravity in human nature" ("Melville's *Redburn*," 568). On Jackson's role in firing Allan Melvill's father, Major Thomas Melvill, from his position as officer of the port of Boston and on Gansevoort Melville's role as a Jacksonian, see Rogin, *Subversive Genealogy*, chap. 2, 42–76, esp. 54–55.

11 Parker notes that no source for Bolton has been identified and he conjectures that Harry was a late addition to the manuscript ("Historical Note," *R*, 326, 332). But Gilman found that a Henry Gill had signed up for Melville's return voyage from Liverpool (*Melville's Early Life*, 144). Robert Sattlemeyer suggests that Bolton was modelled on H in J. Ross Browne's *Etching of a Whaling Cruise*, which Melville reviewed in the *Literary World*, March 6, 1847 ("Origin of Harry Bolton in *Redburn*," 23–25).

12 Rogin argues that after Redburn "finds community among the democratic outcasts; Harry is the discarded identity he leaves behind (*Subversive Genealogy*, 70).

13 James H. Justus calls Harry a doubling figure and "the objectification of unresolved sexuality that we see in the protagonist" explains why the "truncated tale" of Harry's demise "veers awkwardly between intense concern and casual, almost playful, report" ("*Redburn* and *White-Jacket*," 52). On Bolton as Redburn's double, see Merlin Bowen, "Angle of Vision," 107–08; James Schroeter, "Failure of Mythic Criticism" 293–96; Pops, *Melville Archetype*, 57; William Dillingham, 58.

14 Melville invented the fever for dramatic effect. See Parker, "Historical Note," *R*, 330.

15 William Charvat believes that *Redburn* and *White-Jacket* were "conceived in a mood of contempt for his readers" (*Profession of Authorship*, 236). Douglas develops Charvat's argument: "Melville reveals his increasing distrust of his audience by withholding his book, by refusing to perform the authorial tasks of development and reconciliation" (367).

16 It is significant that Carlo comes on the scene immediately after the spontaneous combustion of the sailor. Jackson believes "the body-snatching crimp had knowingly shipped a corpse on board" (245). This would seem the ultimate commercialization of death.

17 Bell observes that Redburn transforms symbols of authority into "emblems of a raw power and social injustice" ("Melville's *Redburn*," 561).

18 In Victorian American representations of bereavement the face of the mourner was characteristically averted. See Halttunen, *Confidence Men and Painted Women*, 172. Rogin points out that "the image of the dead Nelson [actually he is dying], resting on slaves, associates his father's ideal Liverpool with death and internal corruption." Redburn identifies with the Liverpool outcasts "that the image of his father's Liverpool had hidden" (*Subversive Genealogy*, 69). I am emphasizing how Redburn alerts us to the social codes that also victimized his father, although this may well be an evasion from targeting his anger against his father.

19 It is significant that Redburn's exposure occurs while on the riverboat to New York. Allan Melvill incurred his last illness after he walked across a frozen

Hudson River on his way home from New York. See Howard, *Herman Melville: A Biography*, 7.

20 On the similarities between the process of mourning and that of social change, see Peter Marris, *Loss and Change*. Bell notes that Redburn associates the crew both with depravity and with the "true sources of social power" ("Melville's *Redburn*," 568). Justus takes an opposing view: Redburn never overcomes his "social alienation" (*"Redburn* and *White-Jacket*," 54).

CHAPTER 5: BURIED GRIEFS

1 Charles Anderson notes that Melville observed 163 of his fellow sailors flogged (*Melville in the South Seas*, 425). Rogin links naval floggings to the slavery crisis (*Subversive Genealogy*, 90). Also see H. Bruce Franklin, *Victim as Criminal and Artist*.

2 On Shenly's real life model, see Anderson, *Melville in the South Seas*, 350. However, Howard P. Vincent points out that Shenly's death scene was not taken from Melville's experience (*Tailoring of Melville's White-Jacket*, 174).

3 Anderson notes that Melville's ship was well supplied with pea jackets. He inserted the jacket into his narrative "to unify an otherwise disjointed" performance. The jacket was "a coat-of-arms for the Gansevoort-Melville sense of family pride" (417–18). Nevertheless, Melville wrote to Dana that he actually wore the jacket (*L*, 107). Vincent calls *WJ* a documentary, not a novel: "Disjunctive, spasmodic," it moves about "at random." Vincent views the jacket as a symbol, among other things, of Melville's debacle in *Mardi*, which nearly destroyed Melville's reputation (*Tailoring of Melville's White Jacket*, 19–20). E. H. Miller views the jacket as a prop, one which "avoids exploration of emotional depths" (*Herman Melville: A Biography*, 168). Wai-Chee Dimock perceives in *WJ* the covert presence of "a morose, sardonic Melville, the exact opposite of his sociable self" ("*White-Jacket*: Authors and Audiences," 296–317). Rogin takes an opposing view to mine. White-Jacket does not wear an "inherited jacket" like Redburn, but rather a "self-made garment." His jacket announces his exile in the world: his rejection of "the class stratification which is replacing the failed family" (*Subversive Genealogy*, 89).

4 Robert C. Albrecht views the jacket as an "idealized external self" ("White-Jacket's Intentional Fall," 17–26). Thompson argues that Melville's "disappointments" in the wake of Allan's death caused him to question the moral organization of the universe, leading Melville to blame God for Allan's death. Thompson, though, believes death obsessed Melville only in his later thought (*Melville's Quarrel With God*, 124, 123). Vamik Volkan, *Linking Objects*, 211.

5 Gilman, *Melville's Early Life*, 41.
6 Anderson discovered that White-Jacket's fall reworked a scene from Nathaniel Ames (*Melville in the South Seas*, 415). Vincent argues for the influence of Schiller's poem, "The Diver" (*Tailoring of Melville's White-Jacket*, 217–8). Rogin observes that it is "as if Melville, excising his brother from the remembered family, were following him to his grave" (*Subversive Genealogy*, 97).
7 Anderson claims that Melville invented *WJ*'s "most powerful scenes" (361). But Vincent found sources for Cuticle in Smollet and for the "Massacre" in the national scandal surrounding the Fruitlands' community's Joseph Palmer, who responded to a demand that he cut off his beard: " 'You shan't"—the apparent source for Melville's Ushant (*Tailoring of Melville's White-Jacket*, 136, 185–86).
8 Adler points out that "Cuticle" connotes dead skin (*War in Melville's Imagination*, 48).
9 Vincent on the horned woman (*Tailoring of Melville's White-Jacket*, 138–40). Miller calls the jacket a "simulated breast," but it also performs a "concealed death-wish . . . Lovingly he creates a breast, and snuggles into it . . . but his creation cannot restore . . . the mother" (*Herman Melville: A Biography*, 164).
10 See Henry Murray, ed., *Pierre, or, The Ambiguities*, 431.
11 Chase is "a gentleman," marked by "grace and self-possession," and "amusingly intent on egotistically mending our manners and improving our taste, so that we might reflect credit upon our tutor" (14, 94, 15). White-Jacket is saved from his flogging by the "mild, firm, but extremely deferential manner" of the "remarkably handsome and gentlemanly corporal of marines," Colbrook, who intercedes for him (280, 281).

Charvat believes Melville's "proper level was the upper middle class" (*Profession of Authorship*, 262). Justus points out that White-Jacket's real affinities are with the natural aristocrats, Chase and Colbrook ("*Redburn* and *White-Jacket*," 61). Rogin notes that Melville "brought a rebellious sensibility into his family, a sensibility on which he could not act" (*Subversive Genealogy*, 99). Dennis Berthold argues that Melville "subtly establishes authorial superiority to both his persona and his audience" by having White-Jacket cite erroneous information ("Factual Errors," 236).

Writing to Dana to ask him to come to *WJ*'s defense, should it be attacked in the press, Melville genteelly fears that his novel is "in some parts rather man of warish in style—rather aggressive I fear" (Letter of Oct. 6, 1849, *L*, 93). Shortly before his death, Melville scored in Schopenhauer: "if he is a man of genius, he will occasionally feel like some noble prisoner of state condemned to work in the galleys with common criminals" (cited in Leyda, *Melville Log*, vol. 2, 832).

Larry Reynolds discusses how White-Jacket's double vision of the crew reflects Melville's own divided nature. White-Jacket manifests "aristocratic pretensions" and Melville insufficently distances himself from them ("Anti-Democratic Emphasis," 15, 19). Priscilla Zirker argues that White-Jacket and Melville reflect the ideology of the Democratic party in the 1830s and 1840s, in which slavery was not an issue of egalitarianism but of property ("Evidence of the Slavery Dilemma," 478–49). Robert Caserio finds that in replacing "the fiction of hierarchy with flat, factual reporting," White-Jacket fails to find a plot "for his attempt at a written act of rebellion" (*Plot, Story, and the Novel*, 159). James Duban offers a fine reading of *WJ*'s divided tone. What Vincent calls its "disjunctive and spasmodic form," "aptly coincide[s] with the narrator's shifting and sometimes contradictory sentiments on the nature of democracy." White-Jacket's inconsistencies mirror those reflected in "republican notions of liberty and democracy," while his radicalism may in part derive from the novel's sources (*Melville's Major Fiction*, 70, 79, 68).

12 The master-at-arms, Bland, is "an organic and irreclaimable scoundrel" (188). But, after a long-winded, transcendentalist critique of sin as something that "widely prevails among men of warped understanding and unchristian and unchristianable hearts," White-Jacket writes of his just stated position—"evil was but good disguised": it was "sorely jarred . . . by events that took our philosophy aback. For after all, philosophy—that is, the best wisdom that has ever in any way been revealed . . . —is but a slough and a mire, with a few tufts of good footing here and there" (184).

Evert Duyckinck warned his friend in a review of the novel "lest he get into a bewildering, barren, and void scepticism" (in Watson G. Branch ed., *Melville: The Critical Heritage* 228). Intriguingly, Melville underlined Exod. 15:3: "The Lord is a man of war" (see Wilson W. Cowen, "Herman Melville's Marginalia,", vol. 3, 108. On Melville's complex religious attitudes see esp. Anderson, *Melville in the South Seas*, 429; Thompson, *Melville's Quarrel with God*, 95; and Braswell, *Melville's Religious Thought*, 50–51. Wright observes of Melville's religiosity that "no strict system of thought seems ever to have taken hold of him" (*Melville's Use of the Bible*, 96).

13 Zirker takes this as imagery that portends regional and class conflict ("Evidence of the Slavery Dilemma," 491).

CHAPTER 6: A THING WRIT IN WATER

1 Melville cites the "Deep and Secret grief" quote from Bacon in notes, probably made in the summer of 1849, on the flyleaf of vol. 7 of his edition of Shakespeare, which contained *Lear, Othello*, and *Hamlet*. Olson reproduces only part of these notes (*Call Me Ishmael*, 39, 52). For the Bacon quote see Mansfield and Vincent eds., *MD*, 643–44. In their invaluable notes, they

also cite DeQuincey, whom Melville read shortly before he began *MD*, on the "mysterious handwritings of grief" in the brain, which "are not dead, but sleeping. . . . In some potent convulsion of the system, all wheels back into its earliest elemental stage" (704). On the Harvard study, see Ira Glick, et al., *First Year of Bereavement*, chap. 13, 261–82, esp. 263–65, 271.

2 On antebellum reviewers' detestation of what they called "morbidity," see Nina Baym, *Novels, Readers, and Reviewers*, 142. For instance, *House of Seven Gables* was found "morbid" by one reviewer (Baym, *Novels, Readers, and Reviewers*, 177). Melville seems to be playing on this popular prejudice when he identifies Ahab as poisoned by " 'a half-wilful overruling morbidness at the bottom of his nature' " (*MD*, 111). Melville's crony, Evert Duyckinck, mockingly objects to *MD's* "association of whaling and lamentation," which seemed to him "why blubber is popularly associated with tears." *Southern Quarterly Review* (Jan. 1852) calls Ahab "a monstrous bore"; and the *London Morning Advertiser* (Oct. 24, 1851) complains of Ahab's madness: " 'Somewhat too much of this!' " (in Mansfield and Vincent, eds., *MD*, xvii, xx; and Branch, ed. *Melville: The Critical Heritage* 252).

For an exploration of monomania in Melville's culture, see Henry Nash Smith, *Democracy and the Novel*, chap. 3, 35–55; and Vieda Skultans, *Madness and Morals*.

See Mansfield and Vincent's introduction for a good survey of attitudes of early twentieth-century critics to Ahab. After the 1920s, when critics identified Ahab with Melville, the tendency was to identify Ahab with the various bogeymen of the critic's political moment. However, critics such as William Ellery Sedgwick (1944) could speak of "Ahab's noble madness that sprang from an excess of humanity" (Mansfield and Vincent eds., *MD*, xxvii).

3 Mansfield and Vincent note that the aspect of the biblical Ahab's story which most interested Melville's contemporaries was Ahab's usurpation of Naboth's paternal inheritance, his vineyard (*MD*, n. to 637). Melville might have been unconsciously drawn to Ahab in part by the way this appropriation mirrored how his mother's bereaved image of his father displaced his own sense of paternal identification and inheritance. For the way Ahab's story was used in antebellum political rhetoric, see Rogin, *Subversive Genealogy*, chap. 4, 102–54. Rogin gives a fine precis of the earlier political readings and he goes beyond them by transforming the political allegories of these critics into a sense for how *MD's* language is "deeply enmeshed in the crisis of 1850," i.e., the slavery issue in the U.S. and the failed revolutions abroad (*Subversive Genealogy*, 107). Rogin draws attention especially to how "Melville's family connections to Indian dispossession and slavery" left their mark on his art (*Subversive Genealogy*, 107, 143). The scholarship Rogin summarizes includes Willie T. Weathers, "*Moby-Dick* and the Nineteenth Century

Scene," 477–501; Charles H. Foster, "Something in Emblems," 3–35; and Alan Heimert, "*Moby-Dick* and American Political Symbolism," 498–534.

In the source that Mansfield and Vincent suggest for Fedallah—*1001 Days, Persian Tales*—a dervish, who possesses the power of " 'reanimating a dead body, by flinging my own Soul into it,' " revives a dead nightingale to assuage a queen's grief (*MD*, 732). For a different view of Ahab's claim to a "queenly personality," see Robert Zoellner: "This is superb rhetoric, but it is false fact. Ahab has willfully destroyed his 'personality,' and obliterated its 'queenly' freedom" (*The Salt Sea Mastodon*, 100).

Herbert argues that in his grief for his father Melville simultaneously absolved him and identified with his mother's probable damnation of him from her Dutch Reformed perspective. Allan's death shattered a tenuous balance in which Melville had been able to harmonize his parents' respective Unitarian and Dutch Reformed views. See Chap. 1 for my reading of Maria's idiosyncratic Calvinism, one more mixed with genteel codes than Herbert implies (*Moby-Dick and Calvinism*, chap. 3, 57–68, esp. 60–61).

As noted in Chapter 1, given that Allan Melvill appeared in her life shortly after her heroic father, General Peter Gansevoort, died, Maria may have turned Allan into a living linking object to her father. If so, this may illuminate Ishmael's need to imbue Ahab with excessive heroic qualities, at the same time that Ahab's damnation suggests that he is being viewed from Maria's Dutch Reformed perspective.

Wright points out that the biblical Ahab is already a figure of doubleness: he is a composite of two sources, one of which found him able and the other viewed him as a dangerous innovator (*Melville's Use of the Bible*, 62).

4 Putting the stress on the cultural context of what he finds to be Melville's religious crisis, Herbert argues that by allowing "spiritual dislocations" and their attendant "feverish excitement" to surface, Melville "became convinced that his true creativeness lay in braving this tumult, winning the articulation of a 'vital truth,' in contention with apparent madness." Herbert links Ahab to Allan insofar as both could be described as liberal heretics as depicted by Calvinist rhetoric (*Moby-Dick and Calvinism*, 18, 40).

Richard Chase reads Ahab as "both father and son" (cited in Mansfield and Vincent eds., *MD*, xxix). Newton Arvin characterizes Moby Dick as an "archetypal Parent . . . the mother also, so far as she becomes a substitute for the father." Moby Dick also evokes "the violently contradictory emotions that prevail between parent and child" (*Herman Melville*, 173). E. H. Miller calls *MD* "a study of the rivalry of the 'son' (Ishmael) with the father (Ahab)"; and he finds that "Ahab fathers Ishmael," in as much as the latter writes the former's story (*Herman Melville: A Biography*, 182, 210).

5 See Francis Parkman, "Occasions and Remedy of Excessive Grief," in *Offer-*

ing of Sympathy to the Afflicted, 109–17. Baym argues that antebellum reviewers viewed the novel as "an agent of social control" (*Novels, Readers, and Reviewers*, 170). One contemporary reviewer, conflating Ishmael and Melville, describes the novel's narrator as performing with "the ease and polish of a finished gentleman" (*Philadelphia American Saturday Courier* (Nov. 22, 1851), cited in Hershel Parker and Harrison Hayford, eds. *Moby-Dick as Doubloon*, 52).

Critics rarely view Ishmael negatively. Zoellner, though, notes that the verbal resolutions which satisfy Ishmael do not satisfy Melville (*Salt Sea Mastodon*, 216). Deploying Sacvan Bercovitch on the jeremiad, James Duban subtly argues that "the exclusive tendencies of the covenant psychology under-girding all jeremiads lead Ishmael to betray the abolitionist egalitarianisms he purports to champion." "Ishmael . . . is the American child who trips over his own conceptual shoestrings while seeking to flee the brutality of his nation's past" (*Melville's Major Fiction*, 108, 137).

6 Cited in David Perkins ed., *English Romantic Writers* (NY: Harcourt Brace Jovanovich, 1967), 1115. See Mansfield and Vincent eds., *Moby-Dick*, 827. They also suggest that the biblical Moab, a possible source for *Moby*, in Hebrew means "seed of the father," while *Ahab* in Hebrew means "the brother of the father," or "uncle or father of the brother" (*Moby-Dick* 695, 637). This last etymology bears on Edinger's suggestion that Maria did not commit herself emotionally to her husband but remained attached to her family, esp. her brother: "making the psychic atmosphere of Melville's family that of a matriarchy in which the mother is the central figure and the masculine authority resides not with the father but with the maternal uncle" (*Melville's Moby-Dick*, 7–8). In his letters, Allan addresses Peter Gansevoort as brother.

7 Sophia Hawthorne cited in Eleanor Metcalf Melville, *Cycle and Epicycle*, 106.

8 The important difference between Ahab and the bereaved parent is that Ahab is acting consciously and willfully. My point is that the effect is the same: the transference of emotion.

9 A desire to reunite with the deceased underlies the suicidal urges of some victims of pathological mourning (see Bowlby, *Loss*, 301–06). Significantly, Ishmael next describes the Manhattanite water-gazers: the harbor they gravitate toward must have been strongly associated in Melville's memory with his father's fall, because Allan Melvill's import firm was in lower Manhattan. Zoellner observes that "Ishmael's off-hand tone is a screen deliberately thrown up to distract us from certain terrible urgencies of his being" (*Salt Sea Mastodon*, 119).

10 Douglas notes that in *MD* women are "the mourners and losers: they have no other role" (*Feminization of American Culture*, 367).

11 Zoellner calls Queequeg "the very figure and image of death." In befriending Queequeg, Ishmael gets on friendly terms with death. But, "as a figure of death, he is a source of life" because the coffin which saves Ishmael "is really Queequeg transmogrified" (*Salt Sea Mastodon*, 217, 220, 234).

12 The scary night spent alone with Queequeg may gesture towards Melville's memory of spending a night alone with his father at the Courtland Street dock after the rest of the family removed to Albany in the wake of Allan's bankruptcy (Gilman, *Melville's Early Life*, 42). Rogin also argues that Melville's coat imagery evokes Allan Melvill (*Subversive Genealogy*, passim).

13 Of Queequeg's deathbed scene, James Grove argues: "Queequeg facing death seems to mock the sentimental literature's depictions of death," because it is a cannibal, not a Christian, who serenely faces death. While noting that Ishmael narrates sentimentally here, Grove maintains that Queequeg's failure to die "trivializes" the sentimental conventions of the deathbed scene. However, Grove admits that Melville "might have wanted the scene to be read straight" ("Melville's Vision of Death," 185, 186, 187).

14 If Queequeg's characterization gestures towards Allan Melvill, then Ishmael, as partially shaped by Maria Melville's bereavement, is his wife. John Seelye suggests the "supernatural hand" belongs to Ishmael's dead mother (*Ironic Diagram*, 61). Melville may here register his sense of losing Maria to her grief for Allan. Further, after Allan's death she may have seemed changed to him, like a stepmother.

15 See Zirker, "Evidence of the Slavery Dilemma," 480.

16 The survival of Ishmael's morbidity may perhaps best be seen in chap. 94, "Squeeze of the Hand," in which Ishmael needs to squeeze the sperm to feel "divinely free of all ill-will, or petulance, or malice" (348). In chap. 69, "The Funeral," Ishmael's anger surfaces as he sardonically observes of the whale carcass set adrift: "There's a most doleful and most mocking funeral. The sea vultures all in pious mourning . . . In life but few of them would have helped the whale, I ween; if peradventure he had needed it" (262). Yojo's Ramadan trance seems to invert the circumstances of Allan Melvill's death, in which sleeplessness led to mania, not to Queequeg's Ramadan meditation.

17 Grove argues that the sinking of the Pequod inverts the deathbed scene of "consolation-graveyard" literature ("Melville's Vision of Death," 185).

18 Halttunen, *Confidence Men and Painted Women*," 172.

19 Mansfield and Vincent cite Byron and Carlyle as Melville's sources for the notion of grief as a conduit to wisdom (*MD*, 800). Given that Hawthorne was writing *The House of the Seven Gables*, with its morbid interest in questions of social inheritance, while Melville was writing *MD*, one imagines that the Ahab's ideas about the inheritance of grief could have formed part of the two authors' discussions. Brodhead, *Hawthorne, Melville, and the Novel*, 17.

20 This may be another allusion to Melville's sense of his mother's transformation by the loss of Allan.

21 Olson, *Call Me Ishmael*, 54. Also see Melville on Charles Fenno Hoffman's madness: "in all of us lodges the same fuel to light the same fire. And he who has never felt, momentarily, what madness is has but a mouthful of brains" (letter to Evert A. Duyckinck, April 5, 1849, *L*, 83).

22 Because it was Fanny Kemble's Shakespearean readings, especially of Lady Macbeth, in Boston on Feb. 1849 that re-ignited Melville's interest in Shakespeare, while writing *MD* he may have associated the bard with a female presence (Howard, *Herman Melville: A Biography*, 165; and his "Melville's Struggle with the Angel," 201).

23 Thomas Vargish believes that this imagery derives from the Gnostic myth of the fallen mother ("Gnostic Mythos in *Moby-Dick*," 272–77).

24 Halttunen, *Confidence Men and Painted Women*, 132.

25 An important link between Ahab's mania and Allan's is that while Allan's was brought on by overwork and sleeplessness, Ahab, in the last part of the novel, becomes a sleepless figure, obsessively driven in his quest for revenge. Even early in the novel Ishmael speaks of "the sleeplessness of his [Ahab's] vow" (173).

The characterization of Maria Melville is from Puett, "Melville's Wife," 101. Mrs. Glendinning in *Pierre*, believed to be in part modeled on Maria Melville, is also described as "queenly" ("Introduction," in Murry ed., *Pierre, or, The Ambiguities*, xli–xlii).

26 Ishmael evinces one way of managing the anxieties Ahab provokes when he genially observes, "we are all somehow dreadfully cracked about the head, and sadly needing mending" (78). "Here goes for a cool, collected dive at death and destruction," he elsewhere blithely suggests (197).

Ishmael also presents two other maniacs: Elijah and Gabriel. Elijah is a "crazy man" who accosts Ishmael in New Bedford and offers him cryptic warnings against shipping out with Ahab (88). Ishmael is "riveted with the insane earnestness of his manner"; later, "the ragged Elijah's diabolical incoherences uninvitedly [were] recurring to me, with a subtle energy I could not have before conceived of" (86, 109). Of Gabriel, Ishmael observes that in his "sleepless, excited imagination [were] all the preternatural terrors of real delirium" (266). Starbuck and Melville share at least one thing in common: both had lost a father and a brother (104).

27 For evidence that Melville read a pietistic children's magazine, see Robert Sattlemeyer and James Barbour, "A Possible Source and Model," 577–83. The reviewer for the *Spectator* (Oct. 1851) commented on the "magazine article writing" in *MD*. Perth's story may also parody Longfellow's "The Village Blacksmith"; and Perth's "virtuous elder brother" possibly alludes to Gansevoort (Mansfield and Vincent eds. *Moby-Dick*, xx, 815, 816).

28 Sharon Cameron observes that when Ahab orders Pip below this indicates a "refusal to allow grief and rage to face each other when they will not reduce to an identity" (*Corporeal Self*, 19).

29 The coat factory imagery once more appears when Stubb says of the bereaved Gardiner that he looks as though "'some one in that missing boat wore off . . . [his] best coat" (434). In a possible source for the seals—Captain James Colnett's *A Voyage to the South Atlantic*—their cries are compared to the "shrieks and lamentations so like those produced by the female voice" (Mansfield and Vincent eds., *MD*, 824).

30 Mansfield and Vincent claim Ahab's "topmost grief" echoes Carlyle's "Man's Unhappiness . . . comes of his greatness" (*MD*, 828). Raphael, *Anatomy of Bereavement* (NY: Basic Books, 1983), 40.

31 Melville may also be parodying his culture's theatrical sense of grief by alluding to the actress Rachel, well-known for her emotional performances. While in Paris, Melville attempted to see "Madame Rachel" (Eleanor Melville Metcalf, ed. *Melville's Journal of a Visit to London and the Continent*, 57).

For the biblical Rachel see Jer. 31:15. A contemporary poem, R.S. Chilton's "Burial at Marshfield," contains the lines: "Ay, well may'st thou mourn, like a RACHEL, today, / Dear Goddess of Freedom, and weep by his grave" (373).

CHAPTER 7: CUNNING PURPLENESS

1 E. L. Grant Watson argues that *Pierre* is at "the center of Melville; if we would understand him, we must understand this book before all others" ("Melville's *Pierre*," 233). For a survey of *Pierre's* critical history, see Hershel Parker, "Historical Note," *P*, 379–91 and 396–407. I abbreviate "Historical Note," *P*, as "HN" hereafter. Parker concludes that "Critics are still confused" by virtually every aspect of the novel; "there is no consensus as to either the value or the success of *Pierre*" ("HN," 406–07). Also, see Ralph Willet's survey of the criticism, "Preface," *Merrill Studies*, *vii–ix*. Henry Murray's introduction and notes still remain the essential starting point for criticism of Melville's "literary monster" (*Pierre*, 1949, xcii). For an updated introduction to the novel, see Brian Higgins and Hershel Parker, "Introduction," *Critical Essays on Pierre*, 1–27.

2 Michael Rogin notes that Pierre's "reciprocal devotion to his mother, by being all too faithful to antebellum cultural prescriptions, calls attention to the anxieties behind them" (*Subversive Genealogy*, 162, 163). Nina Baym argues that the "connection between family and fiction is the one most frequently on the [antebellum] reviewers' minds." "'The novel, at present,'"

one reviewer reported in 1858, ". . . becomes a household book, and in some sort a member of the family'" (*Novels, Readers, and Reviewers*, 49).

3 Jay Fliegelman argues that "It is a parent's grief, not anger, authority, or indifference, that is feared in the postpatriarchal family" (*Prodigals and Pilgrims*, 262). Eric Sundquist observes that "for Pierre, the father is . . . so internalized by Pierre's actions as to be his haunting double" (*Home as Found*, 157). The most influential reading of Isabel is that of Henry Murray, who argues that she is "the personification of Pierre's unconscious"; and I am building on his insight that "she embodies . . . the grief and self-pity which have been bottled up . . . the open expression of which has been barred by culture" (*Pierre*, liii).

4 With the exception of *Godey's Lady's Book* and *Putnam's Monthly*, Melville's contemporary reviewers mistook the parody for lameness (see Parker, "HN," 388, 391, 393). The notion of *Pierre's* serious substratum dates from Raymond Weaver's remark that *Pierre* is "half satirical, half of the utmost seriousness" (*Herman Melville: Mariner and Mystic*, 114). Also see Howard, "HN," 373; Carol Strickland, "Coherence and Ambivalence in Melville's *Pierre*," 308; Raymond Nelson, "Art of Herman Melville," 214. Sundquist argues that Pierre "only properly becomes parody in retrospect"; "we should be . . . alert to the peculiar and real powers generated by scenarios in the book that are overly theatrical, farcical, or parodic" (*Home as Found*, 181, 157). Newton Arvin observes, "There are whole passages that waver back and forth between absurdity and genuine power." Melville felt "a bitter distaste and disbelief in his own book in the process of writing it" (*Herman Melville*, 231, 225, 231).

Melville began *Pierre* while his wife and his mother were absent from home—Lizzie was in Boston for a month (Puett, "Melville's Wife," 81). Parker observes that as *Pierre* was vilified in the press, his family "evidently held nervous councils," in which they concluded "that his literary career was finished" and agreed to help him secure a foreign consulship ("HN," 392). Puett Emmers discovered the letter which strongly suggests that Melville's father sired an illegitimate daughter ("Melville's Closet Skeleton," 339–43. Reprinted in Higgins and Parker eds., *Critical Essays on Pierre*, 237–40). Henry Murray has recently identified Allan Melville's illegitimate daughter and her mother ("Allan Melvill's By-Blow," 1–6). Lewis Mumford calls *Pierre* "a blow, aimed at" Melville's family (cited in Willet ed., *Merrill Studies*, 8). "It is significant that after *Pierre*, Melville's mother, particularly, was determined that he should give up writing" (Puett, "Melville's Wife," 91).

5 On the biographical parallels, see Murray, *Pierre*, xli–xlii, 438, 450. In discussing Maria Melville's patrician descent, Murray observes that her "sudden decline of social status" after her husband's death and bankruptcy "caused her to tighten the hold upon . . . her relics of buried family glory."

This attitude was transmitted to Herman and "never wholly outgrown" (*Pierre*, 437). John Logan observes that "Mrs. Glendinning is modelled on Melville's mother, whose wishes for upper class splendor are gratified by" *Pierre* ("Psychological Motifs," 326).

The women in the Melville household read sentimental literature aloud in the evening (Puett, "Melville's Wife," 55).

William Ellery Sedgwick notes that *Pierre* "issues from intolerable tensions and uncertainties . . . it is the expression of a grief-stricken man" (*Tragedy of Mind*, 156). Weaver believes that "after *Pierre*, Melville was without internal urging to write" (*Mariner and Mystic*, 343–44). F. O. Mathiessen observes that *Pierre* "gives the sense of having been wrenched" from Melville (*American Renaissance*, 474).

In a June 3, 1926 letter to Henry Murray, George Eustic Corcoran claims, "An old friend of mine, who is dead now, knew Herman Melville & told me that Herman Melville told him that 'Pierre' was a true! story & very closely connected with him!" (in BA).

If Parker is correct about Melville's extensive additions to *Pierre* by the third week of Jan. 1852, then Melville would have been adding to *Pierre* during the time of year that his father had died, thus suggesting a kind of anniversary reaction—a revival of grief during the time of year when a loved one died. Allan Melvill died Jan. 28, 1832, after two-and-a-half weeks of intermittent deathbed mania ("Why *Pierre* Went Wrong," 7–23; Murray, *Pierre*, 453–54).

6 See Murray on Pierre's unresolvable moral conflict, which obstructs psychic integration (*Pierre*, xv).

7 John P. McWilliams, Jr., argues Pierre's make-up reveals that Melville's "ideal American character is made up of self-destructive and incompatible parts," comprised of "democratic Christianity" and extreme individualism (*Hawthorne, Melville, and the American Character*, 171).

More recent critics of *Pierre's* style and tone have not gotten much further than the novel's contemporary reviewers, who complained of its "chaotic state of authorship." "Mr. Melville's style of writing in this book is probably the most extraordinary thing that an American press ever beheld" (cited in Branch, ed., *Melville: The Critical Heritage*, 299, 318). As Baym points out, antebellum reviewers were rarely able to appreciate stylistic experimentation (*Novels, Readers, and Reviewers*, 130, 132, 13). On *Pierre's* complex tone, also see E. L. Watson, "Melville's *Pierre*," 216, Willet ed., *Merrill Studies* viii; A. R. Humphreys, *Herman Melville*, 87; Charles Feidelson, *Symbolism and American Literature*, 206; Leslie Fiedler, *Love and Death in the American Novel*, 455; Edgar Dryden, *Melville's Thematics of Form*, 141; Sundquist, *Home as Found*, 153; Rogin, *Subversive Genealogy*, 178. E. H. Miller discusses the influence on *Pierre's* style of the strain of writing *MD*, the birth of Stanwix, and the departure of Hawthorne (*Herman Melville: A Biography*, 232–33). Seelye believes that after *Pierre* sheds his early idealism the novel's style changes "from scornful schmaltz to symphonic thunder" (*Melville: The Ironic Diagram*, 77). Parker, implausibly, claims that the first half of *Pierre* is "the most objective and tightly controlled piece of writing Melville had yet achieved." But after Melville's publishers refused his request for an advance in Jan. 1852, Melville added 150 angry and unbalanced pages, in which he turned Pierre into a writer and attacked the New York publishing scene ("Why *Pierre* Went Wrong," 9). Duban may well be the lone critic who perceives stylistic unity in the novel, as the subjective transcendentalism of the novel's beginning leads to Pierre's literary transcendentalism (*Melville's Major Fiction*, 181). However, *Pierre* has found two ideal readers. Picasso is reported to have said, "*Pierre* was the only American book worth reading" (cited in Willet ed., *Merrill Studies*, viii). And Maurice Sendak confesses that he borrowed Melville's title for his *Pierre* (cited in Jonathan Cott, *Pipers at the Gates of Dawn*, 65).

On *Pierre's* style as self-punitive, see Charles Haberstroh, *Melville and Male Identity*, 104; E. H. Miller, *Herman Melville: A Biography*, 231; Nelson, "Art of Herman Melville," 204. Logan comments on Pierre's "terrific need for punishment ("Psychological Motifs," 328). In "Shelley's Vision," Melville wrote: "In elf-caprice of bitter tone / I too would pelt the pelted one: / At my shadow I cast a stone" (*CP*, 233).

8 Schorsch, *Mourning Becomes America*. For different perspectives on Isabel's origin, see Murray on a Berkshire legend of "lovely Isabel," who was saved from being burnt by Indians at the foot of a Pittsfield elm (*Pierre*, 430); Franklin associates Isabel with the savage or primitive mind (*Wake of the Gods*, 166–67); Duban argues that Pierre's "early encounter with Isabel conforms to a conversion experience" (*Melville's Major Fiction*, 179).

On Maria Melville's needlepoint mourning art, see Kenney, *The Gansevoorts*, 173.

9 Rogin: "Twelve-year-old Herman Melville was abandoned by his father; that may have contributed to Pierre's identification with the abandoned Isabel." "Pierre sees in Isabel that part of himself abandoned when his father died" (*Subversive Genealogy* 171, 173).

10 Joshua C. Taylor notes of the female mourning figure that she is "at once a *muse*, a virtue, and fashionable young woman." (*America As Art*, 30, my emphasis.) In Melville's "Hawthorne and His Mosses," the Virginian refers to Hawthorne's Isabelian "wild, witch voice" ringing through him (*MD*, 536). Seelye links Isabel's cottage to Hawthorne's Lenox home (*The Ironic Diagram*, 438). Judith Fryer calls Isabel "the source of" Melville's "creativity" (*Faces of Eve*, 54). Logan believes that Isabel is modelled on

Melville's sister Augusta, his principal copyist, who had the same name as "the figure in a celebrated nineteenth century incestous affair," i.e., Byron's sister ("Psychological Motifs," 326).

The novel pervasively associates the "pregnant fact" of Isabel with birth imagery (104). See *P*, 53, 54, 106. Murray argues that Pierre fulfills a maternal role toward Isabel (*Pierre*, lxxxii).

11 E. H. Miller observes that Pierre is subject "to fainting fits, not unlike those of Melville's mother in periods of emotional stress" (*Herman Melville: A Biography*, 231).

12 Earlier, in her Plant prayer, Isabel had prayed " 'for the feeling of myself, as of some plant" (49). After listening to this "prayer," Pierre felt "caught as fast-bound in some necromancer's garden" (128). Jane Tompkins suggests sentimentalists were evangelicals who believed that events were controlled by prayer (*Sensational Designs*, 147–85).

13 In a letter of Nov. 24, 1854, Maria Melville writes of her return home: "there to my great delight, as I was stepping down, Herman received me in his arms—by the light of lantern I saw him, for it was pitch dark, and the rain falling heavily" Leyda (*Melville Log*, vol. 1, 493).

E. L. Watson argues that Pierre's attraction to Isabel is "a disguised incest-tendency towards his mother" ("Melville's *Pierre*," 228). Also see William Braswell, *Melville's Religious Thought*, 102; Richard Chase, *Herman Melville: A Critical Study*, 104; E. H. Miller, *Herman Melville: A Biography*, 227; Rogin, *Subversive Genealogy*, 173.

14 Weaver calls Allan Melvill "a model of rigid decorum" and quotes Allan's dedications in the behavior manuals he gave his wife (*Mariner and Mystic*, 59). Allan Melvill advised his nephew, who was about to ship out, "to blend the graces & courtesy of the Gentleman, with the frankness & sincerity of the Sailor" and that his "great object with God's blessing must ever be, to preserve the Family name unsullied in Social intercourse with the World" (cited in Murray, *Pierre*, 433). Rogin notes that Maria saved her letters from Allan and that she "probably showed them to her children" (*Subversive Genealogy*, 172). Also see discussions of Allan in Eleanor Metcalf, *Cycle and Epicycle*; Gilman, *Melville's Early Life*; Kenney, *The Gansevoorts*; and Herbert, *Moby-Dick and Calvinism*.

Metcalf discusses the family legend that Maria Melville used a " 'steering oar' " to marry Herman to Lizzie (*Cycle and Epicycle*, 42). Maria's granddaughter noted she was " 'stern' " and of a " 'dignified stateliness.' " Sealts observes that " 'according to family tradition his mother was persistently critical' " (cited in Puett, "Melville's Wife," 102). Weaver claims that Maria was "remembered in such terms as 'cold,' 'worldly,' 'formal,' 'haughty,' and 'proper'; as putting the highest premium on appearances. . . . She preserved to death a remarkable regality of appearance." Between Melville and his mother "there existed a striking personal resemblance" (60, 61).

15 Jean-Jacques Mayoux: "The mother has taken over the dead father as a part of what she herself represents; and she imposes the worship of his sanctified image which reverts to her" (*Melville*, trans. John Ashbery, 102).

Both portraits of Mr. Glendinning are modelled closely on portraits of Allan Melvill (Murray, ed., *Pierre*, 454–55). Arvin discusses the portrait as a "favorite Gothic device," deriving from *Castle of Otranto*, in which there is also a character named Isabella (in Willet, ed., *The Merrill Studies*, 13–14).

16 Murray points out these are the "shapes" of thieves (*Pierre*, 455).

17 His brother Thomas describes the frightening image of Allan Melvill on his deathbed: " 'I found him very sick, under great mental excitement—at times fierce, even maniacal' " (cited in Arvin, *Herman Melville*, 23).

18 The narrator elsewhere remarks, "Yet let me here offer up three locks of my hair, to the memory of . . ."(267). See Murray's discussion of Isabel's "death-wish" (*Pierre*, lxxxix, li).

19 Isabel claims that she left the asylum when she was between nine and eleven years of age. Pierre, as well as Melville, lost his father when he was twelve. Melville may be implying here that the real anguish—what felt like living in an asylum—was watching his father's world fall apart and that his father's death was in some sense a release from this "insane" state of affairs.

20 Much of the narrator's philosophizing about "The Ambiguities" implicitly exonerates the fathers of both Pierre and Melville. For instance, "one can never be entirely certain whether another person, however carefully and cautiously conscientious, has acted in all aspects conceivable for the very best" (53).

21 John Bowlby observes that a mourner may "oscillate between treasuring" reminders of the dead and "throwing them out" (*Loss*, 92).

22 Porte notes that in his trance Pierre produces "the romance that eludes his waking skill" (*Romance in America*, 183).

23 Barbara Blansett links the Mount of the Titan's to Mardi's Peak of Ofo, which a god fell off of and to which he could not return. Ofo was located on the island of Maramma, which clearly parodies Maria Melville's Calvinist faith ("From Dark to Dark" 223).

24 Murray notes that Bunyan's Delectable Mountain afforded a view of the Celestial City (*Pierre*, 499). John Owen King III observes that "whether conceived externally as wilderness or desert or internally as bewilderment and desertion, the landscape of America and its historically various forms of alienation . . . have been found by authors to be ideal places to make an attempt at personal transformation" (*Iron of Melancholy*, 2).

25 Paula Miner Quinn maintains that Pierre's "apparent attempt to emulate his

long-dead father can be interpreted as a rejection of the Oedipal role in order to act out unconsciously homosexual desires." Sexuality becomes death-like because "all females stand for 'mother,'" and such daring incest would result in death" ("Pierre's Sexuality," 116). See Bowlby on the stages of grief (*Loss*, 86–93).

26 Raymond Nelson argues that "*Pierre* is the book he [Pierre] is writing" ("Art of Herman Melville," 202). Sundquist calls the dream "a fantasy of self-fathering": "the landscape that begins as the mons of the Mother is transfigured into a Medusan nightmare" (*Home as Found*, 170, 169). Rogin: "Pierre's failure to write *Pierre* becomes Melville's central subject" (*Subversive Genealogy*, 179). Charvat argues that "Through *Pierre*, Melville is looking back at his experience with himself and with the literary world between 1846 and 1849" and that Pierre is writing *Mardi* (in Matthew J. Bruccoli, ed., *Profession of Authorship* 283).

   Lacan's early work on female paranoia may illuminate the relationship between Pierre and his mother. Catharine Clement notes that "Lacan's paranoiacs lash out because they are too close to a threatening female figure and too far from other figures." All of the doubling in *Pierre* may relate to Lacan's "mirror stage," which is "the moment when one becomes oneself because one is no longer the same as one's mother." The paranoid was arrested in this stage; she "identified herself with her various doubles in order to destroy them," much as Pierre destroys his double, Glen Stanly, and Melville destroys his parodic double, Pierre (*Lives and Legends of Jacques Lacan*, 76).

27 Brook Thomas uses post-structuralist notions to claim that for Melville "the creative process itself is incestuous" ("The Writer's Procreative Urge in *Pierre*," 422). This view is anticipated in Braswell, *Melville's Religious*, 103. Mumford views the incest motif as symbolic of a "shrinkage" in Melville's emotional growth due to his supposedly unhappy marriage. More generally, Mumford reads the novel's sexual symbolism as an "unconscious revelation of his dilemmas as a writer" (in Willet ed., *Merrill Studies* ed., 8).

28 Imagery of dismemberment also pervades the narrator's musings on the nature of creativity: "all the great books are but mutilated shadowing-forths"; and the "profounder emanations of the human brain . . . have no proper endings" but are "as mutilated stumps" (284, 141).

29 Murray points out that the scene Pierre views is also the one Melville viewed from his writing desk in Pittsfield (*Pierre*, 429). Murray notes that in 1848 the South Baptist Church in New York City was turned into office space (*Pierre*, 484).

30 The original of the Memnon Stone is the Balance Rock, just north of Pittsfield (Murray, ed., *Pierre*, 462). Also see Murray's discussion of Melville's

neighbor putting a music box under the rock, thus causing its association with Memnon, who was also a "favorite figure of the Romantics" (464).

31 Farrell notes that boulders with name plates were indeed used in garden cemeteries (*Inventing the American Way of Death*, 126).

32 For the lack of critical consensus on whether or not Melville identifies with Plinlimmon, see Parker, "HN," 406; and Floyd Watkins, "Melville's Plotinus Plinlimmon and *Pierre*," in Willet ed., *Merrill Studies*, 93–94. Watkins notes that most critics who argue that Melville views Plinlimmon negatively include Braswell, *Melville's Religious Thought*, 83; Wright, *Melville's Use of the Bible*, 176; Brian Higgins, "Plinlimmon and the Pamphlet Again," 34; E. H. Miller, *Herman Melville: A Biography*, 238; Lawrance Thompson, *Melville's Quarrel with God*, in Willet ed., *Merrill Studies*, 29; McWilliams, *Hawthorne, Melville, and the American Character*, 174. Mary E. Dichman argues that Melville agrees with "EI" ("Absolutism in Melville's *Pierre*," 713). Feidelson subtly calls Plinlimmon "the embodiment of the problematic," while noting that "EI" is "one more instance of the problem, not Melville's 'solution' " (*Symbolism and American Literature*, 204).

33 "Plinlimmon" is a mountain in Wales (Murray, ed., *Pierre*, 475); see Murray's discussion of its literary sources (475–76). He links Plinlimmon's nonresponsiveness to Hawthorne's cool reaction to Melville (*Pierre*, lxxvii–iii, 476, 491). I find suggestive the fact that Melville first met Hawthorne during the summer of 1850 while the latter was in a state of bereavement for his mother and composing *The Scarlet Letter*. See E. H. Miller, *Herman Melville: A Biography*, 244.

"Repell" links Plinlimmon to Mrs. Glendinning, who found the chair-portrait "repelling" (*P*, 72). Her displaced image—the palisade—also possesses a "hideous repellingness" (344). Plinlimmon is a confidence-man, "capable of assuming a very off-hand, confidential . . . air," or of having "tacitly pretended" to Pierre's friend, Charlie, that they are on intimate terms (292).

34 Feidelson observes that " 'difficult' is too mild a word for Pierre's situation, which comes closer to bankruptcy" (*Symbolism and American Literature*, 199). The immediate literary source for "Glendinning" is Scott's *Monastery*, in which Halbert Glendinning marries Mary Avenel (Murray, ed., *Pierre*, 431).

35 Melville's wife comments on his reaction to *Pierre's* poor reception: " 'in fact it was a subject of joke with him, declaring that it [*Pierre's* critical trashing] was but just, and I know that however it might have affected his literary reputation, it concerned him personally but little' " (Elizabeth Melville's 1901 letter to Mrs. Mary L. D. Ferris, in Dorothy V. B. D. R. McNeilly, "The Melvilles and Mrs. Ferris," *Extracts*, cited in Higgins and Parker, *Critical Essays on Pierre*, 20). Higgins and Parker believe his joking "must

have concealed misery"; he failed to complete his next two books, "Agatha" and the Tortoise book (*Critical Essays on Pierre*, 20).

36 "Cunning purpleness" may be a version of the "cunning glimpses" that Truth reveals as it is "forced to fly like a scared white doe" (*HHM*, 542). Many of the novel's critics would agree with Sundquist that *Pierre's* parody has "no place to go," except to perform "a mocking of" Melville's own "authorial desires" (Sundquist, *Home as Found*, 178). Also see Murray, ed., *Pierre*, xcvi; Bell, "Glendinning Heritage," 230; Jane Mushabac, *Melville's Humor*, 152, 149. Those critics who view the novel as a deliberate and controlled parody include Braswell, *Melville's Religious Thought*, 437–38; Donald Phelps, "Holy Family in *Pierre*," 110; Fiedler, *Love and Death*, 420; Robert Milder, "Melville's Intentions in *Pierre*," 187; Charvat, *Profession of Authorship*, 249. Merlin Bowen straddles both views, arguing that the novel is "more carefully designed" than it is usually taken to be, but then concluding that "There are too many Pierres" (*Long Encounter*, 159). Brodhead gives the shrewdest reading of Melville's use of form: "Hawthorne and Melville do not simply include different literary modes in their works; they play them off against each other; and they do so in such a way that each mode reveals the imaginative basis of the other's fictions and tests their capacities as vehicles of truth" (*Hawthorne, Melville, and the Novel*, 22–23).

For the novelistic genres Melville was parodying, see Baym, *Novels, Readers, and Reviewers*, chap. 10, 196–223. *Pierre* would appear to parody the genres she calls "Highly Wrought Novels" and "Metropolitan Novels" (208, 209). She also usefully notes that "Gothic" never appears as a term in the period; and "romance" was used "so broadly and inconsistently" that we cannot fix its meaning (201, 226). Charvat argues that *Pierre* was a deliberate attempt to write a mass market novel that would also have the depth of a Renaissance tragedy. He identifies such popular culture influences on *Pierre* as Mrs. Rowson's "misery novel" and the *New York Ledger* stories of such writers as Mrs. E. D. E. N. Southworth (*Profession of Authorship*, 251, 276, 274). Kenney notes that Maria Melville's brother, Peter Gansevoort, criticized her letters for their "'affected coyness of expression,'" which he thought derived from her love of reading popular fiction. (*Gansevoorts*, 173).

Pierre himself early on was the sentimental author of the "'The Tear'" (263). One might also argue that Melville possesses a feminist side which takes domestic fiction so seriously that it taps into a substratum of anger and alienation implicit in the form. Mary Kelley, for instance, argues for the ambivalence of the domestic writer (*Private Woman, Public Stage*).

In *Clarel*, Derwent comments about Vine's song that it is "'Like purple in a royal mourning'" (Walter Bezanson, ed., *Clarel* Part III, xiv, I.46).

The riot in the police house may have been inspired by a review of *Typee* in the *New York Evangelist* 18 (Jan. 28, 1847):13, entitled "Beware of Bad Books": "foul and exciting romance [which] . . . familiarizes the reader with characters, sentiments and events, that should be known only to the police. Licentious scenes and obscene imagery are unblushingly introduced" (cited in Herbert, *Marquesan Encounters*, 183).

37 For a provocative discussion of parody in early American art, see Bryan Jay Wolf, *Romantic Revision*, 17–18. "The parodic imagination invested the work of art with an awareness of its status within a signifying system, using the status as a means of qualifying and often contradicting those meanings traditionally associated with the content" (17). Douglas believes *Pierre* critiques those genteel forces which curtail "genuine masculinity." Instead of repudiating his father, Pierre "is shielding . . . precisely his father's 'sin' . . . against his mother's censorious standards" (*Feminization of American Culture*, 355, 375). Karcher argues that *Pierre* dramatizes how Melville came "to recognize the disparity between the democratic and religious ideals his peers and mentors profess and the poverty, exploitation, and injustice they sanction" (*Shadow Over the Promised Land*, 102).

AFTERWORD

1 On the textual history of *Billy Budd*, see "Editors' Introduction," in Harrison Hayford and Merton M. Sealts, Jr., eds., *BB*, 1–23. For an overview of the critical history of the text, see *BB*, 24–39. All further references to this work are given in my text. Michael Rogin observes that Melville began *Billy Budd* "within weeks" of Stanwix's death. Rogin also argues that Melville began his last novel before the national press revived the Somers case (*Subversive Genealogy*, 287, 295). Peter L. Hays and Richard Dillworth Rust argue that Billy killing Claggart rewrites Melville's son Malcom's suicide ("'Something Healing,'" 330). Robert Wallace maintains that the Somers affair was revived by the Haymarket controversy ("*Billy Budd* and the Haymarket Hangings," 108–12). For the mourning customs I mention, see Farrell, *Inventing the American Way of Death*, 81–82.

2 For readings of the novel as social critique, see Sacvan Bercovitch, who argues that Billy "personifies the spirit of America's baby and budding age; the ship into which he is thrust is Melville's contemporary America.'" Billy lashes out at Claggart/America's "lies" ("Melville's Search for National Identity," 226–27). Also see Alan Trachtenberg, who argues that *Billy Budd* reflects the way "Americans must reckon with ragged edges, the cunning currents and deceits of history" (*Incorporation of America*, 206–07).

3 For the genetic history of *Billy Budd*, see Hayford and Sealts, eds., *BB*, 1–12. Nathaniel M. Floyd calls Claggart, Billy's "shadow-figure" ("A Psychologi-

cal Autopsy," 47). Milton Stern notes that "Claggart becomes the other facet of Budd" ("Introduction," *Billy Budd: Sailor,* 26).

Miriam Cheiken notes that "Vere participates not only in Claggart's nature, but in Billy's as well" ("Captain Vere," 308–09). H. Bruce Franklin argues that "Vere is Claggart in the most subtle form." Franklin also identifies "vere" as a nautical term for "shifting before the wind" (*Victim as Criminal and Artist,* 68, 67). Rogin argues that Melville "purified Billy and Vere of bad motives" by inventing Claggart (*Subversive Genealogy,* 304). Harold Beaver argues that Claggart "forms a commentary on Vere; Vere partly mirrors Claggart." Further, "Vere" is a compound of "'vir' (man)" and "'veritas' (truth)" (Beaver, ed., *Billy Budd,* 48, 45).

4 See A. F. Gaskins, "Symbolic Nature of Claggart's Name," 56.

5 See Herbert, *Moby-Dick and Calvinism.*

6 E. H. Miller links Claggart with Gansevoort, Melville's older brother. Claggart accuses the "younger son or brother of plotting the father's overthrow" (*Herman Melville: A Biography,* 362–63).

7 Sacvan Bercovitch, "Ideological Context of the American Renaissance," 1–20. I cite pp. 13, 17. Also see Bercovitch's "Rites of Assent," 5–42; and "Ritual of Consensus," chap. 5, 132–75. For an incisive critique of the early Bercovitch, see Kenneth S. Lynn, review of *Puritan Origins of the American Self,* 67–69. For Turner on Bercovitch see "Commentary on the Essays," 75–78.

8 On the source of "liminality" in Van Gennep, see Huntington and Metcalf, *Celebrations of Death,* 12. On "irreparable conflicts," see Turner, *Ritual Process.* And for his important qualifications to the application of liminality to modern cultures, see "Liminal to Liminoid," 53–92. For the phases of grief, see Bowlby, *Loss,* 85–102. Peter Marris studies the similarities between the processes of social change and mourning in *Loss and Change.*

9 On "fluid liminality," see Halttunen, *Confidence Men and Painted Women,* 30. Sophia Hawthorne is cited in Metcalf, *Cycle and Epicycle,* 106. On the dangers of the margin, see Mary Douglas, *Purity and Danger,* 97–98.

Bibliography

MELVILLE BIBLIOGRAPHIES

Boswell, Jeannetta. *Herman Melville and the Critics: A Checklist of Criticism, 1900–1978.* Metheun, N.J.: Scarecrow Press, 1981.

Bryant, John. *Melville Dissertations, 1924–1980; An Annotated Bibliography and Subject Index.* Westport, Conn.: Greenwood Press, 1983.

ARCHIVAL SOURCES

Melville Collection. Berkshire Athenaeum, Pittsfield, Mass.

Melville Family Papers. Gansevoort-Lansing Addition, Rare Books and Manuscripts Division, The New York Public Library, Astor, Lenox and Tilden Foundations.

Melville Family Papers. Gansevoort-Lansing Collection, Rare Books and Manuscripts Division, The New York Public Library, Astor, Lenox and Tilden Foundations.

MELVILLE CRITCISM

Abrams, Robert. *"Typee* and *Omoo:* Herman Melville and the Ungraspable Phantom of Identity." *Arizona Quarterly* 31 (1975): 33–50.

Adler, Joyce Sparer. *War in Melville's Imagination.* New York: New York University Press, 1981.

Albrecht, Robert C. "White-Jacket's Intentional Fall." *Studies in the Novel* 4 (1972): 17–26.

Anderson, Charles. *Melville in the South Seas.* New York: Columbia University Press, 1939.

Arvin, Newton. *Herman Melville.* New York: William Sloane, 1950.

Babin, James. "Melville and the Deformation of Being: From *Typee* to Leviathan." *Southern Review* 7 (1971): 89–114.

Baym, Nina. "The Erotic Motif in Melville's *Clarel.*" *Texas Studies in Literature and Language* 16 (1974): 315–28.

———. "Melville's Quarrel with Fiction." *PMLA* 94 (1979): 902–23.

Bell, Michael D. *The Development of American Romance: The Sacrifice of Relation.* Chicago: University of Chicago Press, 1980.

———. "The Glendinning Heritage: Melville's Literary Borrowings in *Pierre.*" *Studies in the Novel* 12 (1973): 741–62.

———. "Melville's *Redburn*: Initiation and Authority." *New England Quarterly* 46 (Dec. 1973): 558–72.

Bercovitch, Sacvan. "Melville's Search for National Identity: Son and Father in *Redburn, Pierre,* and *Billy Budd.*" *College Language Association Journal* 10 (Mar. 1967): 217–28.

Bergler, Edmund. "A Note on Herman Melville." *American Imago* 11 (1954): 385–97.

Berthold, Dennis. "Factual Errors and Fictional Aims in *White-Jacket.*" *Studies in American Fiction* 11.1 (Autumn 1983): 233–39.

Blansett, Barbara. "From Dark to Dark: *Mardi,* a Foreshadowing of *Pierre.*" *The Southern Quarterly* 1 (Apr. 1963): 213–27.

Blau, Richard. *The Body Impolitic: A Reading of Four Novels by Herman Melville.* Amsterdam: Rodopi, 1979.

Bowen, Merlin. *The Long Encounter: Self and Experience in the Writings of Herman Melville.* Chicago: University of Chicago Press, 1960.

———. "*Redburn* and the Angle of Vision." *Modern Philology* 52 (Nov. 1954): 100–09.

Branch, Watson G. *Melville: The Critical Heritage.* London: Routledge and Kegan Paul, 1974.

Braswell, William. *Melville's Religious Thought.* Durham, N.C.: Duke University Press, 1943.

Breitwieser, Mitchell. "False Sympathy in Melville's *Typee.*" *American Quarterly* 34.4 (Fall 1982): 396–417.

Brodhead, Richard. *Hawthorne, Melville, and the Novel.* Chicago: University of Chicago Press, 1973.

Cameron, Sharon. *The Corporeal Self: Allegories of the Body in Melville and Hawthorne.* Baltimore: Johns Hopkins University Press, 1981.

Carothers, Robert. "Herman Melville and the Search for the Father: An Interpretation of the Novels," Ph.D. diss., Kent State University, 1969.

Caserio, Robert. *Plot, Story, and the Novel.* Princeton: Princeton University Press, 1979.

Chaffee, Patricia A. "The Lee Shore: Volition, Time, and Death in the Fiction of Herman Melville." Ph.D. diss., Indiana University, 1971.

Charvat, William. *The Profession of Authorship in America.* Ed. Matthew J. Bruccoli. Columbus: Ohio State University Press. 1968.

Chase, Richard. *Herman Melville: A Critical Study.* New York: Macmillan, 1949.
———. *The American Novel and Its Tradition.* 1957. Reprint. Baltimore and London: Johns Hopkins University Press, 1980.

Cheiken, Miriam. "Captain Vere: Darkness Made Visible." *Arizona Quarterly* 34 (1978): 293–310.

Clark, Michael. "Melville's *Typee*: Fact, Fiction, and Esthetics." *Arizona Quarterly* 34 (1978): 351–70.

Davis, Merrell. *Melville's Mardi: A Chartless Voyage.* New Haven: Yale University Press, 1952.

Davis, Merrell, and William H. Gilman, eds. *Melville's Letters.* New Haven: Yale University Press, 1960.

Dichman, Mary. "Absolutism in Melville's *Pierre*." *PMLA* 67 (1952): 702–15.

Dillingham, William. *An Artist in the Rigging: The Early Work of Herman Melville.* Athens: University of Georgia Press, 1972.

Dimock, Wai-Chee. "*White-Jacket*: Authors and Audiences." *Nineteenth-Century Fiction* 36 (Dec. 1981): 296–317.

Douglas, Ann. "Herman Melville and the Revolt Against the Reader." Chap. 9 in *The Feminization of American Culture.* New York: Knopf, 1977.

Dryden, Edgar. *Melville's Thematics of Form.* Baltimore: Johns Hopkins University Press, 1968.

Duban, James. *Melville's Major Fiction: Politics, Theology, and Imagination.* Dekalb: Northern Illinois University Press, 1983.

Durand, Regis. " 'The Captive King': The Absent Father in Melville's Text." In *The Fictional Father: Lacanian Readings of the Text,* edited by Robert Con Davis, 49–72. Amherst: University of Massachusetts Press, 1981.

Edinger, Edward. *Melville's Moby-Dick: A Jungian Commentary: An American Nekyia.* New York: New Directions, 1975.

Eigner, Edward. *The Metaphysical Novel in England and America.* Berkeley: University of California Press, 1978.

Ellis, William. *Polynesian Researches.* 1829. Reprint. London: Dawsons of Pall Mall, 1967.

Emmers, Amy Puett. "Melville's Closet Skeleton: A New Letter About the Illegitimacy Incident in *Pierre*." In *Critical Essays on Herman Melville's Pierre,* edited by Brian Higgins and Hershel Parker, 237–39. Boston: G. K. Hall, 1983.

Fieldelson, Charles. *Symbolism and American Literature.* Chicago: University of Chicago Press, 1953.

Fiedler, Leslie. *Love and Death in the American Novel.* Rev. ed. New York: Stein and Day, 1966.

Firebaugh, Joseph. "Humorist as Rebel: The Melville of *Typee*." *Nineteenth-Century Fiction* 9 (Sept. 1954): 108–20.

Fletcher, Richard. "Melville's Use of Marquesan." *American Speech* 39 (1964): 135–38.

Floyd, Nathaniel M. "*Billy Budd:* A Psychological Autopsy." *American Imago* 34 (1977): 28–49.

Foster, Charles, "Something in Emblems: A Reinterpretation of *Moby-Dick.*" *The New England Quarterly* 34 (Mar. 1961): 3–35.

Franklin, H. Bruce. *The Victim as Criminal and Artist: Literature from the American Prison.* New York: Oxford University Press, 1978.

———. *The Wake of the Gods: Melville's Mythology.* Stanford: Stanford University Press, 1963.

Fryer, Judith. *The Faces of Eve: Women in the Nineteenth Century American Novel.* New York: Oxford University Press, 1976.

Gaskin, A. F. "Symbolic Nature of Claggart's Name." *American Notes and Queries* 6 (1967): 56.

Gilman, William H. *Melville's Early Life and* Redburn. New York: New York University Press, 1951.

Giltrow, Janet. "Speaking Out: Travel and Structure in Herman Melville's Early Narratives." *American Literature* 52.1 (Mar. 1980): 18–32.

Gredja, Edward. *The Common Continent of Man: Racial Equality in the Writing of Herman Melville.* Port Washington, N.Y.: Kennikat Press, 1974.

Grove, James. "Melville's Vision of Death in *Moby-Dick:* Stepping Away from the 'Snug Sofa.'" *New England Quarterly* 52 (June 1979): 177–96.

Haberstroh, Charles. *Melville and Male Identity.* Cranbury, N.J.: Associated University Press, 1980.

Hayford, Harrison. "The Significance of Melville's 'Agatha Letters.'" *Journal of English Literary History* 13 (Dec. 1946): 299–310.

Hayford, Harrison and Hershel Parker. Moby-Dick *as Doubloon: Essays and Extracts (1851–1970).* New York: Norton, 1970.

Hays, Peter and Richard Dillworth Rust. "'Something Healing': Fathers and Sons in *Billy Budd.*" *Nineteenth-Century Fiction* 34 (Dec. 1977): 326–36.

Herbert, T. Walter. Moby-Dick *and Calvinism: A World Dismantled.* New Brunswick, N.J.: Rutgers University Press, 1977.

———. *Marquesan Encounters: Melville and the Meaning of Civilization.* Cambridge, Mass.: Harvard University Press, 1980.

Herzog, Kristin. "Women and Savages in Melville." Chap. 2 in *Women, Ethnics, and Exotics: Images of Power in Mid-Nineteenth-Century American Fiction.* Knoxville: University of Tennessee Press, 1983.

Higgins, Brian. "Plinlimmon and the Pamphlet Again." *Studies in the Novel* 4 (1972): 27–38.

Higgins, Brian and Hershel Parker, eds. *Critical Essays on Herman Melville's* Pierre. Boston: G. K. Hall, 1983.

Houghton, Donald. "The Incredible Ending of Melville's *Typee.*" *Emerson Society Quarterly* 22 (1961): 28–31.

Howard, Leon. *Herman Melville: A Biography.* Berkeley: University of California Press, 1951.

———. "Melville's Struggle with the Angel." *Modern Language Quarterly* 1 (June 1940): 195–206.

Humphreys, A. R. *Herman Melville.* New York: Grove Press, 1962.

Joswick, Thomas. "*Typee:* The Quest for Origin." *Criticism* 17 (Fall 1975): 335–54.

Jubak, James. "The Influence of Travel Narrative on Melville's *Mardi.*" *Genre* 9 (1976): 79–83.

Justus, James H. "*Redburn* and *White-Jacket:* Society and Sexuality in the Narrators of 1849." In *Herman Melville: Reassessments,* edited by A. Robert Lee, 41–67. Totowa, N.J.: Barnes and Noble, 1984.

Karcher, Carolyn. *Shadow Over the Promised Land: Slavery, Race, and Violence in Melville's America.* Baton Rouge: Louisiana State University Press, 1980.

Kennedy, Joyce, and Frederick Kennedy. "Elizabeth and Herman (Part Two)." *Melville Society Extracts* 34 (May 1978): 3–8.

———. "Elizabeth Melville and Samuel Hay Savage, 1847–1853." *Melville Society Extracts* 39 (Sept. 1979): 1–7.

Kenney, Alice. *The Gansevoorts of Albany: Dutch Patricians in the Upper Hudson Valley.* Syracuse: Syracuse University Press, 1969.

Lebowitz, Alan. *Progress into Silence: A Study of Melville's Heroes.* Bloomington: Indiana University Press, 1970.

Leyda, Jay. *The Melville Log.* 2 vols. 1951. Reprint with new material. New York: Gordian Press, 1969.

Logan, John. "Psychological Motifs in Melville's *Pierre.*" *Minnesota Review* 7 (1967): 325–35.

Mansfield, Luther S. "Melville's Comic Articles on Zachary Taylor." *American Literature* 9 (Jan. 1938): 411–18.

Mathiessen, F. O. *American Renaissance: Art and Expression in the Age of Emerson and Whitman.* New York: Oxford University Press, 1941.

Mayoux, Jean-Jacques. *Melville.* Trans. John Ashbery. New York: Grove Press, 1960.

McCarthy, Paul. "Facts, Opinions, and Possibilities: Melville's Treatment of Insanity Through *White-Jacket.*" *Studies in the Novel* 16 (1984): 167–79.

McNeilly, Dorothy V. B. D. R. "The Melvilles and Mrs. Ferris." *Melville Society Extracts* 28 (Nov. 1976): 1–9.

McWilliams, John P. Jr. *Hawthorne, Melville, and the American Character: A Looking-Glass Business.* Cambridge: Cambridge University Press, 1984.

Meldrum, Barbara. "The Artist in Melville's *Mardi.*" *Studies in the Novel* 1 (1969): 459–67.

Melville, Allan. Journal of July 16, 1843. Melville Collection, Berkshire Athenaeum, Pittsfield, Mass.

Melville Family Bible. *The Holy Bible.* Philadelphia: Carey, 1810. Gansevoort-Lansing Collection, Rare Books and Manuscripts Division, The New York Public Library, Astor, Lenox and Tilden Foundations.

Melville, Herman. *Battle-Pieces and Aspects of War.* Ed. Sidney Kaplan. Amherst: University of Massachusetts Press, 1972.

———. *Billy-Budd: An Inside Narrative.* Eds. Harrison Hayford and Merton Sealts. Chicago: University of Chicago Press, 1962.

———. *Billy-Budd: An Inside Narrative.* Ed. Milton Stern. Indianapolis: Bobbs-Merrill, 1975.

———. *Billy Budd and Other Stories.* Ed. Harold Beaver. London: Penguin, 1972.

———. *Clarel: A Poem and a Pilgrimage in the Holy Land.* Ed. Walter Bezanson. New York: Hendricks House, 1960.

———. *Collected Poems of Herman Melville.* Ed. Howard P. Vincent. New York and Chicago: Hendricks House, 1947.

———. *The Confidence-Man: His Masquerade.* Ed. Elizabeth S. Foster. New York: Hendricks House, 1954.

———. "The Death Craft." *The Democratic Press and Lansingburgh Advertiser* (Nov. 16, 1839). In Martin L. Pops, *The Melville Archetype,* appendix, 256–60. Kent, Ohio: Kent State University Press, 1970.

———. "Fragments From a Writing Desk 1." *The Democratic Press and Lansingburgh Advertiser* (May 4, 1839). In *Billy Budd and Other Prose Pieces,* edited by Raymond Weaver, 382–90. New York: Russell and Russell, 1963.

———. "Fragments From a Writing Desk 2." *The Democratic Press and Lansingburgh Advertiser* (May 18, 1839). In William H. Gilman, *Melville's Early Life and Redburn,* appendix B, 271. New York: New York University Press, 1951.

———. *Israel Potter: His Fifty Years of Exile.* Introduction by Alfred Kazin. New York: Warner Books, 1974.

———. *Melville's Journal of a Visit to London and the Continent, 1849–1850.* Ed. Eleanor Melville Metcalf. Cambridge: Harvard University Press, 1948.

———. *Journal of a Visit to Europe and the Levant, Oct. 11, 1856–May 6, 1857.* Ed. Howard C. Horsford. Princeton: Princeton University Press, 1955.

———. *Mardi and A Voyage Thither.* Eds. Harrison Hayford et al. Historical note by Elizabeth S. Foster. Evanston: Northwestern University Press, 1970.

———. *Moby-Dick.* Eds. Harrison Hayford and Hershel Parker. New York: Norton, 1967.

———. *Moby-Dick*. Eds. Luther Mansfield and Howard P. Vincent. New York: Hendricks House, 1952.

———. *Pierre, or, The Ambiguities*. Eds. Harrison Hayford et al. Historical note by Leon Howard and Hershel Parker. Evanston: Northwestern University Press, 1971.

———. *Pierre*. Ed. Henry Murray. New York: Hendricks House, 1949.

———. *Redburn*. Eds. Harrison Hayford et al. Historical note by Hershel Parker. Evanston: Northwestern University Press, 1969.

———. *Typee*. Eds. Harrison Hayford, et al. Historical note by Leon Howard. Evanston: Northwestern University Press, 1968.

———. *White-Jacket, or, The World in a Man-of-War*. Eds. Harrison Hayford et al. Historical note by Willard Thorp. Evanston: Northwestern University Press, 1970.

Metcalf, Eleanor Melville. *Herman Melville: Cycle and Epicycle*. Cambridge: Harvard University Press, 1953.

Milder, Robert. "Melville's Intentions in *Pierre*." *Studies in the Novel* 6 (1974): 186–99.

Miller, Edwin Haviland. *Herman Melville: A Biography*. New York: Braziller, 1975.

Miller, Perry. *The Raven and the Whale*. New York: Harcourt, Brace and World, 1956.

Mitchell, Lee. "Melville's Cannibals and Christians." Chap. 7 in *Witnesses to a Vanishing America: The Nineteenth-Century Response*. Princeton: Princeton University Press, 1981.

Murray, Henry. "Dead to the World: The Passions of Herman Melville." In *Endeavors in Psychology*, edited by Edwin Schneidman, 498–577. New York: Harper and Row, 1981.

Murray, Henry, et al. "Allan Melvill's By-Blow," *Melville Society Extracts* 61 (Feb. 1985): 1–6.

Mushabac, Jane. *Melville's Humor*. Hamden, Conn.: Archon Books, 1981.

Nelson, Raymond. "The Art of Herman Melville: The Author of *Pierre*." *Yale Review* 59 (1970): 197–214.

Olson, Charles, *Call Me Ishmael*, San Francisco: City Lights Books, 1947.

Osborne, Frances Cuthbert Thomas. "Recollections." In *The Early Lives of Melville*, edited by Merton M. Sealts, 179–85. Madison: University of Wisconsin Press, 1974.

Parker, Hershel. "Evidence for 'Late Insertions' in Melville's Works." *Studies in the Novel* 7 (1975): 407–24.

———. "Why *Pierre* Went Wrong." *Studies in the Novel* 8 (1976): 7–23.

Parker, Hershel and Donald Yanella, eds. *The Endless Winding Way in Melville: New Charts by Kring and Carey*. Glassboro, N.J.: The Melville Society, 1981.

Patterson-Black, Gene. "On Herman Melville." In *American Novelists Revisited: Essays in Feminist Criticism*, edited by Fritz Fleischman, 107–40. Boston: G. K. Hall, 1982.

Petrullo, Helen. "The Neurotic Hero of *Typee*." *American Imago* 12 (1955): 317–23.

Phelps, Donald. "The Holy Family in *Pierre*." *Prose* 5 (1972): 99–113.

Puett, Amy. "Melville's Wife: A Study of Elizabeth Shaw Melville," Ph.D. diss., Northwestern University, 1969.

Pops, Martin L. *The Melville Archetype*. Kent, Ohio: Kent State University Press, 1970.

Porte, Joel. *The Romance in America: Studies in Cooper, Poe, Hawthorne, Melville, and James*. Middletown, Conn.: Wesleyan University Press, 1969.

Pry, Elmer. "*Redburn* and the 'Confessions.'" *American Transcendental Quarterly* 43 (Summer 1979): 181–88.

Pullen, Faith, ed. *New Perspectives on Melville*. Edinburgh: Edinburgh University Press, 1978.

Quinn, Paula Miner. "Pierre's Sexuality: A Psychoanalytic Interpretation of Herman Melville's *Pierre, or, The Ambiguities*." *University of Hartford Studies in Literature* 13 (1981): 111–21.

Reynolds, Larry. "Anti-Democratic Emphasis in *White-Jacket*." *American Literature* 48.1 (March 1976): 13–28.

Rogin, Michael P. *Subversive Genealogy: The Politics and Art of Herman Melville*. New York: Knopf, 1983.

Rosen, Bruce. "*Typee* and *Omoo*: Melville's Literary Apprenticeship." Ph.D. diss., New York University, 1965.

Rosenheim, Frederick. "Flight from Home: Some Episodes in the Life of Herman Melville." *American Imago* 1 (1940): 1–30.

Ruland, Richard. "Melville and the Fortunate Fall: *Typee* as Eden." *Nineteenth-Century Fiction* 23 (Dec. 1968): 312–23.

Samson, John. "The Dynamics of History and Fiction in Melville's *Typee*." *American Quarterly* 36.2 (Summer 1984): 276–90.

Sattlemeyer, Robert. "The Origin of Harry Bolton in *Redburn*." *American Transcendental Quarterly* 31 (Summer 1976): 23–25.

Sattlemeyer, Robert and James Barbour. "A Possible Source and Model for the Story of China Aster in Melville's *The Confidence-Man*." *American Literature* 48.4 (January 1977): 577–83.

Schneidman, Edwin. "A Literary Example of Partial Death: The Deaths of Herman Melville." Chap. 14 in *Deaths of Man*. New York: Quadrangle, 1973.

Schroeter, James. "*Redburn* and the Failure of Mythic Criticism." *American Literature* 39 (Nov. 1967): 293–96.

Sealts, Merton, Jr. *Melville as Lecturer*. Cambridge, Mass.: Harvard University Press, 1957.

——. *Melville's Reading*. Madison: University of Wisconsin Press, 1966.

——. *Pursuing Melville, 1940–1980*. Madison: University of Wisconsin Press, 1982.

Sedwick, William Ellery. *Herman Melville: The Tragedy of Mind*. Cambridge: Harvard University Press, 1944.

Seelye, John. *Melville: The Ironic Diagram*. Evanston, Ill.: Northwestern University Press, 1970.

Sherrill, Rowland. *The Prophetic Melville: Experience, Transcendence, and Tragedy*. Athens: University of Georgia Press, 1978.

Smith, Henry Nash. "The Madness of Ahab." Chap. 3 in *Democracy and the Novel*. New York: Oxford University Press, 1978.

Stern, Milton. *The Fine Hammered Steel of Herman Melville*. Urbana: University of Illinois Press, 1957.

Stern, Milton, ed. *Critical Essays on Herman Melville's Typee*. Boston: G. K. Hall, 1982.

Strickland, Carol. "Coherence and Ambivalence in Melville's *Pierre*." *American Literature* 48 (November 1976): 302–11.

Sundquist, Eric. *Home as Found: Authority and Genealogy in Nineteenth Century American Literature*. Baltimore: Johns Hopkins University Press, 1979.

Thomas, Brook. "The Writer's Procreative Urge in *Pierre*: Fictional Freedom or Convoluted Incest." *Studies in the Novel* 11 (1979): 416–30.

Thomas, Russell. "Yarn for Melville's *Typee*." *Philological Quarterly* 15 (Jan. 1936): 16–29.

Thompson, Lawrance. *Melville's Quarrel with God*. Princeton: Princeton University Press, 1952.

Tolchin, Neal. "The Mourning Figure in Melville's Art." *SEASA 85, Proceedings of the Southeastern American Studies Association Conference: Ritual in the United States: Acts and Representations*. Ed. Donald Harkness. Tampa, Fla.: American Studies Press, 1985. 3–6.

Trachtenberg, Alan. *The Incorporation of America: Culture and Society in the Gilded Age*. New York: Hill and Wang, 1982.

Vargish, Thomas. "Gnostic Mythos in Moby-Dick." *PMLA* 81 (1966): 272–77.

Vincent, Howard P. *The Tailoring of Melville's White-Jacket*. Evanston, Ill.: Northwestern University Press, 1970.

Wadlington, Warrick. *The Confidence Game in American Literature*. Princeton: Princeton University Press, 1975.

Waite, Robert. "Melville's *Memento Mori*." *Studies in American Fiction* 5.2 (Autumn 1977): 187–98.

Wallace, Robert. "*Billy Budd* and the Haymarket Hangings." *American Literature* 47 (Mar. 1975): 108–12.

Warren, Joyce W. "The Masculine Sea: Herman Melville." Chap. 5 in *The American Narcissus: Individualism and Women in Nineteenth-Century Fiction.* New Brunswick: Rutgers University Press, 1984.

Watson, Charles N., Jr. "Melville's Jackson: Redburn's Heroic 'Double.'" *Emerson Society Quarterly* 62 (Winter 1971): 8–10.

Watson, E. L. Grant. "Melville's *Pierre.*" *New England Quarterly* 3 (Dec. 1930); 195–234.

Weathers, Willie T. "*Moby-Dick* and the Nineteenth-Century Scene." *Texas Studies in Literature and Language* 1 (Winter 1960): 477–501.

Weaver, Raymond. *Herman Melville: Mariner and Mystic.* New York: George H. Doran Co., 1921.

Wenke, John. "Melville's *Mardi* and the Isles of Man." *American Transcendental Quarterly.* 53 (Winter 1982): 25–41.

Willet, Ralph, ed. *The Merrill Studies in Pierre.* Columbus, Ohio: Merrill, 1971.

Williams, David P. "Peeping Tommo: *Typee* as Satire." *Canadian Review of American Studies* 6 (1975): 36–49.

Witherington, Paul. "The Art of Melville's *Typee.*" *Arizona Quarterly* 2 (1970): 136–50.

Wright, Elizabeth. "The New Psychoanalysis and Literary Criticism: A Reading of Hawthorne and Melville." *Poetics Today* 3.2 (Spring 1982): 89–105.

Wright, Nathalia. *Melville's Use of the Bible.* Durham, N.C.: Duke University Press, 1949.

Zirker, Priscilla. "Evidence of the Slavery Dilemma in *White-Jacket.*" *American Quarterly* 18 (Fall 1966): 477–92.

Zoellner, Robert. *The Salt Sea Mastodon: A Reading of* Moby-Dick. Berkeley: University of California Press, 1973.

ON MOURNING: PRIMARY SOURCES

Bryant, William Cullen. *The Poetical Works of W. C. Bryant.* Ed. Parke Godwin. New York: D. Appleton and Co., 1883.

Chilton, R. S. "The Burial at Marshfield." In *The Knickerbocker Gallery*, 373. New York: Samuel Hueston, 1854.

Davey, Richard. *A History of Mourning.* London: Jay's, 1890.

"Deceased People Whom We Meet Every Day." *Littel's Living Age* 3 (Apr. 11 to Aug. 1844): 222–24.

Dewey, Orville. *Discourses on Human Nature, Human Life, and the Nature of Religion.* In *The Works of Orville Dewey.* Boston: American Unitarian Association, 1883.

————. *The Problem of Human Destiny*. In *The Works of Orville Dewey*. Boston: American Unitarian Association, 1883.

Duyckinck, Evert. "Authorship." *Arcturus* 3 (1841): 22–23.

Fellowship, Letters Addressed to My Sister Mourners. New York: Anson D. F. Randolph and Co.

"The House of Mourning." *Littel's Living Age* 2 (Apr.–Aug. 1844): 435–36.

Irving, Washington. "Strewing Flowers Upon Graves." In *The Mourner's Gift*, edited by M. A. Patrick, 190–92. New York: Van Nostrand and Dwight, 1837.

Keese, John. *The Mourner's Chaplet*. Boston: Gould, Kendall and Lincoln, 1844.

Mathews, Cornelius. *The Career of Puffer Hopkins*. New York: D. Appleton and Co., 1842.

————. "Deceased People Whom We Meet Every Day." *Littel's Living Age* 3 (Apr. 11–Aug. 1844): 222–24.

————. "The Solemn Vendue." *Arcturus* 1 (1841): 36–38.

————. "Tickets for Greenwood." *The Dollar Magazine* 8 (July–Dec. 1851): 84–85.

————. "The UnRest of the Age." *Arcturus* 3 (1841): 133–37.

On the Duties of Consolation and the Rites and Customs Appropriate to Mourning. Boston, 1826.

Parkman, Francis. *An Offering of Sympathy to the Afflicted . . .* 3d ed. Boston: James Monroe & Co., 1842.

Poe, Edgar Allan. "The Premature Burial." In *The Other Poe; Comedies and Satires*, edited by David Galloway, 161–75. New York: Penguin Books, 1983.

Richmond, Rev. Leigh. "Letters on the Death of His Mother and Father." In *The Mourner's Book: By a Lady*, 71. Phil.: W. Marshall, 1836.

Story, Justice Joseph. "Address on the Dedication of Mt. Auburn Cemetary." In *The Picturesque Pocket Companion, and Visitor's Guide, through Mt. Auburn*. Boston: Otis, Broaders, 1839.

Wellington's Funeral Procession. *The Illustrated Magazine of Art*. 1 (1853).

Young Man's Own Book. Phil.: Key, Mielke and Biddle, 1832.

ON MOURNING: SECONDARY SOURCES

Aaron, Daniel. "The Etiquette of Grief: A Literary Generation's Response to Death." In *Prospects: An Annual of American Cultural Studies*. Vol. 4 Ed. Jack Salzman. New York: Cambridge University Press, 1979.

Bernstein, Stephen et al. "Changes in Patients with Gender-Identity Problems after Parental Death." *American Journal of Psychology* 138.1 (1981): 41–45.

Bowlby, John. *Loss: Sadness and Depression*. New York: Basic Books, 1980.

De Spelding, Lynne A., and Albert L. Strickland. *The Last Dance: Encountering Death and Dying.* Palo Alto, Calif.: Mayfield, 1983.

Deutsch, Helene. "Absence of Grief." *Psychoanalytic Quarterly* 6 (1937): 12–23.

Douglas, Ann. "The Domestication of Death." chap. 6 in *The Feminization of American Culture.* New York: Knopf, 1977.

Farrell, James J. *Inventing the American Way of Death, 1830–1920.* Philadelphia.: Temple University Press, 1980.

Freud, Sigmund. "Mourning and Melancholia." In *The Collected Papers of Sigmund Freud.* Vol. 14. Ed. Ernest Jones. Trans. Joan Riviere. New York: Basic Books, 1959.

———. "Splitting of the Ego in the Defensive Process." In *The Collected Papers of Sigmund Freud.* Vol. 5. Ed. John Strachey. New York: Basic Books, 1959.

———. *Totem and Taboo.* Ed. John Strachey. New York: Norton, 1950.

Fulton, Robert, ed. *Death and Identity.* New York: John Wiley and Sons, 1965.

Furman, Edna. *A Child's Parent Dies.* New Haven: Yale University Press, 1974.

Glick, Ira et al. *The First Year of Bereavement.* The Harvard Study of Bereavement. New York: John Wiley and Sons, 1974.

Habenstein, Robert, and William M. Lamers. *The History of American Funeral Directing.* 2d rev. ed. Milwaukee: National Funeral Directors Assoc., 1981.

Halttunen, Karen. "Mourning the Dead: A Study in Sentimental Ritual." Chap. 5 in *Confidence Men and Painted Women: A Study of Middle-Class Culture in America, 1830–1870.* New Haven: Yale University Press, 1982.

Hilgard, Josephine et al. "Strength of Adult Ego Following Childhood Bereavement." In *Death and Identity,* edited by Robert Fulton. 259–72.

Huntington, Richard, and Peter Metcalf. *Celebrations of Death: The Anthropology of Mortuary Ritual.* Cambridge: Cambridge University Press, 1979.

Jackson, Charles. "Death Shall Have No Dominion: The Passing of the World of the Dead in America." *Omega* 8.3 (1977): 195–203.

———, ed. *Passing: The Vision of Death in America.* Westport, Conn.: Greenwood Press, 1977.

Jones, C. R. *Memento Mori: 200 Years of Funerary Art and Customs of Concord, Mass.* Concord, Mass.: Concord Antiquarian Society, 1967.

Kastenbaum, Robert J. *Death, Society, and Human Experience.* St. Louis: C. V. Mosby Co., 1977.

Kübler-Ross, Elisabeth. *On Death and Dying,* New York: Macmillan, 1969.

Lacquer, Thomas. "Bodies, Death, and Pauper Funerals." *Representations* 1 (Feb. 1983): 109–31.

Lindemann, Erich. "Symptomatology and Management of Acute Grief." In *Death and Identity,* edited by Robert Fulton, 186–200. New York: John Wiley and Sons, 1965.

Merloo, Joost. "Delayed Mourning in Victims of Extermination Camps." In *From a Ruined Garden: The Memorial Books of Polish Jewry*, edited and translated by Jack Kugelmass and Jonathan Boyarin. New York: Schocken Books, 1983.

Pike, Martha V. "In Memory Of: Artifacts Relating to Mourning in Nineteenth-Century America." In *Rituals and Ceremonies in Popular Culture*, edited by Ray B. Browne, 296–315. Bowling Green, Ohio: Bowling Green University Press, 1980.

Pike, Martha V., and Janice Armstrong, eds. *A Time to Mourn: Expressions of Grief in Nineteenth-Century America.* New York: The Museums at Stony Brook, 1980.

Pollock, George. "Mourning and Adaptation." *International Journal of Psycho-Analysis* 42 (1961): 344–45.

Ragon, Michael. *The Space of Death.* Trans. Alan Sheridan. Charlottesville: University Press of Virginia, 1983.

Raphael, Beverly. *The Anatomy of Bereavement.* New York: Basic Books, 1983.

Rosaldo, Renato. "Grief and a Headhunter's Rage: On the Cultural Force of Emotions." In *Text, Play, and Story: The Construction and Reconstruction of Self and Society*, edited by Edward M. Bruner, 178–95. N.p.: Proceedings of the American Ethnological Society, 1984.

Rosenblatt, Paul C. *Bitter, Bitter Tears: Nineteenth-Century Diarists and Twentieth-Century Grief Theories.* Minneapolis: University of Minnesota Press, ·1983.

Rosenblatt, Paul C., et al. *Grief and Mourning in Cross-Cultural Perspective.* New Haven: Human Relations Area Files Press, 1976.

Sagan, Eli. *Cannibalism: Human Aggression and Cultural Form.* New York: Harper and Row, 1974.

Saum, Lewis. "Death." Chap. 4 in *The Popular Mood of Pre-Civil War America.* Westport, Conn.: Greenwood Press, 1980.

———. "Death in Pre-Civil War America." In *Death in America*, edited by David Stannard, 30–48. Philadelphia: University of Pennsylvania Press, 1975.

Schorsch, Anita. *Mourning Becomes America: Mourning Art in the New Nation.* Clinton, N.J. Main Street Press, 1976.

Taylor, Lawrence. "Symbolic Death: An Anthropological View of Mourning Ritual in the Nineteenth Century." In *A Time to Mourn: Expressions of Grief in Nineteenth-Century America*, edited by Martha V. Pike and Janice G. Armstrong. New York: Museums at Stony Brook, 1980.

Volkan, Vamik. *Linking Objects and Linking Phenomena: A Study of the Forms, Symptoms, Metapsychology, and Therapy of Complicated Mourning.* New York: International University Press, 1981.

Volkart, Edmund, and Stanley Michael. "Bereavement and Mental Health." *In Death and Identity*, edited by Robert Fulton. 272–93. New York: John Wiley and Sons, 1965.

CULTURAL AND SOCIAL HISTORY

Allen, Gay Wilson. *Waldo Emerson: A Biography*. New York: Viking Press, 1981.

Auerbach, Nina. *Woman and the Demon: The Life of a Victorian Myth*. Cambridge, Mass.: Harvard University Press, 1982.

Barker-Benfield, G. J. *The Horrors of the Half-Known Life*. New York: Harper and Row, 1976.

Baym, Nina. "Melodramas of Beset Manhood: How Theories of American Fiction Exclude Women Authors." *American Quarterly* 33.2 (Summer 1981): 123–39.

———. *Novels, Readers, and Reviewers: Responses to Fiction in Antebellum America*. Ithaca: Cornell University Press, 1984.

Bercovitch, Sacvan. *The American Jeremiad*. Madison: University of New Mexico Press, 1981.

———. "The Ideological Context of the American Renaissance." In *Forms and Functions of History in American Literature*, edited by Winifred Fluck et al., 1–20. Berlin: Erich Schmidt Verlag, 1981.

———. "The Rites of Assent: Rhetoric, Ritual, and the Ideology of American Consensus." In *The American Self: Myth, Ideology and Popular Culture*, edited by Sam B. Girgus, 5–42. Albuquerque: University of New Mexico Press, 1981.

Bettleheim, Bruno. *Symbolic Wounds: Puberty Rites and the Envious Male*. Rev. ed. New York: Collier Books, 1962.

Bonaparte, Marie. *The Life and Works of Edgar Allan Poe*. 1933. Reprint. London: Imago, 1949.

Brown, Charles H. *William Cullen Bryant*. New York: Charles Scribner's Sons, 1971.

Cameron, Sharon. "Representing Grief: Emerson's 'Experience.'" *Representations*. 15 (Summer 1986): 15–41.

Carroll, Peter N., and David W. Noble. *The Free and the UnFree: A New History of the U.S.* Hammondsworth: Penguin Books, 1977.

Cott, Jonathan. *Pipers at the Gates of Dawn: The Wisdom of Children's Literature*. New York: Random House, 1981.

Cott, Nancy, F. *The Bonds of Womanhood: "Woman's Sphere" in New England 1780–1835*. New Haven: Yale University Press, 1977.

Ehrlich, Gloria C. *Family Themes and Hawthorne's Fiction*. New Brunswick, N.J.: Rutgers University Press, 1984.

Ferguson, Robert. *Law and Letters in American Culture.* Cambridge, Mass.: Harvard University Press, 1984.

Fliegelman, Jay. *Prodigals and Pilgrims: The American Revolution Against Patriarchal Authority, 1750–1800.* Cambridge: Cambridge University Press, 1982.

Forgie, George B. *Patricide in the House Divided: A Psychological Interpretation of Lincoln and His Age.* New York: Norton, 1979.

Gay, Peter. *The Bourgeois Experience: Victoria to Freud,* Vol. 1. *The Education of the Senses.* New York: Oxford University Press, 1984.

Griffith, Elisabeth. *In Her Own Right: The Life of Elizabeth Cady Stanton.* New York: Oxford University Press, 1984.

Handy, E. S. C. *The Native Culture in the Marquesas.* Honolulu, Hawaii: Bernice P. Bishop Museum, 1923.

———. *Polynesian Region.* Honolulu, Hawaii: Bernice P. Bishop Museum, 1927.

Higham, John. *From Boundlessness to Consolidation: The Transformation of American Culture, 1848–1860.* Ann Arbor, Mich.: William L. Clements Library, 1969.

Howe, Daniel Walker. "Victorian Culture in America." In *Victorian America,* Ed. Daniel Walker Howe. 3–28. Philadelphia: University of Pennsylvania Press, 1976.

Kardiner, Abram, *The Individual and His Society: The Psychodynamics of Primitive Social Organization.* New York: Columbia University Press, 1939.

Kelley, Mary. *Private Woman, Public Stage: Literary Domesticity in Nineteenth-Century America.* New York and Oxford: Oxford University Press, 1984.

Kenney, Alice. *Stubborn for Liberty: The Dutch in New York.* Syracuse: Syracuse University Press, 1975.

Kett, Joseph. *Rites of Passage: Adolescence in America.* New York: Basic Books, 1977.

King, John Owen, III. *The Iron of Melancholy: Structures of Spiritual Conversion in America from the Puritan Conscience to Victorian Neurosis.* Middletown, Conn.: Wesleyan University Press, 1983.

Kolodny, Annette. *The Lay of the Land: Metaphor as Experience and History in American Life and Letters.* Chapel Hill: University of North Carolina Press, 1975.

Lebeaux, Richard. *Young Man Thoreau.* New York: Harper and Row, 1975.

Linton, Ralph. "Marquesan Culture." Chap. 5 in Abram Kardiner, *The Individual and His Society: The Psychodynamics of Primitive Social Organization.* New York: Columbia University Press, 1939.

Longford, Elizabeth. *Victoria, R. I.,* London: Weidenfeld and Nicolson, 1964.

Lynn, Kenneth. Review of *The Puritan Origins of the American Self,* by Sacvan Bercovitch. *ELN* 14.1 (Sept. 1976): 67–69.

Mellow, James R. *Nathaniel Hawthorne In His Times*. New York: Houghton Mifflin, 1980.

Messerli, Jonathan. *Horace Mann: A Biography*. New York: Alfred A. Knopf, 1972.

Meyers, Marvin. *The Jacksonian Persuasion: Politics and Belief*. Stanford: Stanford University Press, 1957.

Miller, Perry. "Afterword." In *The Sketch Book*, by Washington Irving. New York: Signet, 1961.

Nye, Russell B. *Society and Culture in America, 1830–1860*. New York: Harper and Row, 1974.

Pugh, David. *Sons of Liberty: The Masculine Mind in Nineteenth-Century America*. Westport, Conn.: Greenwood Press, 1983.

Rogin, Michael P. *Fathers and Children: Andrew Jackson and the Subjugation of the American Indian*. New York: Random House, 1975.

Roheim, Geza. "Marquesan Culture." Chap. 7 in *Psychoanalysis and Anthropology: Culture, Personality and the Unconscious*. New York: International University Press, 1950.

Schlesinger, Arthur. *Learning How to Behave: A Historical Study of American Etiquette Books*. New York: Macmillan, 1947.

Sklar, Kathryn Kish. *Catharine Beecher: A Study in American Domesticity*. New Haven: Yale University Press, 1973.

Skultans, Vieda. *Madness and Morals: Ideas on Insanity in the Nineteenth Century*. London: Routledge and Kegan Paul, 1975.

Smith-Rosenberg, Carroll. "Sex and Symbol in Victorian America." In *Prospects: An Annual of American Cultural Studies*. Vol. 5. Ed. Jack Salzman. New York: Cambridge University Press, 1980.

Stafford, John. *The Literary Criticism of "Young America"*. Berkeley: University of California Press, 1952.

Taylor, Joshua. *America As Art*. New York: Harper and Row, 1976.

Tompkins, Jane. *Sensational Designs: The Cultural Work of American Fiction, 1790–1860*. New York: Oxford University Press, 1985.

Turner, Victor. "Commentary on the Essays by Roland A. Delattre and Carroll Smith-Rosenberg." *Prospects: An Annual of American Cultural Studies*. Vol. 5. Ed. Jack Salzman. New York: Cambridge University Press, 1980.

Wilentz, Sean. *Chants Democratic: New York City and the Rise of the American Working Class, 1788–1850*. New York: Oxford University Press, 1984.

Wolf, Bryan Jay. *Romantic Revision*. Chicago: University of Chicago Press, 1982.

Ziff, Larzer. *Literary Democracy: The Declaration of Cultural Independence in America*. New York: Viking Press, 1981.

Zwieg, Paul. *Walt Whitman: The Making of the Poet*. New York Basic Books, 1984.

THEORY

Bakhtin, Mikhail. "Discourse in the Novel. "In *The Dialogic Imagination: Four Essays*. 259–422. Ed. Michael Holquist. trans. Michael Holquist and Caryl Emerson. Austin: University of Texas Press, 1981.

Chodorow, Nancy. *The Reproduction of Mothering: Psychoanalysis and the Sociology of Gender*. Berkeley: University of California Press, 1978.

Clark, Katerina, and Michael Holquist. *Mikhail Bakhtin*. Cambridge: Harvard University Press, 1984.

Clement, Catharine. *The Lives and Legends of Jacques Lacan*. Trans. Arthur Goldhammer. New York: Columbia University Press, 1983.

Derrida, Jacques. *Of Grammatology*. Trans. Gayatri Spivak. Baltimore: Johns Hopkins University Press, 1974.

Douglas, Mary. *Purity and Danger: An Analysis of the Concepts of Pollution and Taboo*. London: Routledge and Kegan Paul, 1966.

Erikson, Erik. *Childhood and Society*. Rev. ed. New York: Norton, 1963.

Johnson, Barbara. "Teaching Deconstructively." In *Writing and Reading Differently*, edited by G. Douglas Atkins and Michael L. Johnson, 15–41. Lawrence, Kans.: University of Kansas Press, 1985.

Jung, C. G. *Analytical Psychology: Its Theory and Practice*. New York: Random House, 1968.

Klein, Melanie et al., eds. *New Directions in Psychoanalysis*. New York: Basic Books, 1957.

Kovel, Joel. *The Age of Desire; Case Histories of a Radical Psychoanalyst*. New York: Pantheon Books, 1981.

Kuhns, Richard. *Psychoanalytic Theory of Art: A Philosophy of Art on Developmental Principles*. New York: Columbia University Press, 1983.

LaCapra, Dominick. *Rethinking Intellectual History: Texts, Contexts, Language*. Ithaca: Cornell University Press, 1983.

Levi-Strauss, Claude. *Tristes Tropiques*. Trans. John and Doreen Weightman. New York: Pocket Books, 1977.

Marris, Peter. *Loss and Change*. London: Routledge and Kegan Paul, 1974.

Mitchell, Juliet. *Psychoanalysis and Feminism*. New York: Pantheon Books, 1974.

Rowe, John Carlos. *Through the Custom-House: Nineteenth-Century American Fiction and Modern Theory*. Baltimore: Johns Hopkins University Press, 1982.

Segal, Hanna. *Introduction to the Work of Melanie Klein*. 1963. Reprint. New York: Basic Books, 1973.

Skura, Meredith Anne. *The Literary Use of the Psychoanalytic Process*. New Haven: Yale University Press, 1981.

Turner, Victor. "Comments and Conclusions." In *The Reversible World*, edited by Barbara Babcock. Ithaca: Cornell University Press, 1978.

————. *Dramas, Fields, Metaphors: Symbolic Action in Human Society*. Ithaca: Cornell University Press, 1974.

————. "Liminal to Liminoid in Play, Flow and Ritual: An essay in Comparative Symbology." *Rice University Studies* 60 (Summer 1974): 53–92.

————. *The Ritual Process: Structure and Anti-Structure*. Ithaca, New York: Cornell University Press, 1969.

Van Gennep, Arnold. *Rites of Passage*. Trans. Monika B. Vizedom and Gabrielle L. Caffee. Chicago: University of Chicago Press, 1960.

Williams, Raymond. "Culture." In *Marx: The First One Hundred Years*, edited by David McLellan, 15–56. New York: St. Martin's Press, 1985.

Index